Translated Texts fo

This series is designed to meet the needs of students of ancient and medieval history and others who wish to broaden their study by reading source material, but whose knowledge of Latin or Greek is not sufficient to allow them to do so in the original languages. Many important Late Imperial and Dark Age texts are currently unavailable in translation and it is hoped that TTH will help to fill this gap and to complement the secondary literature in English which already exists. The series relates principally to the period 300-800 AD and includes Late Imperial, Greek, Byzantine and Syriac texts as well as source books illustrating a particular period or theme. Each volume is a self-contained scholarly translation with an introductory essay on the text and its author and notes on the text indicating major problems of interpretation, including textual difficulties.

Editorial Committee

Sebastian Brock, Oriental Institute, University of Oxford
Averil Cameron, Keble College, Oxford
Henry Chadwick, Oxford
John Davies, University of Liverpool
Carlotta Dionisotti, King's College London
Peter Heather, University College London
Robert Markus, University of Nottingham
John Matthews, Queen's College, Oxford
Raymond Van Dam, University of Michigan
Michael Whitby, University of Warwick
Ian Wood, University of Leeds

General Editors

Gillian Clark, University of Liverpool
Mary Whitby, Royal Holloway, London

Front cover: Representation of Childeric's seal ring.

A full list of published titles in the Translated Texts for Historians series is printed at the end of this book.

Translated Texts for Historians
Volume 23

Venantius Fortunatus: Personal and Political Poems

Translated with notes and introduction by
JUDITH GEORGE

Liverpool
University
Press

First published 1995 by
LIVERPOOL UNIVERSITY PRESS
Senate House
Abercromby Square
Liverpool
L69 3BX

Copyright © 1995 Judith George

All rights reserved. No part of this
book may be reproduced in any form
without permission in writing from the
publishers, except by a reviewer in
connection with a review for inclusion
in a magazine or newspaper.

British Library Cataloguing-in-Publication Data
A British Library CIP Record is available
ISBN 0-85323-179-6

**The publishers gratefully acknowledge the
generous financial support provided towards
the publication of this book by the Open
University's Regional Academic Services.**

Printed in the European Union by
Page Bros, Norwich, England

In memory of

Margaret Gibson

CONTENTS

Abbreviations	xi
Genealogical table of the Merovingian Royal Family	xv
Map of Europe at the time of Fortunatus	xvi
Introduction	xvii

Book Three[1]   1
Poem 3.13:   to Vilicus, Bishop of Metz
Poem 3.13
    a - d: to Vilicus, Bishop of Metz

Book Four   5
Poem 4. 16:   *epitaph for Atticus*
Poem 4. 17:   *epitaph for the young man, Arcadius*
Poem 4. 19:   *epitaph for Aracharius*
Poem 4. 20:   *epitaph for Brumachius*
Poem 4. 22:   *epitaph for the innocents*
Poem 4. 35:   *epitaph for Queen Theudechild*
Poem 4. 26:   *epitaph for Vilithuta*
Poem 4. 28:   *epitaph for Eusebia*

Book Five   17
Poem 5. 2:   to Martin, Bishop of Galicia
Poem 5. 8:   to Bishop Gregory, after a journey
Poem 5. 8a: to the same
Poem 5. 8b: to the same for the gift of a book

---

[1] The titles to the poems are later additions and subject to scribal error. Where they appear particularly inaccurate or are of the "more of the same (*item aliud*)" variety, alternative titles have been substituted. These are indicated ad loc.

Poem 5. 13:	to the same for the apples and the grafting slips	
Poem 5. 17:	a greeting to the same	

Book Six   25
Poem 6. 1:	on the king, Lord Sigibert, and the queen, Brunhild
Poem 6. 1a:	on King Sigibert and Queen Brunhild
Poem 6. 2:	on King Charibert
Poem 6. 3:	on Queen Theudechild
Poem 6. 5:	on Galswinth
Poem 6. 6:	on Ultrogotha's garden
Poem 6. 7:	on the villa Cantusblandus, on the subject of apples
Poem 6. 8:	about the cook who took the poet's boat
Poem 6.9:	to Dynamius of Marseilles

Book Seven   57
Poem 7. 1:	to Gogo
Poem 7. 7:	on Duke Lupus
Poem 7. 8:	to Duke Lupus
Poem 7. 16:	on Conda, the domesticus
Poem 7. 24 a - g:	verses on a salver and for festive occasions

Book Eight   69
Poem 8. 2:	on the subject of his journey, when he should have journeyed to Lord Germanus, and was held back by the Lady Radegund
Poem 8. 6:	to Lady Radegund about violets
Poem 8. 7:	to Lady Radegund and Agnes about the flowers upon the altar
Poem 8. 18:	to Bishop Gregory in greeting
Poem 8. 19:	to Bishop Gregory for the present of a villa
Poem 8. 21:	to Bishop Gregory for the skins he sent

Book Nine		73
Poem 9. 1:	to King Chilperic on the occasion of the synod at Berny-Riviere	
Poem 9. 2:	to Chilperic and Queen Fredegund	
Poem 9. 3:	to Chilperic and Fredegund	
Poem 9. 4:	epitaph on the tomb of Lord Chlodobert	
Poem 9. 5:	epitaph on Dagobert	
Poem 9. 6:	to Bishop Gregory on the Sapphic verses	
Poem 9. 7:	to Bishop Gregory	
Book Ten		97
Poem 10. 8:	in praise of King Childebert and Queen Brunhild	
Poem 10. 9:	on his voyage	
Book Eleven		103
Poem 11. 6:	to Agnes	
Poem 11. 8:	to Agnes	
Poem 11. 11:	a poem about flowers	
Poem 11. 13:	to Lady Radegund and Agnes, for the chestnuts	
Poem 11. 14:	to Agnes, for the milk	
Poem 11. 19:	for the other delicacies and for the milk	
Poem 11. 23:	verses composed after a feast	
Poem 11. 25:	to Lady Radegund and Agnes about his journey	
Poem 11. 26:	to Lady Radegund	
Appendix		111
Appendix 2:	to Justin and Sophia, Augusti	
Appendix 3:	to Artachis	
Appendix 5:	on King Childebert	
Appendix 6:	on Queen Brunhild	
Appendix 10:	to Lady Radegund and Agnes	
Appendix 11:	another poem	
Appendix 15:	to Radegund and Agnes	

Appendix 26:   to Radegund and Agnes
Appendix 31:   to Lady Radegund

Biographical notes   123

Select bibliography   133

Index   151

Abbreviations

The following are sources referred to frequently; other source material is listed in the select bibliography.

Primary sources

Baudonivia	VR	Baudonivia, *De vita S. Radegundis 2*, ed. B. Krusch, MGH SRM 2 (Hanover, 1888)
Fortunatus	Poems	Venantius Fortunatus, *Opera poetica*, ed. F. Leo, MGH AA 4.1 (Berlin, 1881)
	VM	-, *Vita S. Martini*, ed. F. Leo, MGH AA 4 (Berlin, 1881)
	VR	-, *De vita S. Radegundis*, ed. B. Krusch, MGH SRM 2 (Hanover, 1888)
Gregory of Tours	HF	Gregory of Tours, *Historia Francorum*, ed. W. Arndt, MGH SRM 1 (Hanover, 1885)
	GC	-, *Liber in gloria confessorum*, ed. W. Arndt, MGH SRM 1 (Hanover, 1885)
MGH		Monumenta Germaniae Historica
	AA	Auctores Antiquissimi
	SRL	Scriptores rerum Langobardicarum et Italicarum, saec. VI-IX
	SRM	Scriptores rerum Merovingicarum
Paul the Deacon	HL	Paul the Deacon, *Historia Langobardorum*, ed. L. Bethmann and G. Waitz, MGH SRL (Berlin, 1878)
PL		Patrologiae cursus completus, series Latina, ed. J.-P Migne
SCr		Sources Chrétiennes (Paris)

Secondary sources

Blomgren   *SF*   S. Blomgren, *Studia Fortunatiana* (Uppsala, 1933)

(1941) - , "De duobus epitaphiis episcoporum, utrum Venantio Fortunato attribuenda sint necne", *Eranos* 39 (1941), pp. 82-99

(1944) - , "De Venantio Fortunato Vergilii aliorumque poetarum priorum imitatore", *Eranos* 42 (1944), pp. 81-88

(1950a) - , "De P. Papinii Statii apud Venantium Fortunatum vestigiis", *Eranos* 48 (1950), pp. 57-65

(1950b) - , "De Venantio Fortunato Lucani Claudianique imitatore", *Eranos* 48 (1950), pp. 150-156

Brennan (1983) B. Brennan, "Bishop and community in the poetry of Venantius Fortunatus", PhD thesis (Melbourne, 1983)

(1984) - , "The image of the Frankish kings in the poetry of Venantius Fortunatus", *Journal of Medieval History* 10, 1 (1984), pp. 1-11

(1985) - , "Senators and social mobility in sixth century Gaul", *Journal of Medieval History* 11 (1985), pp. 145-161

Caron   M. L. Caron, *Le poète Fortunat et son temps* (Mémoire de l'Academie des Sciences et des Lettres et des Arts d'Amiens, ser. 3, 10, 1883), pp. 225-303

Curtius   E. R. Curtius, *European literature and the Latin Middle Ages,* tr. W. R. Trask (New York, 1953)

Duchesne   L. Duchesne, *Fastes épiscopaux de l'ancienne Gaule,* 1-3 (Paris, 1907-1915)

George		J. W. George, *Venantius Fortunatus: a poet in Merovingian Gaul* (Oxford, 1992)
Godman		P. Godman, *Poets and emperors* (Oxford, 1987)
James	(1982)	E. James, *The origins of France* (London, 1982)
	(1988)	-, *The Franks* (Oxford, 1988)
Koebner		R. Koebner, *Venantius Fortunatus: Seine Persönlichkeit und seine Stellung in der geistigen Kultur des Merowingerreiches* (Beitrage zur Kulturgeschichte des Mittelalters und der Renaissance, 22, Leipzig, 1915)
Le Blant		E. Le Blant, *Inscriptions chrétiennes de la Gaule anterieure au VIIIe siècle*, 1-2, (Paris, 1856-1865)
MacCormack	(1972)	S. MacCormack, "Change and continuity in late antiquity: the ceremony of *adventus*", *Historia* 21 (1972), pp. 721-752
	(1975)	-, "Latin prose panegyrics", in T. Dorey (ed.), *Empire and aftermath* (London, 1975)
	(1981)	-, *Art and ceremony in late antiquity* (Berkeley, 1981)
Meyer		W. Meyer, *Der Gelegensheitsdichter Fortunatus* (Abhandlungen der Königlichen Gesellschaft der Wissenschaften in Göttingen, phil.-hist. Klasse, N. F. no. 4.5, Berlin, 1901)
Nisard		M. C. Nisard, *Venance Fortunat: poésies mêlées traduites en français pour la première fois* (Paris, 1887)
Reydellet	(1981)	M. Reydellet, *La royauté dans la litterature latine de Sidoine Apollinaire à Isidore de Seville* (Rome, 1981)
	(1994)	-, *Venance Fortunat: Poèmes*, 1 (Paris, 1994)

Riché	P. Riché, *Education and culture in the barbarian west: from the sixth through the eighth century*, tr. J. J. Contreni (South Carolina, 1976)
Salin	E. Salin, *La civilisation mérovingienne d'après les sepulture, les textes et la laboratoire*, 1-4 (Paris, 1949-1959)
Stroheker	K. F. Stroheker, *Die senatorische Adel im spätantiken Gallien* (Tübingen, 1948)
Tardi	D. Tardi, *Fortunat: Étude sur un dernier représentant de la poésie latine dans la Gaule mérovingienne* (Paris, 1927)
van Dam (1985)	R. van Dam, *Leadership and community in late antique Gaul* (Berkeley, 1985)
(1993)	- , *Saints and their miracles in late antique Gaul* (Princeton, 1993)
von Moos	P. von Moos, *Consolatio, 1-4: Darstellung, Anmerkungen, Testimonien, Index* (Munich, 1971)
Wemple	S. Wemple, *Women in Frankish Society* (Philadelphia, 1981)
Wood	I. Wood, *The Merovingian kingdoms: 450-751* (New York, 1994)

Genealogical table of the Merovingian Royal Family

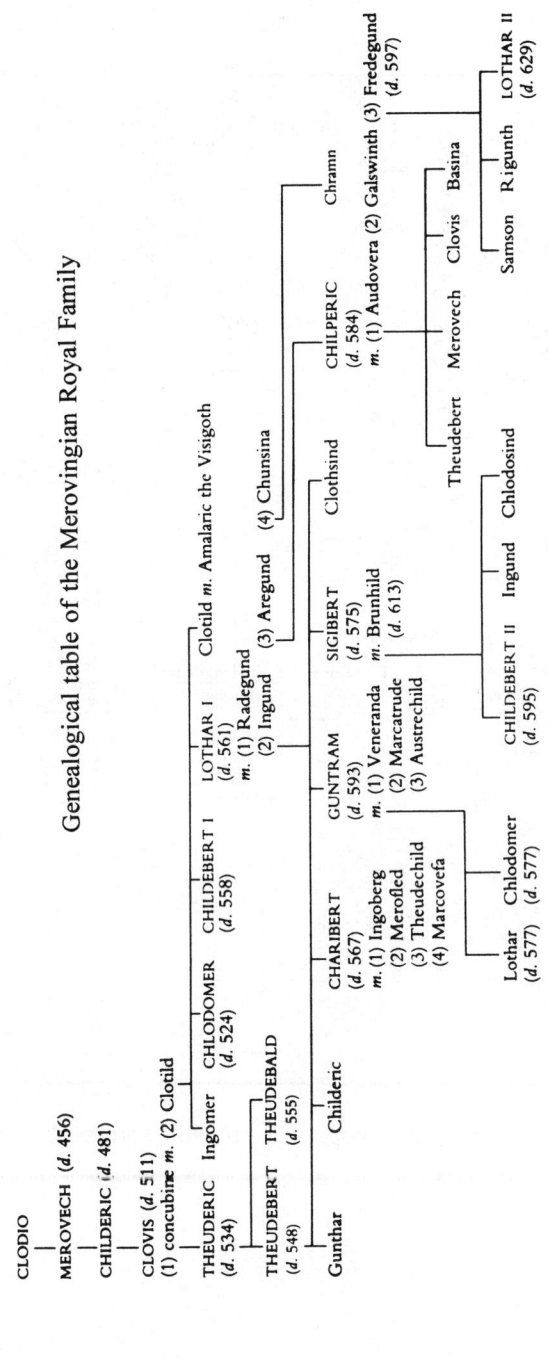

Map of Europe at the time of Fortunatus

Introduction

The late sixth century in Gaul was a time of military and political turbulence, and of considerable social and cultural change: not unusual characteristics of many ages and times, but significant in that these fifty years or so can be seen as the central span of the bridge between a world in the early years of the century which still could be seen and see itself as an extension of the classical world, and a period which witnessed the beginnings of a different and medieval world. These years are documented by inscriptions and archaeological evidence, charters and diplomata, letters, hagiographies and histories, and especially by the rich resource of Gregory of Tours' *Historia Francorum*.

Interweaving amongst these are the works of Venantius Fortunatus: not only a number of valuable hagiographies, but also occasional poetry, a critically different dimension of writing, which almost performs for this age the sort of service which the works of Cicero do for the late Roman Republic. That is not to claim the artistic brilliance of a Cicero for Fortunatus. But as Cicero's speeches bring to life the political cut and thrust of the law-courts, so Fortunatus' panegyric to King Chilperic, *Poem* 9.1, for example, makes us spectators of the poet's fighting speech for the defence of his friend and patron, Gregory of Tours, against the deadly charges of his political adversaries. As Cicero's letters put flesh on the dry bones of the recorded names and places, so Fortunatus' encomia can bring to life the stiff Gallo-Roman aristocrat, Bishop Leontius of Bordeaux, and his blue-blooded wife, Placidina, with their classical villas and fountains; or Duke Lupus, in the first triumphant flush of appointment to that post by King Sigibert; or cultured magnates, ambitious administrators, and a host of others. The poems also fill in the interstices left in the more formal and public records. They show us the lives of energetic women, busy building churches and administering to the poor of the parish; the festive occasions - the flowers, the food, the verses guests had to contribute as their "party piece"; the inscriptions on tombstones or silver salvers. And, above all, in reflecting Fortunatus' relationship with Gregory, and with the ex-queen Radegund, and Agnes, Mother Superior at the community Radegund had established, the poems contribute vivid insights into those lives and characters.

All that is to regard Fortunatus merely as a purveyor of evidence about a period and a culture. But he himself contributed not insignificantly to major events and developments. Above all, he contributed as a Latin poet, the epitome of the tradition the Gallo-Romans strove to maintain and the Franks to achieve; a Janus-figure, who looked back to and embodied for his generation the literary greatness of the classical past, but also, for ages to come, set the benchmarks and influenced writers on the continent and in the Irish and Anglo-Saxon world; a poet whom Meyer could term both the last Latin poet and the first French. His skills were used by Radegund to maintain her network of national and international contacts. He was closely identified with Gregory in the bishop's pastoral and political activities. He visited and corresponded with the major political and ecclesiastical figures of his time.

So, in sum, for modern literary scholars, study of Fortunatus' poetry gives us insight at a general level into an important link in the transmission of the Latin literary tradition: what elements the poet preserved, why and how he adapted what he inherited and brought north to Gaul. Working in closer focus, we can assess in detail the poet's own style, his poetic purpose and competence. But at the same time, the poems reflect for us the occasions and the patrons for which they were written. Used carefully and systematically, they thus provide a rich and unique source of historical information about the individuals Fortunatus wrote for, and the society within which he worked.

The poet's life and writing

Venantius Honorius Clementianus Fortunatus was born near Treviso in north Italy about 540; he received a formal classical education in Ravenna, and then travelled north into Merovingian Gaul. At the time of his arrival, the Merovingian lands were divided between the four sons of Lothar 1: Charibert, Guntram, Sigibert, and Chilperic. On Lothar's death, Chilperic had seized his father's treasury at Berny-

Rivière, and occupied Paris, the former capital of Lothar's brother, Childebert 1. His brothers promptly united to effect a more equable division of territory: Charibert's kingdom centred on Paris, Guntram's on Orleans, Sigibert's on Reims and Metz, and Chilperic's on Soissons.

Probably through letters of introduction to the bishops in the east of the kingdom, Fortunatus contrived to arrive at the court of Sigibert in Metz for the grand occasion of the marriage of Sigibert to the Spanish Visigothic princess Brunhild in 566. His delivery of a panegyric and an epithalamium for the royal couple provided him with a dramatic entrée to the wide circle of secular and ecclesiastical notables assembled in Metz for this event. Taking the best advantage of this flying start in royal patronage, Fortunatus wrote intensively and travelled widely over the next few years. He addressed poems to Sigibert and to notable members of his court; he delivered a panegyric to Charibert, whose court was based in Paris; he developed strong ties with the bishops of both kingdoms; he travelled as far as Toulouse, and kept up a literary correspondence with patrons and friends he had met in Metz in 566/7.

Through an introduction from Bishop Eufronius of Tours, the poet then made his way to Poitiers and met the formidable and charismatic ex-queen, Radegund, who had established the community of the Holy Cross there. Fortunatus became involved immediately in Radegund's diplomatic exchanges with the Emperor Justin and the Empress Sophia in Byzantium to secure important relics for the community, writing *Poem* 8.1 and *Appendix* 1 and 3 to establish her religious and cultural credentials. Her success, and the ceremonial installation of a fragment of the Holy Cross and other relics, were celebrated by Fortunatus' two great hymns, *Pange lingua* and *Vexilla regis,* and the emperor and empress thanked by his formal panegyric, *Appendix 2.*

From that time onwards, the poet's home was Poitiers and the community there, and his writing reflects his involvement with their concerns, as well as his deep friendship with Gregory of Tours, the great bishop and historian of the period.

Charibert had died shortly after Fortunatus' arrival, in 567/8, and his kingdom, with the exception of Paris, which was treated as neutral ground, had been divided between the remaining brothers. There was continuing tension and strife between all three; but that between Sigibert and Chilperic gained particular bitterness when Chilperic, emulating Sigibert's dynastic alliance with the Visigoths, married Brunhild's sister, Galswinth, only to have her murdered a few weeks after the event. Fredegund promptly took her place, and open hostilities broke out between the two families. In 575, when Sigibert was on the point of defeating Chilperic, he was assassinated, probably at Fredegund's instigation. From this dangerous situation, Brunhild worked hard and successfully to create and maintain a position of power for herself and her son, Childebert. After the assassination of Chilperic in 584 (by Fredegund herself, it was suggested), the Treaty of Andelot was signed between Guntram and Childebert ll, making provision for the peaceable division of territory, for the position of Childebert as Guntram's heir, and for the security of the women and children of the royal family. Matters were somewhat more settled from that point onwards, though the feud between the two branches of the family was only finally resolved by Brunhild's gruesome death at the hands of Lothar ll, son of Fredegund, in 613.

Throughout this period of savage feuding, Fortunatus served Radegund's commitment to peacekeeping between the warring factions, and, after her death in 587, continued to work with Gregory for peace between the kingdoms and the diplomatic solution of tensions. He wrote and travelled widely, especially on Radegund's behalf in the early years, his skill and standing as a major Latin poet serving her purposes as well as those of any court poet. But his poems also reflect the routine of daily life in the community, and the warm and loving relationship between the poet and the two women who headed the community - Radegund, its founder, and Agnes, its first Mother Superior. His deep and lasting friendship with Gregory is also reflected in his verse, on literary, diplomatic and on practical topics. Gregory became his patron to the extent of gifts of a villa and land, and other necessities; patronage which Fortunatus repaid by the stalwart and successful defence of the bishop in his panegyric to King Chilperic at the synod of Berny-Rivière in 580. He was in all likelihood ordained priest in the 590s, possibly by Gregory himself; and served the last days of his life as Bishop of Poitiers, dying in the early 600s.

As for Fortunatus' style and versification, his writing bears witness to his rhetorical training, to his thorough grounding in the classical authors as well as in the bible and the church fathers, and to the taste of the age for elaborate verbal virtuosity. The epitaph to Dagobert (*Poem* 9.5), for example, is an acrostic on the prince's name; other poems, not in this selection, are in the shape of a cross or in serpentine form. The more formal poems not only have the traditional rhetorical structure, say, of a panegyric, but are rich in rhetorical imagery and *topoi*; classical allusion and biblical reference abound in Fortunatus' writing.

Fortunatus most commonly writes in the classical elegaic couplet, a hexameter followed by a pentameter, though with certain non-classical irregularities. *Poem* 9.7 is the exception in this selection, being written at Gregory's request in Sapphic stanzas (though the poet complains, not without justification, that this metre does not come easily to him).

The collection and publication of Fortunatus' poems

Though debate continues on this subject[1], it is probable that the poems were published in three collections. The first collection was made by Fortunatus of poems written over the first ten years of his life in Gaul, dedicated to Gregory of Tours and published in 576 or thereabouts. This collection comprised Books 1 - 7, and within the collection the books are arranged by recipient and order of social precedence. Book 1 contains poems written to bishops or about their churches; Book 2 includes the poems on the Holy Cross, with verse relating to clergy in Toulouse and Paris; Book 3 contains poems to bishops and clergy, in that order, over a wide range of dioceses; Book 4 collects epitaphs for bishops, clergy and lay-people; Book 5 reverts to poems to bishops; Book 6 addresses lay people, starting with members of the royal family; and Book 7 addresses lay people of lesser rank.

The second collection, Books 8 and 9, was published shortly before Radegund's death in 587. Book 8 contains the more public and formal poems to Radegund and the community of the Holy Cross in

---

[1] For a brief summary of this discussion, see George, pp. 207-211. See also Koebner, *Excursus* 2.1, pp. 125-128; Leo, *Prooemium*; Meyer, pp. 25-29, 108; M. Reydellet, *Venance Fortunat: Poèmes 1-IV* (Paris, 1994), pp. lxviii-lxxi; Tardi, pp. 92-96.

Poitiers; and Book 9 addresses a wider range of people than any other book, both living and dead, but still in the same order of social rank.

It appears likely that the final collection, Books 10 and 11, was assembled by the poet at some time in the 590s, after the deaths of Radegund and Agnes, though the impression of disorder and lack of finish in Book 10 might well point to a collection made by friends of the poet after his death. Book 11 comprises smaller, informal poems, reflecting life in the community in Poitiers, whilst Book 10 ranges from a prose dissertation on the Lord's Prayer to poems to lay people, ordered in the familiar sequence of status.

The poems presently gathered in the Appendix derive from Σ, the Paris MS 13048. This manuscript contains a random and unsystematic collection of Fortunatus' poems; but it often offers a better text for some of the poems present in other manuscripts, and also a number of poems which are not found elsewhere, but which are undoubtedly genuine.

The selection of poems

This particular selection of poems in translation focuses on the secular poetry of Fortunatus, personal and political, complementing the companion volume by Brian Brennan, which concentrates on the poet's sacred and ecclesiastical writings. Within the constraints of a selection from the considerable works of the poet, this volume attempts to convey a sense of the range of Fortunatus' writing in formal and informal genres - epithalamium, consolation, and panegyric; and, at the same time, to include poems which offer insights into characters and relationships, into ways of life and work, and into details of daily life not otherwise available to us.

Some of the poems are written to clergy, but touch on aspects of general interest: the verses written for Bishop Vilicus of Metz for recitation at a meal (*Poem* 3.13), for example, or the description of the wonderful golden apples Fortunatus came upon on his visit to Aregius of Limoges (*Poem* 6.7). Other poems reflect friendships and links of patronage - with Conda, Sigibert's *domesticus* (*Poem* 7.16), or Gogo, the king's counsellor (*Poems* 6.8, 7.1); some long lasting ties (*Poems* 7.7 and 8 to Duke Lupus), some more transitory (*Poem* 6.9 to Dynamius of Marseilles). A variety of epitaphs records the lives and deaths of young and old, male and female; and a long consolation mourns the death in childbirth of the young Frankish woman, Vilithuta (*Poem* 4.26).

Most of Fortunatus' formal court poems are included here: the early epithalamium and panegyric to Sigibert and Brunhild in Metz (*Poem* 6.1 and 1a), the panegyric to Charibert in Paris (*Poem* 6.2), and a delicate consolation to the king's widowed aunt, Ultrogotha (*Poem* 6.6). There is the dramatic consolation for Galswinth, Brunhild's sister, married to Chilperic and murdered within weeks (*Poem* 6.5). A group of poems written in 580/1 also centre on Chilperic: the panegyric to the king, in effect defending Gregory of Tours from a charge of treason at the synod of Berny-Rivière (*Poem* 9.1), followed a few months later by consolations to the king and queen for the death of their two young sons in a dysentery epidemic, and by epitaphs for the princes (*Poems* 9.2-5). By 587 Chilperic was dead, and Fortunatus was addressing diplomatic eulogies to Childebert ll and Brunhild, now queen regent (*Poems* 10.8-9, *Appendix* 5-6).

Fortunatus' close friendship with Gregory of Tours, and with Radegund and Agnes is reflected in many of his poems. He thanks the bishop for gifts of apples and grafting slips, of skins and of a villa (*Poems* 5.13, 8.19 and 21), is thankful for his safe return (*Poems* 8.17-18), and writes Sapphic verses at Gregory's request (*Poem* 9.6-7).

The poet writes formally on Radegund's behalf to thank the Emperor Justin and the Empress Sophia for the relic of the Holy Cross (*Appendix* 2); *Appendix* 3 concludes correspondence with relatives at the Byzantine court. Other poems reflect her network of ecclesiastical contacts - Martin of Braga's advice about the adoption of the Rule of Caesarius (*Poem* 5.2), Fortunatus' rough winter journey to visit Domitianus of Angers, amongst others (*Poem* 11.25). Informal verses give vignettes of the daily life of the community and the friends; flowers on the altar at Easter (*Poem* 8.7), small gifts to each other (*Poems* 8.6, 11.13-14), celebratory meals (*Poems* 11.11 and 23, *Appendix* 10-11), and the verses written for these meals, not only by Fortunatus (*Appendix* 31).

Finally, two poems, written nearly twenty years apart, reflect Fortunatus' own perception of his standing and worth. *Poem* 6.8, written in somewhat unnerving surroundings soon after his arrival in Metz, stakes a claim for the importance of poetry and poet as part of civilised court life, contrasting interestingly with his assured declamation in the entourage of Childebert ll and Brunhild, as they sail down the Moselle in 587/8 (*Poem* 10.9).

The constraints of selection have meant that many interesting poems have had to be excluded, but I hope that readers will suffer no significant loss as a result. I have excluded poems to less central characters (such as Sigoald and Galactorius), and further poems to patrons who are already represented, where the poems add little further to our knowledge of that person or to our understanding of the poet's technique (such as *Poems* 8.2-4 to Gogo). The main difficulty was to select from the poems to Gregory, and to Radegund and Agnes. I would hope that the omissions in the case of Gregory will be largely rectified by Brian Brennan's volume, and that the 17 poems to the women which I have translated serve to give an adequate flavour of their lives and characters.

The text used is that of Leo in MGH AA 4.1, with indications given where I have differed from this myself or incorporated emendations from Reydellet's recent revised text and French translation of Books 1 - 4.

The annotations to the translation are intended to explain the nature of the texts translated and the relevant context, in historical, personal or literary terms. The purpose of this series of texts in translation is to make valuable source material more widely available. Being mindful of that purpose, I was also conscious that it is not only lack of facility with the language, but also lack of familiarity with the cultural roots of a text like this which can make it inaccessible to many a modern student - or inaccessible except at the most superficial level. So a classicist may feel impatient at the detail of the note on the poet Horace, or a biblical scholar at the notes on the Old Testament kings; but, given the centrality and resonance of such references for the poet, it seemed important to me to ensure that students from any academic background and experience should be able to gain insight into the whole range of what, for the poet and his readers at the time, lay behind his words, whether this stemmed from classical literature, biblical parables, Merovingian politics, Byzantine economics or whatsoever.

I have included a map and genealogy; and a selected bibliography of primary and secondary source material, which in some cases ranges more widely than the sources quoted in the text, for the convenience of readers who may want to explore certain topics further. The sources referred to frequently are listed in the Abbreviations at the front of the volume. In addition, I have included brief biographical details of the major characters referred to in the poems.

My warm thanks are due to Margaret Gibson and Robert Markus for their prompting and encouragement to undertake this work: to John Cowan and Inga Mantle for their patient support and advice: to Allan Hood and Jan Zwolkowski for their thoughtful and inspiring reflections on the draft version - the remaining mistakes and false judgements are entirely mine: and to Tim Slaughter for his technical assistance.

Edinburgh, September 1995   J.W.G.

Book Three

Poem 3.13: To Vilicus, Bishop of Metz[1]

With its dark stream the Moselle spreads forth its main[2], and the river softly rolls along its great waters; it laps the banks, scented with the verdant sward, and the wave gently washes the grassy blades. (5) Here, from the right, flows the river called the Seille, but it bears its waves along in a gentler stream; here, where it enters the Moselle with its clear course, it increases the other's force and itself comes to an end.
    Metz, established at this point, gleaming with splendour, (10) rejoices, both sides besieged by fish. The delightful domain is bright with flourishing fields; here you see tended crops, and there you behold roses. You look forth on hills clothed in shady vines, fertile growth of all kinds strives for place.
    (15) O city, exceedingly well fortified, girt with wall and river, you stand to flourish all the more through the merit of your bishop; Vilicus, who fights so well with heaven's weapons, prostrate on the ground, through his bended knee raises you on high. You cast yourself humbly to the earth for this reason, bountiful priest, (20) by praying you guide your country's capital[3] to the stars from here; by constant lamentation you win joy for your people; the sheep are gladdened by the tears of their shepherd[4]. However much the wicked

---

1 Vilicus was Bishop of Metz; see Duchesne, 3, p.55; N. Gauthier, *L'Évangelisme des pays de la Moselle* (Paris, 1980), pp. 209-211. The Bishop gave welcome support to the newly arrived poet; see *Poem* 6.8.22. Fortunatus may well have arrived in Gaul with letters of introduction from Italian bishops to their Gallic counterparts; see George, pp. 26-27.
2 The style echoes classical Latin nature writing, a compliment to the recipient, also emphasising Fortunatus' provenance and literary standing.
3 Metz was the capital of Sigibert's kingdom.
4 The following catalogue lists the conventional virtues of a good bishop, which reflect his role in Merovingian, as in other, times; protection and leadership of his people materially and spiritually, and charity towards strangers and the less fortunate. For the bishop's role, see Brennan (1983), ch. 2-4; Wood, pp. 71-87; van Dam, passim. For the literary reflection of

threatens with his vain blows, they for whom you are a wall fear no hurt, (25) and, though the wolf should lie in ambush for the encircling sheepfold[5], yet with you as protector of the flock no robber will do harm there. You delight the people with your serene and cloudless countenance, and pleasing kindness nourishes the spirits of all. If a new guest asks for sustenance, you offer food; (30) and he finds a home of his own under your roof. As you satisfy his needs, the exile[6] becomes all the less mindful of the wealth he has in his own country. You take lamentation from the lips of him who tells you his hurts, and, bringing back joyfulness, you banish all sorrows. (35) Here you clothe the naked, there you feed the needy; the beggar gives nothing to you in return, God gives it in love. You lay up granaries ready in advance better than by hoarding the stored grain; the wealth you thus bestow Paradise grants you[7]. You have restored the lofty places of the temples, Vilicus the builder; (40) when the Lord comes, behold your labours stand forth. I see that you have not buried the talent which was entrusted to you[8], but rather the task has been taken on and multiplied. May you continue such worthy works long throughout the years as they stretch ahead, and may your name remain for ever, noble one.

---

these virtues in Fortunatus' poems, see George, pp. 106-131. The imagery here uses the biblical motif of the shepherd defending his sheep (e.g. John, 10.11-16), but with a classical turn of phrase (see note 4), and a suggestion of the classical rhetorical motif of the wall of defence; for architectural symbolism, see E. Baldwin-Smith, *Architectural symbolism of imperial Rome and the middle ages* (New York, 1978).
5 Cf. Vergil, *Aen.* 11.59.
6 Perhaps a reference to Fortunatus' own condition and an indirect compliment on the bishop's hospitality to him; cf. the poet's reference to himself as an exile in *Poem* 7.9.7.
7 The thought, common in these poems as elsewhere, is that what is given away in charity belongs all the more to the giver, since it secures him a place in heaven and awaits him there; see Matth. 19.21, and cf. e.g. *Poem* 4.26.69-76.
8 For the parable of the talents, see Matth. 25.14-30.

a. to the same[9]

Noble shepherd of the sheep, your sustenance benefits all; how well do you sustain their bodies, who also satisfy their souls! You make your guests so eager for the nectar of your milk, that a bowl must refresh them instead of the usual spoon.

b. to the same

The sheep runs, seeking its pasture from you, O shepherd; you who are wont to be nourishment, grant me the sustenance of bread.

c. about the painting of a vine on his table

The bird luxuriates under the vine shoot with intertwining tendrils, and daintily pecks the painted feast with its beak. The guest deserved a feast of many courses; here he gazes upon the grapes, there he drinks Falernian wine[10].

d. about the fish on this table

Your nets, father, are overflowing with heavy fish; it seems that you have merited the part of Peter[11].

---

9 These short verses may well have been composed for recitation after a meal, for the enjoyment of the guests. *Poems* 11.11 and 23 seem to refer to such occasions; *Poem* 7.24 (c) calls for contributions, and *Poem* 11.23(a), *Appendix* 10, 11, and 31 refer to such verses. They do not have the biting wit and the twist in the ending so characteristic of the great epigrams of Martial, or, to a lesser extent, of the later ones of Ausonius, with which Fortunatus may well have been familiar; but they are neatly rounded expressions of a compliment to the host, of an appropriate moral, or of a humorous play on words.
10 This is a very classical tribute to a Gallo-Roman. Falernian, a famous Italian wine, appears regularly in Roman poetry and epigram. See R. G. M. Nisbet and M. Hubbard, *A commentary on Horace Odes, Book I* (Oxford, 1970), note on *Odes* 1.20.9.
11 Peter, the first apostle, was a fisherman, called by Jesus to follow him and be a "fisher of men"; see Matth. 4.18-19.

Book Four[1]

Poem 4.16: epitaph for Atticus[2]

Though a long life may be led in due course by an old man, when the end comes, nothing can prevail longer[3]. But since no-one escapes the return of dust to dust, one single fate carries off all mankind under this ordinance. (5) In this lowly tomb lies that lofty Atticus, who used to bestow sweet honey with his eloquence, plying his gentle tongue with pleasing harmony; his peace-making speech healed all. Gaul revered his abundant wisdom, (10) and always held this old man in its esteem as a father. Distinguished by his ancestors, the hope of the highest nobility, satisfied with what he had, he was never rapacious; holding doctrine in abundance in his heart, like a chest holding books, anyone drunk of whatever he wished from this brimming fountain; (15) wise in counsel, devout in spirit, of cheerful aspect, so that he was everyone's father in love. He was generous in giving to the venerable temples and to the needy, so that he might send to heaven the wealth he sought to gain[4].

---

1 Book Four contains epitaphs, written for inscription on a tomb or for painting on the wall by a tomb. There is one consolation, *Poem* 4.26, and for that literary tradition, see the note ad loc. For epitaphs of this period, see E. Diehl, *Inscriptiones Latinae Christianae veteres*, 1 (Berlin, 1925); Le Blant, passim; - , *L'epigraphie chrétienne en Gaule et dans l'Afrique romaine* (Paris, 1890); - (ed.), *Nouveau receuil des inscriptions chrétiennes de la Gaule anterieures au Vllle siècle* (Paris, 1892); R. Lattimore, *Themes in Greek and Latin Epitaphs*, Illinois Studies in Language and Literature 28 (Urbana, 1942), pp. 124-5. See also, especially for evidence of skilled craftsmen and use of fine materials at this period, Salin, 2, pp. 131-181; R. Favreau, *Les inscriptions médiévales* (Turnhaut, 1979). For Fortunatus' epitaphs and consolations, see George, pp. 85-105. For the influence on him of earlier writers in the genre, see Blomgren (1973): S. Kopp, *Ein neues Elogium von Venantius Fortunatus* (Wurzburg, 1939).
2 Atticus is not otherwise known. Stroheker, p. 149, no. 44, deduces from the phrase "wise in counsel" that he had occupied some elevated position. But, as Reydellet (1994) observes in note 65 on this passage, the context makes it clear that these tributes are to qualities of character, and not of status.
3 For the common motif of the inevitability of death, see von Moos, *Testimonien*, T526-551, 597-619.
4 See *Poem* 3.13, note 7, for this thought.

Poem 4.17: epitaph for the young man, Arcadius [5].

Everything good passes away speedily with the flight of time; death snatches all the more at what it sees promises delight. Here lies the boy Arcadius, come from senatorial stock[6], snatched from the world by the hastening day. (5) His youthful age had so well taken on self-discipline that a old man was emerging from those tender years[7]. Of flowing eloquence, pleasing with his radiant aspect, even as a boy, a novice in craft, he conquered the practised masters. Beauty, where are you hurrying me in recalling the buried youth? (10) If you bring the various traits to mind, the more you lead me to lament. But since he died unstained by any base act, no-one should mourn him whom Paradise holds[8].

Poem 4.19: epitaph for Aracharius[9]

The earth does not sustain any loss in giving birth; she takes back the body she gave, destined for the dust. Here is laid Aracharius, as his life span declined, who was snatched from the world as he completed thirty years. (5) He was resplendent in glory at the royal court, and merited being held in the king's serene love. He has

---

5 Stroheker, p. 147, no. 30, suggests that Arcadius came from a senatorial family of the Auvergne. G. de Maillé, *Recherches sur les origines chrétiennes de Bordeaux* (Paris, 1959), p.82, argues that he was son of Bishop Leontius of Bordeaux and his wife, Placidina, on the grounds that Placidina's father had the same name. In that case, the boy must have been born by 548/549, the date of Leontius' accession, the bishop having led a celibate life in that elevated status (Fortunatus, *Poem* 1.15.94). He would thus have been about 28 at the time of his death; lines 7-8 suggest he had already received a training in rhetoric, and the young/old motif may put an exaggerated emphasis on his youth.
6 For the title and status of senator, see Brennan (1985); F. Gilliard, "The senators of sixth century Gaul", *Speculum* 54 (1979), pp. 685-697.
7 For the rhetorical motif of young/old, see E. R. Curtius, *European literature and the Latin Middle Ages*, tr. W. R. Trask (New York, 1953), pp. 170 ff.
8 For the motif that mourning is inappropriate, see von Moos, *Testimonien* T625; that heaven is assured, T956-962.
9 Aracharius is not otherwise known. Lines 5-6 suggest that he was one of the youths of noble family, sent to be brought up at court; see Riché, pp. 236-240.

restored to the world all he took from it; yet he possesses alone for himself his good deeds[10].

Poem 4.20: epitaph for Brumachius[11]

You, whoever you are, you wish to know whose ashes are buried in this grave; Brumachius was once glorious and powerful upon this earth. As he performed the task of envoy with discretion and eloquence, hostile fortune carried him off as he was returning home. (5) He died in Italy, but his wife Frigia in her love brought her dear husband's body here. She cared for him as though he were alive, for her husband's shade was dear to her; even the very ashes are treasured by faithful wives. He lived in this world for forty years; (10) then he died and a small tomb covers a great man.

Poem 4.22: epitaph for the innocents

Here in this tomb lie young brothers, who should not be mourned, for a blessed life has made them men without sin. Born of the same womb, they are buried in like fate, and a single light[12] encompasses the two, brought forth together. (5) Bathed in the holy font, he departed first in white garments[13]; the other is led before God as he completes his fifth year. The first was duly named John, the second, Patrick, was of greater accomplishment; many signs declared themselves about his merits; (10) blessed spirits, which offer devout prayers! For their blessed mother rests here, who merited to enjoy the light through their birth[14].

---

10 For this thought, see *Poem* 3.13, note 7.
11 Brumachius is not otherwise known. For an embassy such as Brumachius may have been travelling on, see Gregory, *HF*, 4.40.
12 I.e. the light of heaven.
13 I.e. he had been baptised.
14 For justification of women being their reproductive role, see G. Clark, *Women in Antiquity: pagan and Christian lifestyles* (Oxford, 1993), pp. 119-138; for the wider context of attitude and belief, see P. Brown, *The body and society: men, women and sexual renunciation in early Christianity* (New York, 1988), passim.

Poem 4.25: epitaph for Queen Theudechild[15]

Though she was already guiding her years in the lessening strength of old age, she, who was the hope of many, was yet snatched away abruptly. If prayers could have averted[16] what nature destined, the people would have won her continued existence for them by their tears. (5) What great happiness for the needy has been confined beneath that mound, and how many wishes did a single day steal from the people! Here lies Theudechild, a glorious nobility resplendent with the light of her ancestry, as her last day hastened upon her. Her brother, father, husband, grandfather and forebears[17] (10) were a royal line, of successive eminence. The orphan, the exile, the needy, the widows and the naked, lying prostrate, mourn that they have buried here a mother, food and clothing. One single action pleased her who was a repository of abundant wealth; she gave everything before she was asked for help, (15) concealing her giving from her family lest they should forbid it; but what she gave secretly, she proclaims[18] with the Judge[19] as her witness; builder of the temples of the Lord, bestowing goodly gifts, considering hers to be what the needy had[20]. The one fate is to die and to return, dust to dust[21]; (20) blessed is she whose day is unending for her merits! Zealously devoted to such deeds, translated into eternal light, she lived, an ornament on this earth, for seventy five years.

---

15 For Theudechild, see Biographical Notes.
16 The classical dignity is reinforced by the echo of Vergil here in line 3 (cf.*Aen.* 2.689) and of Ovid in line 6 (cf. *Pont.* 1.2.4).
17 See Biographical Note on Theudechild for their identity.
18 Reydellet (1994), note 87 *ad loc.*, argues convincingly for this reading, against Leo's suggested emendation to *dedit* (gave); the contrast is between her secret action on earth and her open declaration of it in heaven.
19 I.e. God, who will sit in judgement on all men; see, e.g., Romans, 14.10.
20 See *Poem* 3.13, note 7, for this thought.
21 See note 3 above.

Poem 4.26: epitaph[22] for Vilithuta[23]

All good things are swift passing[24], the joys of the world are fleeting; they are made manifest upon the earth and perish, speedily passing away. So that grief may gain intensity as it destroys one who loves, it first creates happiness, and then bears down all the harder. (5) Alas for life's sorrow, alas for man's wretched lot! Why do you create what will bring happiness, when you snatch it away to cause grief? Noble Vilithuta, dear wife of Dagaulf, lies torn from her husband's embrace. Joined with him in body on the marriage bed, she was bound to her husband yet more closely in affection; (10) at the day's end love broke asunder those bonds. For her for whom time could still remain in the prime of life, a bitter end overwhelms the start of life.

Born of noble blood in the city of Paris, she was Roman by upbringing, barbarian by race. (15) She brought a gentle spirit from a

---

22 From this poem's length as well as its structure, it is clearly a consolation, and not an epitaph. For this genre, see R. Cassel, *Untersuchungen zur Griechischen und Romischen Konsolationsliteratur* (Munich, 1958); C. Favez, *La consolation latine chrétienne* (Paris, 1957); R. Lattimore, *Themes in Greek and Latin epitaphs*, Illinois Studies in Language and Literature 28 (Urbana, 1942), especially pp. 215-265. On the motifs and stylistic conventions of consolations, see Curtius, pp. 80-2; von Moos, passim. For discussion of this poem, see George, pp. 93-94. The poem falls into the three formal sections of a consolation: *laudatio* (lines 1-46), *lamentatio* (lines 47-67); *consolatio* (lines 68-160). G. Davis suggests that, whilst the structure of prose lamentation is inflexible and conservative, that of verse lamentation has more flexibility, and can fruitfully be analysed as a dialogue with the bereaved, responding creatively to their emotional state; see *'Ad sidera notus*; strategies of lament and consolation in Fortunatus' *De Gelsuintha"*, *Agon* l (1967), pp. 118-134. This poem significantly develops the third section, almost as a sermon on the rewards in the afterlife for virtue on earth, though the two earlier sections are still substantial.
23 We know nothing else of Vilithuta and her family, unless the Dagaulf of *Appendix* 9.15-18, who wants to drink "bitter beer", is her husband. The reference to Radegund and Agnes in line 97 suggests that the couple were well known to the community at Poitiers. This reference also suggests a date for the poem after the death of Radegund in 587 (Gregory,*HF*, 9.2) and of Agnes before 589 (Gregory,*HF*, 9. 39). The compliment on her Roman upbringing (line 14) and Dagaulf's education (line 40) is reinforced by common motifs of classical consolation (see note 17), and by echoes of classical writers (line 1, cf. Martial, *Ep.* 7.47.11; line 17, cf. Iuvencus, *hist. ev.* 1.165; line 45, cf. Sedulius, *Carm. Pasch.* 2.63; line 91, cf. ibid. 4.165; line 92, cf. Vergil,*Aen.* 9.503; line 144, cf. Vergil,*Aen.* 6.128; line 129, cf. Iuvencus, *hist. ev.* 3.15.
24 For this motif, see von Moos, *Testimonien*, T625.

fierce race; the greater glory was to conquer nature. Never staying downcast, bearing in her expression fresh joys, she was joyful at heart, chasing clouds from her brow. Her aspect, wreathed in beauty, radiated brightness from her face, (20) and her comely shape gave forth its own splendour. In beauty she surpassed the other girls in her lineage, with a milk-white neck and rosy cheeks.

Glorious to behold, she was yet more resplendent in spirit, worthily illustrious in mind and no less in devoutness. (25) Though she had no close relative in this region, by her service she became a unique mother to all, intent upon godly welldoing, ministering food, and by that merit seeing that she had satisfied herself all the more. These gifts bring it about that she who gave them also lives after death[25]; (30) man's form perishes, but his good deeds remain. Bodies will be dust, and a godly spirit flourishes for ever; everything perishes save the love of God.

An orphan, she grew up in the care of her noble grandmother, and, though a granddaughter, was brought up as a daughter. (35) When the thirteenth year of life had first welcomed her, she was united and given into the care of the man she wished, in whose own lineage lofty nobility was resplendent, and a further glory is added through his own merits. He was a gentle youth, joyful, lively and graced with learning; (40) what nature was unable to provide, education readily supplied.

Yet they only merited to remain three years in this union, to enjoy their marriage, their hearts binding them. Both were alike in spirit, wishes, hopes, character and actions, and vied with each other in mind, grace and faith.

(45) Then at full term she came to childbed and gave birth to a child; pregnant with her own doom, she died in labour[26]. Hostile death snatched away unexpectedly her young form, for she had only lived to her seventeenth year. Thus in bearing a life, she was robbed of her own, (50) bringing hope forth to the light as the light failed her. But the childbirth gave a sorrowful example to the parent; the family line failed at the point at which it is wont to move forward. Wishing

---

25 For the assurance of life after death, see von Moos, T1507-1510.
26 For a useful review of perinatal problems, see G. Clark, *Women in late antiquity: pagan and Christian lifestyles* (Oxford, 1993), pp. 81-88. See also B. Rawson, ed., *Marriage, divorce and children in ancient Rome* (Oxford, 1991), pp. 7-17.

to be a father, one of three, alas, he finds himself alone; where the number should have increased, lo, it declined. (55) For the child died with its mother, buried by being born, gaining no hold on life, born in the jaws of death. On their own, they were more, if they had been without offspring then; an added child took away what there was. He was born with illfated auspices through his mother's death (60) and his mother the cause of the child's end. The one was caught up in the doomed fate of the other, and both mutually brought death upon each other. But the father and husband in his grief felt all the more intensely, for in one death he grieved for burying two. (65) He thus wept tears for the burial of a child scarce born, he saw what he should mourn, not what love should possess. To him his wife, snatched from him, bestowed upon him a burden of sorrow; married briefly, she gave him long-lasting tears.

Nevertheless the husband has this consolation[27] for his spouse, (70) that her labour is not without reward. For anything which could be seen as female adornment, she gave readily to the churches and to the poor. She left nothing here of those matters which will come to nothing, so now she has rich treasures laid up in advance[28]. (75) By giving her wealth away, how well did she prevent it from being taken from her! For what she gave generously, she nows reaps in abundance[29]. Thus whatever she handed to a needy person she laid up for herself, and that food which the starving received, that she herself[30] now has.

Blessed are those whom a second death does not oppress[31], (80) and who do not cause their bodies to be subjected to savage punishment! He who does not lay up calamity for himself through sweet temptations, and is unwilling to bury his soul through his body; but abiding in spotless virtue without sin in life, he buys in this light below the prize of that light above. (85) In how short a time does he either gain grievous sorrows or, if his life is glorious, win long happiness!

---

27 For this consolatory motif, see von Moos, *Testimonien*, T510. For this use of *consultum* instead of *consolatio*, see Leo, *Index*, p. 396; S. Blomgren, *SF*, p. 147.
28 For this sentiment, see *Poem* 3.13, note 7.
29 For this sentiment, see *Poem* 3.13, note 7.
30 Reading, with Leo, *ipsa* for *illa*.
31 For a "second death", see Revelation, 20.6.

The sorrow occasioned by this death is trifling; for that is more harrowing, he whom black Tartarus holds whilst he is yet alive. Wretched is any who has practised sinful deeds, (90) who sees himself caught in snares before the Redeemer, when the Judge of the world comes[32], carried on clouds, and the dread trumpet arouses the hosts of heaven[33]! On this chariot comes Elijah[34], on that Enoch[35], here Peter[36] leads his people, and here Stephen[37]; (95) with the flower of maidens encircling her with a crown of roses, Mary[38] is first amongst the choir of virgins; here is our mother[39], here Agnes[40], the bride of Christ, sweet Thecla[41], Agatha[42] and all who have found favour with God by their

---

32 Cf. Matth. 14.36-43; 20.28-30; 24.29-31; 25.31-33. For this motif, see von Moos, *Testimonien*, T881-4; R. Lattimore, op. cit., pp. 313-314.
33 The trumpet which sounds on the last day, to announce the coming of God in judgement.
34 Elijah was one of the great prophets of the Old Testament, precursor of John the Baptist, foretelling the coming of Christ; see 1 and 2 Kings.
35 Enoch was the son of Cain (Genesis, 4.17), and, for his godliness, translated by God, i.e. removed from this life without dying (Genesis, 5.24; Hebrews, 11.5).
36 Peter, first of the apostles, was a fisherman called by Jesus to be a "fisher of men" (Matth. 4.18-19). Originally called Simon, he was given an Aramaic title by Jesus which means "rock", of which the Greek equivalent becomes "Peter". The title is explained by Jesus' statement that Peter was the rock upon which He would build his church, conferring on him "the keys of the kingdom of heaven" and the power of "binding and loosing" (Matth. 16.16-19; 18.18). He was the leader of the early Christian community after Jesus' death (see Acts of the Apostles), making missionary and pastoral visits to Samaria, Antioch and other places. A tradition tells how he eventually went to Rome, and was crucified there.
37 Stephen was the first Christian martyr (Acts of the Apostles, 6.8-7.60).
38 The mother of Christ.
39 I.e. Radegund. This reference suggests a date for the poem after her death in 587.
40 Agnes, died c. 340, was one of the most famous early Christian martyrs. Even the earliest accounts of her are confused and contradictory; but a common thread is that she refused marriage as a young girl, offered herself for martyrdom when persecution broke out, and died by being stabbed through the throat. Her inclusion with Thecla and the others suggest that this is the Agnes referred to; the conjunction with Radegund suggests that Fortunatus also had the Poitiers Agnes in mind. She died shortly after Radegund; see Biographical Notes, and Gregory, *HF*, 10. 15).
41 Thecla, according to an apocryphal *Acts of St. Paul*, was a first century martyr of Iconium, converted by St. Paul. She spent most of her life in seclusion near Seleucia, and was saved from persecution at the age of ninety by the rock of her cave opening to receive her. Veneration of this saint was widespread, and her cave a favourite place of pilgrimage.
42 Agatha, possibly 3rd century, and possibly the virgin martyr from Catania in Sicily who was venerated from an early time. There are various versions of her story, telling, in general, how she was pursued by a man of consular rank, was charged by him of being a Christian when she rejected him, and died after torture.

virginity[43]. Then what fear do the heavens hold there with that senate standing by? (100) What of the soul who will speak in the presence of the Judge? Shortly either punishment awaits the wretched or a palm the blessed; each reaps the seed sown in his life[44]. Some there will be who will say 'Fall, mountain, and crush my body'[45], but the hills at this bidding refuse to afford a tomb. (105) The humblest will be compelled to pay their mite[46]; no-one takes his foot from the paths where his misdeeds lead. Bereft of hope, they will be cast like chaff into the fires[47], our flesh becomes food for the flames to feed upon. They live for punishment in the everlasting fiery furnace[48]; (110) that it may torment the more cruelly, evil death does not die. The flaming stream, alas, affords no water, so that the exhausted folk cannot refresh their souls, burned in the lasting fire.

In another part, dwelling in the heights through blessed merits, the just will be as glorious as the sun in heaven's vault[49]. (115) The worthy have light, the damned bewail the flames, the bright light nourishes those, the heat of the fire roasts these. It is the same substance indeed, but divided into two uses; for it burns the unworthy with the same fire by which it proves the good[50]. The blessed are resplendent in the everlasting light of Paradise, (120) dwelling in His kingdom in the presence of Christ. How great a grace abides for him who has looked upon that countenance! How great an honour for man to be able to see God! (125) Lilies, narcissi, violets, roses, nard and balsam, all the Arab produces with fragrant buds, bloom in the face of the Judge, glorious lights; but the scent of the Lord breathes yet more sweetly than all of these. For by as much as the gleam of gold is better than murky lead, (130) so incense and scent of any kind yield before God. As day is different from night, and the sun from the moon's light, so his creations give place before their Creator. When the just enjoy such glory, they rejoice greatly that they are freed from death.

---

43 On female virginity, see P. Brown, op. cit., passim; G. Clark, op.cit., pp. 119-138; A. Poucelle, tr. F. Pheasant, *Porneia: on desire and the body in antiquity* (Oxford, 1988), pp. 129-159.
44 See Galatians, 6.7.
45 See Hosea, 10.8; Luke, 23.30.
46 See Matth. 5.26; Luke, 12.59.
47 See Matth. 3.12; Luke, 3.17.
48 See Matth. 13.42.
49 See Matth. 13.43.
50 See Malachi, 3.2; 1 Peter, 1.7.

(135) They rejoice in everlasting light that they have come from the darkness, and bewail the fact rather that they have come tardily to so many blessings.

You too must not chafe with tears at the godly fate of your wife[51], for to her we can believe now that better things are here granted. For if you mourn her who lives through the highest merit, (140) you yourself will envy the blessings of your wife, especially since you declare that she who was joined to you in feeling, in mind and in body, had always been joined to Christ in heart. If commanded to return to you after beholding the Lord, she would weep at retracing her path back into this world. (145) She clings to that day with more love which she cannot lose, than that which she feared with its inevitable end. Do not bear heavily the death which Nature brings to all, which the beggar shares with princes[52]. Neither poverty nor abundant means rescue anyone; (150) the rich and the pauper alike have this in common. For boy and old man, black and white, wicked and honourable, weak and strong, gentle and fierce, all die. Wise and foolish, good and bad[53], one and all, stout and small, short and tall, all come to this. (155) That fate touches all, more quickly or more slowly, a single death carries off men with their differing merits. So it is not fitting that you should weep bitterly for your wife, of whose merits you say you yourself have no doubt[54]. Greatly blessed are they who here begin to live without sin[55], (160) who learn all the better how to live after death!

Poem 4.28: *epitaph for Eusebia*[56]

If her parents were able to write down their sufferings through their tears, in place of a picture weeping would here serve as a text. But because the eye does not mark the lover's name with its waters, my

---

51 For this motif of assurance of heavenly happiness, see von Moos, *Testimonien*, T956-62.
52 For the motif that all men must die, see von Moos, *Anmerkungen*, A410; *Testimonien*, 526-551, 597-614.
53 This verse is incomplete in all manuscripts. Brower's text is adopted here, reading *huc sapiens stolidus, (huc et) probus inprobus, omnis* ....
54 For the inappropriateness of grief, see von Moos, *Testimonien* T625.
55 For *praeesse* used in the sense of *prius vivere*, see S. Blomgren, *SF*, p.190.
56 For Eusebia, see Stroheker, p. 169, no. 126.

hand is drawn to follow where grief urges it to go. (5) Here, dark stone, you cover the radiant limbs of noble Eusebia, whose fate is the fearful tomb. By her abilities and the beauty of her form, Minerva[57] was surpassed in dexterity, Venus[58] in grace. Skilled at holding a shuttle[59], and also at marking out the patterns in thread, (10) a web was to her what a sheet of paper is to you. Already promised in marriage to sweet Eusebius, this young girl was fated to live scarce ten years. That you wonder at a young woman, she surpassed a mature woman's sense; she had outstripped herself, as though she was not to remain for long. (15) Her father[60], who has lost daughter and son-in-law, is bowed low; she has died and passed away, he survives and is finished. Yet may it be a comfort, that you are not dead in Christ; a virgin[61], taken to God, you will live beyond the grave.

---

[57] The Roman goddess of skill and knowledge.
[58] The Roman goddess of love and beauty.
[59] Though Riché, p. 222, translates this as "as skilful with the pen as with weaving", this meaning seems more accurate.
[60] Lit. "father-in-law", to emphasise the double loss for him.
[61] Fortunatus, *Poem* 9.2, sects. 4, 13-14, is explicit that the girl in this case, like Eusebia, has avoided the double guilt, of original sin, and of inheriting the sin of Eve's wrongdoing (Genesis, 3), by dying so young. Christ has redeemed all mankind from the former; her virginity has saved her from the latter, and she will thus win eternal life. See note 32 above on female virginity.

Book Five

Poem 5.2: to Martin, Bishop of Galicia[1]

When the single Trinity[2] spread the apostolic light[3] and the earth through this blessing received a new day, so that the light of generation put[4] to flight the darkness of the soul, and the mind, given sight, absorbed clear-shining faith, (5) the capital city of Romulus is restored[5], the tares removed[6], tilled by the plough of the noble leader,

---

1 For Bishop Martin of Braga, see Biographical Notes. Martin had close connections with Gaul, and with the diocese of Tours in particular; he was the author of the verses over the south portal of St. Martin's church in Tours, and gave support to Radegund (see Gregory, *HF*, 5.37: Fortunatus, *Poems*, 5.1.10, 5.2.63-70. Fortunatus' letter to Martin, *Poem* 5.1, was in reply to one from Martin. Their correspondence seems to have been about Radegund's adoption of the Rule of Caesarius for her community, and this poem thanks Martin for his advice (lines 63-70). For the Rule, see note 26 below.
This poem is in the rhetorical tradition of royal panegyrics, and, like *Appendix* 2, is a *gratiarum actio*, a formal thanksgiving. For this tradition, see T. C. Burgess, "Epideictic literature", *Studies in Classical Philology* 3 (1902), pp. 89-142; Alan Cameron, *Claudian: poetry and propaganda at the court of Honorius* (Oxford, 1970); Averil Cameron, *Christianity and the rhetoric of empire. The development of Christian discourse* (California, 1991); Godman, pp. 21- 37; G. A. Kennedy, *Classical rhetoric and its Christian and secular tradition from ancient to modern times* (London, 1980), pp. 3-181; MacCormack (1972); - (1975); - , (1981); T. Nissen, "Historisches Epos und Panegyrikos in der Spätantike", *Hermes* 75 (1940), pp. 298-325; L. B. Struthers, "The rhetorical structure of the encomia of Claudius Claudian", *Harvard Studies in Classical Philology* 30 (1919), pp. 49-81. For discussion of Fortunatus' adaptation of the royal panegyric for episcopal eulogy, see George, pp. 62-79, and for this poem in particular, pp. 67-69.
2 Note the immediate emphasis on Trinitarian orthodoxy, particularly pertinent in addressing a bishop who had achieved the conversion of the king and his entire people to Catholicism from the heresy of Arianism.
3 Note the imagery of light throughout the poem. This is not the sun motif of traditional royal panegyric; see MacCormack (1981), pp. 17, 251, notes 21 and 113. This light is the light of the New Testament, of Christ who is the light of the world; for the use of this imagery in a Christian context, see MacCormack, op.cit, pp. 66, 177, note 53.
4 The image of lifegiving light introduces the motif, found throughout the poem, of growth and fertility, an image which echoes biblical imagery and parables.
5 I.e Rome. See note 2, for the establishment of Trinitarian orthodoxy by Martin, as part of the doctrine of the Catholic Church, centred on Rome.
6 For the parable of the sower, see Matth. 13.18-43. The images of growth lead appropriately into a passage about the great missionary expansion of the Church.

Peter[7]; Paul[8], penetrating through the Scythian frosts to the Illyrians, melted the earth's chill by his fervent doctrine: Matthew[9] cooled the Ethiopian heat with his words (10) and poured forth living waters on the parched earth; the warlike turban of the Persian, bowed by Thomas[10,] might, is made all the stronger, conquered by God; sallow India is given to the far-sighted Bartholomew[11]; Achaia's harvest stands through the guidance of Andrew[12]. (15) To make haste and brook no delay, Gaul of Martin[13] of old took on the arms of light with outstanding faith. Saved by a new Martin, Galicia, give your applause; that man of yours is of apostolic stature. He is a Peter to you in courage, a Paul in doctrine, (20) giving you both the support of a Jacob[14], and also of a John[15]. Coming, they say, from Roman

---

7 For Peter, see *Poem* 4. 26, note 28.
8 Paul, though not one of the apostles, was converted miraculously from being a vigorous persecutor of the early Christians, and become the foremost missionary and evangelist for the faith, travelling to Cyprus, Asia Minor, Syria, Macdonia and Greece. He also wrote extensively to the young Christian communities, though there is debate about the authorship of all the letters in the New Testament traditionally attributed to him.
9 Matthew, apostle, evangelist and gospel writer, is variously reported to have been martyred in Ethiopia, Persia, and elsewhere.
10 Thomas was also one of the apostles, famed as "doubting Thomas" (John 20. 24 - 29). The strongest early tradition about the missionary activities of Thomas, in the 3rd/4th century *Acts of Thomas*, depict him as evangelist of India, and of Kerala in particular. Other sources speak of him evangelizing Parthia (Persia), and in the fourth century his relics were claimed to be at Edessa in Mesopotamia.
11 Nothing certain is known about Bartholomew except that he was called to be one of the twelve apostles (see Matth. 10.3). It is possible that he was the same man as Nathanael (see John 1.45-51, 21.2). He is later associated with evangelism in Lycaonia, in India, but mostly in Armenia, where he is said to have been martyred by being flayed alive.
12 Andrew, the first disciple with his brother, Peter (Mark 1.16-18), is mentioned several times in the gospels, but accounts of his later life are unreliable. He is associated with Scythia and Epirus, and is said to have been martyred in Achaia.
13 For Martin of Tours, see Biographical Notes. Martin was a central influence on all involved in the context of this eulogy; like Martin of Braga, he too was a Pannonian by birth, and, as Fortunatus emphasises, was the forerunner of this further evangelical work in the west; for Gregory of Tours, he was the archetypal bishop, as well as the focus of the great national cult centred in Tours; for Fortunatus himself, he had been the cause of the poet's journey to Gaul in the first place, the poet having been cured of an eye infection by the saint and having decided to make a pilgrimage of thanks to the saint's shrine in Gaul (see Fortunatus, *Vita Martini* 4.630-80, 686-701). Fortunatus wrote a metrical version of Sulpicius Severus' hagiography of Martin, and also wrote poems in celebration of Gregory's work on buildings dedicated to St. Martin (*Poems* 1.5, 2.3, 10.6). See M. Vieillard-Troiekouroff, *Les monuments religieux de la Gaule d'après les oeuvres de Grégoire de Tours* (Paris, 1976), pp. 304-28.
14 Jacob was son of Isaac; see Genesis, 25, 27-37, 42-50.

Pannonia, he was made the salvation of Galicia. He sowed the seeds of life in the barren furrow, where the harvest, come to ripeness, delights with its abundance. (25) Through the merits of an Elijah[16], a second rain falls upon the crop, bringing the blessings of dew, lest drought overcome the fields; and, so that the parched acres do not lie in inert furrows, he waters them with a spring of everlasting running water. He grafted the goodly shoots of faith on the branches of heresy, (30) and the rich olive tree flourishes where was once a wild oleaster[17]. The meagre tree which stood bereft of leaves, now flowers in new glory, to produce sustenance. The sad fig tree, doomed without hope to be put on the kitchen fire, nourished with dung, readies its crannies for fruit. (35) The grapes swelling on the vine, likely to be torn down by the birds' pillaging, with this good guardian are not lost, not one, for the vat. The vine dresser orders the rows in apostolic manner, turning the earth with his hoe, and cutting the shoots back with his pruning hook. He cuts the fruitless wild vines out of the Lord's field, (40) and there are clusters of grapes where once were shrubs. He tore up the bitter tares[18] from God's sowing, and the fruitful harvest springs up evenly.

Applaud[19], Galicia, saved by this new Martin; this man of yours was of apostolic stature. (45) Tracing his steps around his fold with shepherd's zeal[20], he guards over his flock lovingly, lest the wolf come among the sheep; he himself, his arms bearing the sheep, brings

---

15 The reference is probably to John the Baptist, rather than John the Evangelist; cf. *Poem* 9.1.35 - 40. John was the cousin and forerunner of Jesus. Appearing in about 27 A.D. as an itinerant preacher, he called for baptism and the repentance of sins, Jesus being amongst those he baptised. Shortly after he was arrested by Herod and executed at the request of Salome. See Luke 1. 5-23, 7.19-29; John 1.29 -36; Matth. 14.1-12.

16 Elijah was one of the great Old Testament prophets. He foreshadowed the coming of Christ in Old Testament times; he announced to King Ahab God's decision to send drought in response to Ahab's wickedness, and vanquished the false prophets of Baal by summoning up rain through God's help to end the drought (1 Kings 17-18). He was translated (i.e. taken from this life without dying) by a chariot of fire (2 Kings, 2.11), and appeared at Christ's transfiguration (Matth. 17.1-13).

17 These images of fertility have New Testament associations; for the olive tree, see Romans, 11.17; for the fig tree, see Matth. 21.18-22, 7.16-18, Luke 13.6-9; for grapes, Christ spoke of himself as the vine of life, and the kingdom of heaven is likened to a landowner in his vineyard (Matth. 20.1-16); cf. also Matth. 21.33-41.

18 See note 6 above.

19 This apostrophe to Gallicia is repeated, almost as a refrain, in lines 17-18 and 43-4. The call to applaud is a purely literary device, but yet pays the tribute of the panegyric motif of universal acclaim to the great bishop. For the motif of *consensus* see MacCormack (1981), pp. 21, 46-8.

20 For this biblical image, see, for example, Luke 15.3-6,

it to the nourishment of Christ, lest its uncertain wandering over the mountainside bring it to destruction. His voice, overflowing from the fount which brings salvation to the people, (50) offers salt[21] on his lips, that they take in faith by their hearing. Indeed he fulfills the solemn vows made to the Lord, inflicting an injury on the enemy, and returns twofold the talents entrusted to him[22], the goodly workman attending to the voice of the evangelist, that it should be said to him, "Go forth, good servant; (55) insofar as you have been faithful to me in small matters, you will be set over great ones. Behold, now enter in more joyfully upon the delights of your Lord, and the great rewards stored up for you for your small labours!"

You will hear that blessed voice, Martin, (60) but be mindful yourself of your Fortunatus. Pray, I beg you, father, that I witness your joys with you; may you thus be pleasing to the King, as Peter[23] opens the gate. Agnes[24], with humble Radegund[25], in supplication begs you, noble one, that they be commended to you, holy father: (65) and, as the chorus swells with the sisters' holy singing, may they please their Lord, with you as their gentle leader; and may the bountiful Rule of noble Bishop Caesarius[26] from the city of Genesius[27] be adopted and observed by them; Caesarius who became Bishop of Arles from the ranks of Lerins[28], (70) and who remained a monk, a glory to the bishopric.

---

21 Salt is a common biblical and classical metaphor for wit and wisdom.
22 See the parable of the talents, Luke, 19.12-27.
23 See *Poem* 4.26, note 28.
24 Agnes was adopted by Radegund and brought up as her daughter, and then appointed as first Mother Superior of the community of the Holy Cross; see Gregory,*HF* 9.42.
25 For Radegund, see Biographical Notes.
26 For the adoption of the Rule, see Gregory,*HF* 9.40 and 42; *Vitae S. Radegundis* 1.24. The Rule was drawn up by Caesarius, Bishop of Arles, for the guidance of his sister, Caesaria, and her community; Caesaria corresponded with Radegund about the Rule (*Epist. aevi Mer. coll.* p. 452). Radegund was compelled to look for such external regulation by the lack of support from Maroveus, Bishop of Poitiers; see Gregory, *HF* 9. 40. For discussion, see R. Aigrain, "Le voyage de S. Radegonde à Arles",*Bulletin philologique et historique de Comité des travaux historiques et scientifiques* (1926-7), pp. 1-9; Meyer, pp. 97-98, 101-102; F. Prinz, op.cit.; van Dam (1993), p. 32. For the relationship between bishop and community, see W. Klingshern, "Caesarius' monastery for women in Arles and the composition and function of the *Vita Caesarii*", *Revue Bénédictine* 100 (1990), pp. 441-481.
27 Genesius of Arles, martyred in 250, was an official shorthand-writer, who refused to take down an imperial edict against the Christians, fled, but was arrested and beheaded.
28 Lerins, the community founded by Honoratus and Eucherius on the coast of Provence in the early fifth century, was strongly influenced by the eastern tradition of the Desert Fathers.

With a father's zeal may you watch over your own protégées, that whatever good they do may be a blessing to you; then may you gird your noble head with the beautiful diadem, and, as shepherd, give due thanks for your flock.

Poem 5.8: to Bishop Gregory, after a journey[29]

Revered eminence, bountiful grace, noblest glory, shepherd delighting in the love of your apostolic see, you whom I will always embrace, Gregory, holy in your high office, who is never distant from my mind, venerable man; (5) I rejoice that the bishop of Tours has returned in honour and I am overjoyed that you, father, have come back to me. We earnestly applaud that the common prayers are answered, and that you have brought back the light of day for the people and this land. I commend the servant here with myself, O priest, (10) desiring greatly for you to guide your flock.

a: to the same

You who are liberal in devout service, bountiful father Gregory, who seek the stars openly with healing mind, and whoever, ill-protected, is heartened by your guidance, will have the aid of the heavenly host; (5) commending myself, your humble servant, I greet you always with devoted love, a man blessed by God. If this page is small, the zeal of one who loves you is not, for my heart has more devotion than my words express.

It provided candidates for many bishoprics from its ranks, thus disseminating this tradition. Se J. Herrin, *The formation of Christendom* (Blackwell, 1987), pp.68-69.
29 For Gregory of Tours, see Biographical Notes. From the date of his election as bishop of Tours in 573, Fortunatus had already gained his patronage, and wrote an *adventus* panegyric for the new Bishop's arrival in the city (*Poem* 5.3). The two men developed a close friendship, fostered by their joint literary interests. No precise date can be assigned for these poems, but they provide interesting and ample insight into the rich relationship between poet and bishop.

b: to the same, for the gift of a book

Yours is the palm, father, for reading the sacred verses, producing them from your own heart, and sharing them with others. I praise you readily and give you thanks as due for this too, which you had formerly given as a shepherd to your sheep. (5) And may the great blessings of the Thunderer[30] remain with you for this, you who distributed holy riches to the needy. When I am able to peruse them thoroughly, then let my thanks all the more sound from my lips for such a great gift.

(10) I commend in supplication, sweetly loved father, this servant here, Prodomeris, o lofty priest. Granting its gifts to you in the balance of the just scales, may the Lord's palm grow in glory to be yours.

Poem 5.13: to the same for the apples and the grafting slips

Gregory, holy in your high office, generous in your noble kindnesses, in your absence you are present through your gift, highest father; you send me the parents with their offspring, the grafts with the fruit; the slips, together with the apples. (5) May almighty God grant that, abundantly provided with the fruits of your merits, you eagerly pluck the apples[31] which paradise grows.

Poem 5.17: a greeting to the same

The letter, speeding courteously from you, visits me, o holy priest, a man who for his goodness is my father. Receiving this

---

30 This classical title for Jupiter was commonly applied to the Christian God in early Christian literature.
31 The apple, by some traditions, was the fruit Eve picked with such terrible consequences (e.g. *Poem* 10.2.3); but the apple tree also provided the wood for the Cross, which redeemed mankind from Eve's sin (*Poem* 2.1.10), and is one of the trees which grace the gardens of Paradise.

eagerly, I review it with my eyes and with my mind, rejoicing that you are safe and well, as the letter relates to me. (5) May the page sent here from some distance in your name, father Gregory, refresh me with salvation's succour.

Book Six

Poem 6.1: on the king, Lord Sigibert[1], and the queen, Brunhild[2]

As spring comes anew[3], and the land has freed itself of frost, the meadows clothe themselves in painted grass, the mountains stretch further up their leafy peaks, and the shady tree renews its green tresses; the pleasant vine, (5) putting forth grapes in abundance on its fruitful branches, swells with budding shoots. The bee, promising

---

1 For Sigibert and the context for this poem, see Biographical Notes. The king deliberately shunned the casual liaisons of his brothers, and sought a dynastic alliance with the Visigothic royal family of Spain to strengthen his position (*HF*, 4.27; for Merovingian dynastic marriages, see E. Ewig, "Studien zur Merowingischen Dynastie",*Frühmittelalterliche Studien* 8 (1974), pp. 38 ff.). The wedding was held in Metz in the spring of 566, and was celebrated in grand style, with the invitation of the great and good of the kingdom to the celebrations (Gregory,*HF*, 4.27) and with the declamation of a resplendent Latin epithalamium in true classical tradition by Fortunatus, fortuitously arrived in Metz. With this poem, and with the panegyric to Sigibert and Brunhild, *Poem* 6.1a, the poet was brought dramatically to the attention of a wide ring of potential patrons, an opportunity which he seized firmly.
For the tradition of epithalamium, see C. Morelli, "L'epithalamio nella tarda poesia Latina", *Studi Italiani* 18 (1910), pp. 319-432; M. Roberts, "The use of myth in Latin epithalamia from Sidonius to Venantius Fortunatus". *Transactions of the American Philological Association* 119 (1989), pp. 321-348; E. F. Wilson, "Pastoral and epithalamium in Latin literature", *Speculum* 23 (1948), pp. 35-40; see also "epithalamium" in *Reallexikon für Antike und Christentum* 5 (Stuttgart, 1962). For discussion of this poem, see George, p. 153-7.
2 For Brunhild, see Biographical Notes.
3 Fortunatus sets a lush, idyllic background for the wedding, in the best tradition of epithalamium, as advised in the rhetorical handbooks; see Menander Rhetor, edd. and trs. D. A. Russell and N. G. Wilson (Oxford, 1981), *Treatise* 2.6, sect. 411. The general classical tone of the introductory lines is sharpened by two echoes of Ovid (line 4, cf.*Trist.* 3.1.40; line 65, cf. *Fast.* 3.238); see notes 12-17 below for other echoes. But the spring setting is not the mythical one of Venus' paradise in Claudian's epithalamium for Honorius and Maria (*Fesc. de nuptiis Honor. Aug.* 12.1-13); Fortunatus follows the example of Dracontius, Ennodius and others in hymning the beauties of the real springtime of the wedding celebrations (e.g. Dracontius,*Epithal. in fratr. dictum* 6-10; Ennodius, *Epithal. dict. Max.*, 388 (*Carm.* 1. 4), lines 1-12). For the balance between the mythical and nature elements of epithalamium, see Roberts, op. cit.

flowers and charming with its simple humming, stores the delicious honey in the comb; fertile in its chaste bed[4] it gets fresh offspring, and is eager to bear young to be workers with the flowers. (10) The chattering bird, suited in its couplings to its desire for posterity, runs speedily to its young. Each through its seed grows young even as it grows old, and the world rejoices as all return.

(15) Thus now all is propitious, as with blessing from on high the royal palace prepares for Caesar's[5] marriage. In diverse ranks so many glorious Dukes[6] encircle the king on all sides, blessed for all ages. So many eminent lords come together to this one lord; (20) behold, Mars[7] possesses the lords, behold, Peace[8] possesses the glory.

---

4 See Vergil, *Georg.* 4.197-202, for belief about bees' methods of procreation. This prepares the audience for the emphatic declaration in lines 25-36 of Sigibert's freedom from other attachments and his wish to beget legitimate heirs. This can be set in the context of Gregory's statement of the king's wish to avoid the various casual liaisons of his brothers, and provide dynastic stability for his kingdom; see note 1 above. Cf. Amor's exortation to chastity in Ennodius' epithalamium, *Epithal. dict. Max.* 388 (*Carm.* 1.4) lines 19-20, 57-9, for a literary parallel. The emphasis by the Council of Tours in 567 on chastity in clergy and laity alike might also indicate a climate of opinion which would encourage the king to declare this virtue; see *Conc. Turon.* 567, sect. 10-17, *Concilia*, pp. 124-6.

5 Fortunatus uses the adjective *caesarius* only once elsewhere, with factual justification, of Placidina, wife of Bishop Leontius of Bordeaux, who was a descendant of the emperor Avitus (*Poem* 1.15.10). The epithet here underlines the grand ambitions of this union and this occasion. Note also the unique use of *imperare* in reference to a Merovingian king in line 82, and of *triumphare* in lines 76 and 92.

6 Gregory, *HF*, 4.27 for the extraordinary gathering of the kingdom's notables. The *dux* was a companion of the king at court, assisting in administrative or judicial matters, or being sent on special missions, such as an embassy or tax-gathering. For an account of the post, see James (1988), pp. 185-186, 187-188; A. R. Lewis, "The dukes of the Regnum Francorum, A. D. 550-751", *Speculum* 51 (1976), pp. 381-410; F. Lot, *La naissance de la France*, (Paris, 1948), pp. 203-211.

7 Given the imperial tones of this epithalamium, Mars is a more appropriate god here than the bucolic deities who often preside in such surroundings; cf. Dracontius, *Rom.* 6, *Epithal. in fratr. dict.*, 69-71; Patricius, *Epithalamium*, no.118, 37-45, in E. Baehrens, *Poetae Latinae* 1 (Leipzig, 1883), pp. 422-5. See Roberts, op. cit., for the use of the mythical element in this poem.

8 This is an appropriate comment in this context; but Fortunatus emphasises the virtues of peace-making and keeping to such an extent that we may suppose him to have supported Radegund's diplomatic endeavours from personal conviction. For Radegund, see Baudonivia, *VR* 2.10; for other passages, see Fortunatus, *Poems* 6.2.37-44; 9.1.23-32; 10.8.7-12. For the peaceable image of kings, see Brennan, (1984); M. F. Hoeflich, "Between Gothia and Romania; the image of the king in the poetry of Venantius Fortunatus", *Res publica litterarum* 5 (1982), pp. 123-136; J. M. Wallace-Hadrill, "Gregory of Tours and Bede: their views on the personal qualities of kings", *Frühmittelalterliche Studien* 2 (1968), pp.125-133.

With everyone's arrival, the festive palace teems, his people[9] see their heart's desire in the king's marriage. You, whose fountain flows abundantly with water, look on with favour; through your judgement small things are wont to grow.

(25) Spread your blessed light[10], o sun, and scatter your rays with their bright beams, flooding the bridal chamber with pure light; in triumph Sigibert, born to give us joy, wins his desire, he who now, free of any other love[11], submits to the dear bonds. (30) His chaste mind, under the guidance of youth, seeks marriage, beating down licentious ways; he whose age stole nothing from him, turns to the yoke; conducting himself with purity of heart, sole ruler of so many peoples, he applied the rein to himself also; but, as his nature demands, he is satisfied in a sole embrace in legal union. (35) In this love does not sin, but maintaining its chaste bed[12], creates anew from its offspring a home, where an heir will play.

It so happened that Cupid[13] in flight loosed his love-kindling arrows from his whistling bow; he inflames all creatures on earth, and the sea offers no protection with its waters; he soon subdues common hearts, (40) the ordinary throng; then finally the sensibilities of the noble king absorb the licking flames[14] into his peaceful bones; the fire, gently creeping over him, penetrates his very marrow. The king's

---

9 There is perhaps here an echo of the *consensus* of the royal panegyric, of the acclaim of the people for their king; for *consensus*, see MacCormack, (1981), pp. 21, 46-8. See Gregory, *HF*, 8.1 for the acclaim of Sigibert's brother, Guntram; see Fortunatus, *Poem* 10.8.1-14, for a similar picture of the people's delight in a peaceable ruler.
10 Given the triumphal, imperial overtones of this passage, we can see here the light imagery of panegyric; see *Poem* 5.2, note 3.
11 See note 4 above, for this emphasis on chastity. There are echoes in this passage of Amor's exhortation to chastity in Ennodius' epithalamium (*Epithal. dict. Max.*, 388 (*Carm.* 1.4), lines 19-20, 57-9; line 35 - *sed casta cubilia servans* -is a close echo of Vergil, *Aen.* 8.412 - *castum servare cubile*. The specific reassurance in this line was very relevant, given, for example, what happened to Brunhild's sister, Galswinth, shortly after her marriage to Chilperic (see Gregory, *HF*, 4.28). For discussion of this aspect of Merovingian queenship, see J. Nelson, "Royal saints and early medieval kingship", in D. Baker (ed.), *Sanctity and secularity; the church and the world*, Studies on Church History 10 (Oxford, 1973), pp. 34-9.
12 Cf. Vergil, *Aen.*. 8.412, from a passage drawing a picture of dutiful chastity. The intensity of the classical echoes in this and the following lines heighten the evocative power of this mythical passage.
13 Sigibert here suffers the wounds of Love in the best classical tradition. There are close echoes of Vergil: line 42, cf. *Georg.* 3.271; line 43, cf. *Aen.* 6.390; cf. Claudian, *De nuptiis Honor. Aug.*, 5-7, for Honorius' similar affliction.
14 Cf. Verg., *Georg.* 3.271, from a passage about the frenzy of passion.

head raged with fever, there was no rest for his heart in the drowsy night[15], with eye and with mind (45) reviewing the visage Love painted[16], and, wearying his thoughts, oft he dallied in an embrace with an illusory image[17]. Soon, when Cupid with conquering dart saw the gentle king burning with virgin passion, he said in exultation to Venus: "Mother, I have fought my campaign; (50) a second Achilles[18] is defeated by me by his inflamed heart; Sigibert, in love, is consumed by passion for Brunhild; she pleases him, ready for marriage, of sufficient years to be married[19], blooming in the flower of her virginity; she will delight a husband with her first embraces, she suffers no hurtful shame[20], but thus growing in power, is hailed as queen; (55) thus, growing all the more mighty, she is hailed as queen. This too is the maid's desire, though the modesty of her sex holds her back; made love to, she holds off the man with gentler arm, and forgives herself the guilty charges which passion's fire brings. But now come in joy, for they seek your vows."

(60) Soon Venus mingles violets with heavenly balsam, plucks roses with a finger, and stores them in her eager bosom, and together they cleave the clouds with light wings. As they come together to adorn the glorious wedding chamber, here Venus begins to set forth her noble protégée to advantage, (65) there Cupid presents the man; both looking with favour upon the bridal pair, they perform their sacred contest[21].

Then Cupid thus briefly addresses his mother[22]: "This is he whom we promised you, Sigibert, the people's love, born his parents'

---

15 Cf. Vergil, *Aen.* 6.390.
16 Cf. Claudian, *De nupt. Hon.* 6.
17 Cf. Ovid, *Ep.* 17.45.
18 This epic grandeur of reference is reinforced by echoes of Statius'*Achilleid* throughout; see S. Blomgren, "De P. Papinii Statii apud Venantium Fortunatum vestigiis", *Eranos* 48 (1950), pp.57-65.
19 Cf. Vergil, *Aen.* 7.53.
20 Cf. Claudian, *Bell. Gildon.*188.
21 The two deities now enter into the contest (*is*) traditional to this genre, in which each champions one of the bridal pair. For this feature, see the accounts of epithalamium given in notes 1 and 3 above.
22 It is interesting to note that Cupid's eulogy on behalf of Sigibert is in fact a micro-version of a royal panegyric, with the prescribed topics in their traditional order: birth and parentage, early years, virtues in war and in peace, and finally a peroration. For this tradition, see L. B. Struthers, "The rhetorical structure of the encomia of Claudius Claudian", *Harvard Studies*

glory, who has as his lineage kings in lengthy rank from his ancestors, (70) who will be the father of kings, the hope of a noble people[23]; a glorious scion in whom the splendour of his birth has grown brighter, a lofty offspring who arises more nobly from his line and nurtures the renown of his forebears; he spreads abroad the name of his sires with his warring hand[24]; to him came his father's valour[25], (75) which the Naab[26] declares, and conquered Thuringia cries forth, affording a single triumph from two peoples[27]; to him came the devoutness of Theudebert[28], of his uncle's line. He brings back both these, and one man fills the place of two.

Holding sway over the western quarter[29] in the flower of his youth, (80) he already surpasses his elders and his youthful age by his dignity; he has won the right by his deeds to go in advance of the law of nature; although few, yet his years command, second to none. He who rules his feelings maturely and with nobility is he who has been more balanced in times of trouble[30].

(85) Thus he cherishes the people as his reign begins, so that he is a father and king to them, oppresses none, raises all up. No day comes without its harvest; if he does not give what is appropriate, he considers he has lost more, if he has not given generously. He spreads

---

in *Classical Philology* 30 (1919), pp. 49-81. For this classical image of kingship, see also Reydellet, (1981), pp. 321-2.
23 Cf. Sedulius, *Carm. Pasch.* 1.96.
24 Sigibert was indeed the only one of the brothers to fight against foreign enemies; see Gregory, *HF*, 4.23, for his campaign against the Huns. Fortunatus mentions a notable victory against the Saxons and the Thuringians in the panegyric declaimed about this same time, *Poem* 6.1a.11, but there is no other reference to this event; see note 37 below.
25 Lothar fought campaigns against the Thuringians (Gregory, *HF*, 3.7, 4.10), Burgundy (*HF*, 3.11), the Goths (through his son, Gunthar; *HF*, 3.21), Spain (*HF*, 3.29), the Saxons (*HF*, 4.9, 4.14), and the Ripuarian Franks (*HF*, 4.14).
26 *Nablis*, possibly the Naab, which flows into the Danube.
27 Possibly a reference to Lothar's defeat of the allied Thuringians and Saxons in the same year; see Gregory,*HF*, 4.10.
28 The translation is based on Leo's suggested emendation of this line. For Theudebert, see Biographical Notes; see also *Poem* 4.25.9. Sigibert interited the kingdom of Theuderic and his sons; Theudebert was thus the appropriate devout forebear to quote her, as Childebert l is for Charibert in *Poem* 6.2.13-16, 57-60.
29 This exaggerated description of the most easterly of the Merovingian kingdoms, reinforced by an echo of Claudian (*In Rufin.* 2.274), picks up the imperial tones of this address (see note 5 above).
30 There are difficulties with the text here. This translation attempts to convey the general sense given by Leo's emendation.

joy far and wide with the bright light[31] of his countenance; (90) no clouds oppress the people under their glorious king. With mature heart he makes allowance for grievous fault; by forgiving the cause of others' wrong, he triumphs; for, understanding that the first virtue of a ruler is to be dutiful, because he who knows how to forgive always possesses that, (95) he himself first corrects what he demands that another should put right; he who passes judgement on himself, holds others in check by law in sound fashion. As a man in whom all the worthy qualities exist which you would ask of a king, he alone loves all and alone is loved by all[32]."

Then Venus began to recount the praises of the maid: (100) "O maiden, a marvel to me, a delight to be for her husband, more brightly resplendent than the radiant heavens, Brunhild, you have vanquished the splendour of jewels with the splendour of your beauty; a second Venus born, endowed with the power of beauty, no such Nereid (105) swims the Spanish main below the waters of Oceanus, no wood nymph is more beautiful, the very rivers submit their nymphs to your sway. Your milky complexion glows, tinged with red, lilies mingled with roses[33]; if gold gleamed forth among purple[34], in competition they would never come equal to your appearance. (110) Let all yield place - sapphire, pearl, diamond, crystal, emerald, and jasper; Spain has given birth to a new gemstone; worthy was the beauty which could overcome the king".

"Through winter weather, through deep snow, over the Pyrenaean mountains, and through fierce peoples, (115) she has been borne, the glorious king guiding her path, a queen for a foreign bridal bed. Over the mountain peaks you pick a level way; nothing ever baffles lovers[35] whom the gods wish to unite. Who would believe, indeed, that your mistress, Germany, was born a Spaniard, she of great price who united two kingdoms under one bond? (120) No human effort could bring about such a great achievement; for the difficult task requires divine weapons. The generations long past have scarce afforded this to any king; through valiant struggles great achievements

---

31 Note the light imagery of panegyric; see *Poem 5.2* note 3.
32 Sigibert's supreme virtues are those of peace and justice, not those of war; see note 8 above.
33 Cf. Vergil, *Georg.* 3.307.
34 Cf. Claudian, *rapt. Proserp.* 1.184.
35 Cf. Ovid, *Her.* 4.73.

have been wrought. Its lofty nobility shines resplendent, the race of Athanagild[36], (125) who extends his kingdom far away on the bounds of the earth, rich in the wealth the earth contains, and rules the Spaniard under his governance with renowned righteousness. But why should I tell again of the lands of your renowned father, when I see that your parents have increased in honour through your merits? (130) As much as you, a glorious maiden, are seen to outshine the ranks of girls, so you, Sigibert, surpass the husbands".

"Go, long to be joined in body and yoked in heart, both equal in spirit, in merits and in virtues equal, each adorning their sex with their accomplishments beyond price. (135) May your necks be yoked in the one embrace, and may you pass all your days in peaceful diversions. May each wish whatsoever the other desires; may the same salvation be upon both, guarding the two lives, may one love grow, linked by living strength; (140) may the joy of all increase under your auspices, may the world love peace, may concord rule supreme. Thus again may you, as parents, fulfill vows with children, and may you embrace grandchildren, offspring of your children."

Poem 6.1a: on King Sigibert and Queen Brunhild[37]

Conqueror[38], whose fame carries him from the setting to the rising of the sun[39] and makes him a noble and eminent ruler, who

---

36 Brunhild's father, king of the Visigoths.
37 This poem is the earliest of the formal eulogies addressed by Fortunatus to Merovingian kings. The reference in lines 33-4 to Brunhild as queen and recently converted to Catholicism date it to shortly after the royal wedding in 566. Though it is not a full panegyric in sequence and coverage of topics, it builds in many of the traditional features of the royal panegyric, and was perhaps delivered at a formal court occasion - there are no references to the people, as in *Poem* 6.2. For the tradition of royal panegyric, see *Poem* 5.2, note 1. For discussion of this poem, see George, pp. 40-3.
38 The element "Sigi-" in the king's name signifies "victory". (For similar comment on Chilperic's name, see *Poem* 9.1.28) This arresting apostrophe of the king as victor (and one on epic scale - lines 5-6), reinforced by this reference, introduces immediately a virtue essential to Germanic kingship, a motif reinforced by the reference to a winged Victory in lines 9-10. There is no other reference to this defeat of the Saxons and Thuringians in which Sigibert had played a notable part (lines 7-18); see note 24 above. His father, Lothar, inflicted defeat on them both in about 555 (Gregory,*III*, 4.10); reference to this event would necessitate us supposing that Sigibert was present and old enough, if not to have achieved glory, at least to have had it thrust upon him, and that Sigibert was deliberately reviving that

could do you justice? For it is not my ability which thrusts me forward to speak a few words, but love of you which spurs me on[40]. (5) If perchance Vergil were here now, if Homer were at hand, a work about your renown would already be being read[41]. O lordly Sigibert, glorious in splendid triumphs, on one side fresh virtue heralds you, on the other your lineage. Your Victory[42], once won, took wing, (10) and flew, noising your successes abroad. The Thuringian[43] with the Saxon, brooding on their destruction, cry back and forth that so many men have perished to the glory of one man. Because you then went on foot in front of the battle line, ahead of all, now you have cause for kings to follow you. (15) Your wars have granted peace with new-found prosperity, and your sword has brought forth true joy. Yet, that you may delight us all the more, although your Victory may exalt, the more you undertake, the more clement you remain.

You have the highest honour, but your intellect has surpassed the honour[44], (20) so that the highest pinnacle falls short of your character. Fosterer of justice, you are resplendent in your love of righteousness; both virtues dispute which occupies you more. Eloquence, dignity, virtue, goodness, intellect, grace hold sway; any one of your merits would adorn any man. (25) You hold the cares of all in your heart, righteous concern possesses you for the tranquillity of

---

memory in the context of the great gathering for the wedding. If so, this is certainly a point which Fortunatus would be shrewd enough to seize upon and exploit in this fashion.

39 This phrase evokes the sun imagery traditional to royal panegyric; see *Poem* 5.2, note 3.

40 This modesty topos is a common feature of rhetoric; see Curtius, pp. 83-5.

41 Sigibert's rule and virtues are not only in the Roman tradition, they are on an epic scale.

42 At some point in his reign, Sigibert issued coins bearing a winged Victory. They were minted close to Metz, at Trier, and it would be pleasing to suppose that they were struck to commemorate this victory over the Saxons and Thuringians; and that Fortunatus, in true rhetorical tradition, echoed in his poetry the visual motifs of the ruler's triumph. For this aspect of panegyric, see MacCormack, (1981), pp. 11-14; and for the visual context in general, see E. Baldwin-Smith, *Architectural symbolism of imperial Rome and the Middle Ages* (New York, 1978).

43 See note 37 above.

44 Fortunatus here pays the king the classical rhetorical compliment that he is a *rex doctus*, a ruler of civilized accomplishment. For this quality, see A. Alföldi, *A conflict of ideas in the late Roman empire*, tr. H. Mattingley (Oxford, 1952), pp. 112 ff; Brennan, (1984); Curtius, pp. 176-8; Godman, p. 26; Hoeflich, op. cit.. This *topos* of praise for the virtues of peace is in its conventional rhetorical place, after the king's warlike qualities; see Struthers, op. cit., pp. 49-52, 75-82. But see note 31 above for Fortunatus' priority, when he is not constrained by the genre format.

the people. You have been granted as the one salvation[45] for all, to whom in sacred office you restore in present times the joys of old.

Your excellent wife[46] is graced with Catholic ways, (30) the house of the church grows strong through your doing. Christ then joined the Queen Brunhild to Himself in love, for her merits, when He gave her to you, responding all the better to that second wish, since through Christ's gift, she who was first joined by her heart, now gives all the more delight joined legally. (35) Good king, rejoice in so glorious a queen; she is secured twice over who married you but once, beautiful, modest, decorous, intelligent, dutiful[47], beloved, generous, holding sway by her character, her aspect, and her nobility. But though she alone had merited so much grace, (40) before she had pleased only man, however, but now behold she pleases God. May you lead the long ages in splendour with your dear wife, whom divine love has given you as a companion.

---

[45] Praise of Sigibert here gains a religious dimension. For ecclesiastical ideals of kingship, see R. Collins, "Theodebert 1, *Rex Magnus Francorum*", in P. Wormald (ed.) *Ideal and reality in Frankish and Anglo-Saxon society* (Oxford, 1983), pp. 7-33; J. M. Wallace-Hadrill, "Gregory of Tours and Bede: their views on the personal qualities of kings", *Frümittelalterliche Studien* 2 (1968) pp. 125-33. For Fortunatus' development of the ideal, and possible Ravennan influence, see George, pp. 42-3; Reydellet, (1981), pp. 322-30. For Fortunatus' image of kings, see Brennan, (1984), pp. 1-11; M. H. Hoeflich, op. cit., pp. 123 ff; George, pp. 42-3, 47-8, 60-1.

[46] Mention of a queen or empress is given as an option by the rhetorical handbooks, one which is not often taken up; see Menander Rhetor, ed. and trs. D. A. Russell and N. G. Wilson (Oxford, 1981), 2.1, sect. 376. For examples, see Claudian, *Laus Serenae*, and Julian, *Or.* 3.35, and for comment, Struthers, op. cit.. Fortunatus' eulogy reflects Brunhild's importance to Sigibert and his dynastic ambitions; the emphasis on her Catholic orthodoxy underlines the importance, probably to both of them, of being and being seen to be Christian rulers.

[47] Reading, with Leo, *pia*, to fill out the line here.

Poem 6.2: on King Charibert[48]

The resplendent glory of great affairs has gone forth and spread the splendour of the noble king on all sides[49]. The sun in its setting and in its rising proclaims him for his dignity, intellect and understanding, and for his governance of justice; (5) throughout the breadth of the world's four quarters[50] he lays the seeds of praise which faith brings to fruit; the barbarian applauds him on one side, the Roman on the other[51]; a single acclamation resounds in various tongues[52] to this man. O Paris[53], love him who rules in your lofty

---

48 For Charibert, see Biographical Notes. This panegyric was addressed to Charibert in the presence of the people of Paris (line 9), a city he had ruled from the final division of Lothar's kingdom (Gregory, *HF,* 4.22) till his own death in late 567 or early 568. For the chronology, see J. Laporte, " Le royaume de Paris dans l'œeuvre hagiographique de Fortunat", *Études mérovingiennes, Actes des journées de Poitiers* 1952 (Paris, 1953), pp. 169-77. For discussion of this poem, see George, pp. 43-8, Godman, pp. 23-25. The immediate context of this poem is the worsening relationship between the king and the church. Charibert and Bishop Leontius of Bordeaux were at odds (Gregory,*HF,* 4.26); Bishop Germanus of Paris had recently excommunicated the king for his bigamous marriages to Merofled and Marcovefa, a runaway nun; the deaths of the latter, and of the king himself shortly after, were seen by the church as divine judgement (Gregory,*HF,* 4.26). This panegyric must have been delivered in the midst of this troubled situation.
49 This eulogy, unlike *Poem* 6.1a, is a panegyric proper in its structure, and in its delivery to a wider audience - the king himself, the Parisian people (line 9), clergy, and the widowed queen, Ultrogotha, and her daughters (see note 54 below). This suggests that the poem was part of an *adventus* ceremony, a formal welcome of the king into his city by the assembled people, grouped by interest, role, or class (see the typical racial grouping of Franks and Gallo-Romans implicit in line 7); cf. *Poem* 5.3 (Gregory's reception in Tours as its new bishop), *Poem* 9.1.1-4, notes 1 and 2, and Guntram's entry into Orleans (Gregory,*HF,* 8.1). For *adventus,* see MacCormack, (1972); - (1975), pp. 154-159; - , (1981), pp. 17 ff. These opening lines use the traditional sun imagery appropriate to a ruler (cf.*Poem* 6.1a.1; *Poem* 5.2, note 3), and the motif of universal *consensus* for the ruler (cf. *Poem* 6.1a.1, *Poem* 9.1.13-22). For *consensus,* see MacCormack,(1981), pp. 21, 46-8, 240-250.
50 This grandiose image perhaps hints at the fourfold division of Lothar's kingdom, all parts of which acknowledge Charibert's rule.
51 For this attitude to Roman and barbarian, so changed from that, e.g., of Sidonius, see J. Szöverffy, "À la source de l'humanisme chrétien médiéval: "Romanus" et "barbarus" chez Venance Fortunat",*Aevum* 65 (1977), pp. 71-86. See also M. Rouche, "Francs et Gallo-Romains chez Grégoire de Tours" in *Gregorio di Tours,* pp. 141-169, Convegni del Centro di studi sulla spiritualità medievale 12 (Todi, 1979).
52 Latin, Frankish (see James, pp. 31-2), and possibly Celtic (N. Chadwick, *The Celts,* (London, 1971), pp. 43-48).

citadel, (10) and revere the protector who offers you his succour. Him now, in joy and high regard, embrace in eager arms who by right is your lord, but through his goodness your father. Check your long grief for Childebert[54]; a peaceful king has returned, who cherishes your desires. (15) Childebert was gentle, wise and good, the same to all; the uncle has not perished, whilst his nephew stands on this earth. His heir was worthy to take the kingdom for himself, for he is no less great, as his praise tells.

Charibert is at hand; administering public justice to the people (20) he brings back joys of old in present times. So much has he shown himself a successor to his uncle that that nephew is now protector of Childebert's wife[55]; recalling the name of Childebert by his graciousness, he himself is both brother and father to his daughters. (25) They, well protected by the calm governance of the king, rest the hope of a father in their cousin.

O great offspring[56], resplendent with noble refulgence, whose glory springs from lofty forefathers; for whomsoever of his forebears of

---

53 This call for support emphasises Charibert's caring and legitimate rule - "protector", "succour", "by right", "father"; an image which, in light of the conflict with the church, is perhaps persuasive rather than descriptive. For this exhortatory "mirror of princes" technique, see F. Burdeau, "L'empereur d'après les panégyriques latins", in F. Burdeau *et al.* (edd.), *L'aspects de l'empire Romain* (Paris, 1964), pp. 1ff; L.K. Born, "The perfect prince according to the Latin panegyrics", *American Journal of Philology* 53 (1934), pp. 20-35; Alan Cameron, *Claudian: poetry and propaganda at the court of Honorius;* R. Collins, "Theodebert I, *Rex magnus Francorum*", in P. Wormald (ed.), *Ideal and reality in Frankish and Anglo-Saxon society* (Oxford, 1983), pp. 7-33.
54 For Childebert l, see Biographical Notes. On his death in 558, Lothar seized the city, exiled the widowed queen, Ultrogotha, and her two daughters, and held it till his death in 561. Childebert's reign was notable for the number of energetic and distinguished bishops in the cities of his kingdom, and for the extent of royal monastic foundations; Fortunatus elsewhere (*Poem* 2.10.17-24) likens him to Melchisdech, the Old Testament exemplar of royal priesthood; see Hoeflich, op. cit., pp. 128-129, and for the possible Ravennan inspiration for this image, see George, p. 43. In the circumstances, a claim that Charibert was heir to Childebert, rather than to Lothar, was politic (see *Poem* 6.1.77-78 for a similar family attribution of Sigibert's virtue).
55 Ultrogotha, widowed queen of Childebert l, was highly regarded by the church for her saintly devoutness; see *Vita S. Balthildis* 18, ed. B. Krusch, MGH SRM 2 (Hanover, 1888) pp.505-6. It is highly likely that she and her daughters, recalled from exile by Charibert (Gregory, *HF*, 4.20), were present in the audience of this *adventus* panegyric, as living proof of the king's generous succour of the weak and defenceless. The stress on family relationships in the wording of this passage emphasises the position of Charibert as true heir of Childebert. For Ultrogotha, see Biographical Notes, and *Poem* 6.6.
56 Fortunatus continues in the traditional sequence of topics; lineage and early years (lines 27-34), virtues in war and peace (lines 35-104), peroration (lines 105-14).

old I should choose to recall, (30) the royal lineage flows from honourable stock, whose eminence lofty faith led to the stars, and advanced upon the peoples, trampled underfoot the proud, elevated friends, cherished those cast down, and ground down the savage.

(35) But why should I here repeat the high praises of past generations, when your fame even more adorns your family with its glory? They enlarged their country with arms, but with bloodshed; you gain more who rule without slaughter. War wearied them in former times with violent dangers, (40) you now with your love of peace sustain them in safety[57]. Everything in joy sings the blessed times of the king, under whose auspices abundant tranquillity flourishes, and through whom the fruit of the fields abounds in peace; for your loyal people your life is a harvest field. (45) When the age merited your birth as king, the day's light shone with brighter splendour on the earth; your father, beholding at last fresh joy in this new offspring[58], declared he was magnified by the honour of a child. Though as ruler he was on the highest pinnacle, (50) yet when you arrived he bore his head higher still; joyfully resting his hopes in the bosom of his heir, the old man flourished thence all the more with higher hope. Born of royal stock before your other brothers, you were senior in rank, and foremost in piety. (55) Your virtue proclaims you on the one hand, your wisdom acclaims you on the other; between both virtues each claims you for its own. Piety from your uncle[59] is resplendent, a sharp mind from your father; both forebears live in the one countenance. You gather all the praises which both of them had, (60) and alone bring back the two, with the support of the law. You[60] are glorious as the path of justice, and the standard of dignity, and faith beyond price

---

57 Note the prominence given to the king's peaceable virtues; see note 8 above. This idyllic pastoral scene recalls Vergil's Fourth Eclogue and its Christian interpretation as a message of Messianic hope; see S. Benko, " Vergil's Fourth Eclogue in Christian interpretation", in H. Temporini and W. Haase (edd.), *Aufstieg und Niedergang der römischen Welt* 2.31.1 (Berlin, New York, 1980), pp. 646-705; J. Carcopino, *Virgile et le mystère de la IVe Eclogue* (Paris, 1943); P. Courcelle, "Les exégèses Chrétiennes de la quatrième Eclogue", *Revue des Études anciennes* 79 (1957), pp. 294-319; G. Jackmann, *Die Vierte Ekloge Virgils* (Cologne, 1953).
58 This term, *nova progenies*, has particularly optimistic overtones in the Judaeo-Christian tradition.
59 I.e. Childebert; see note 54 above.
60 Note the very Roman catalogue of virtues, again traced to the king's uncle rather than to his father. The "mirror of princes" technique can also be seen here, in the reminder of the family standards Charibert must maintain; see note 53 above.

holds a mirror to your life. Moderation is held firm by your tranquil spirit, you who at all times have a haven within your own breast. (65) Storms never shake your heart with any tumult; the anchor of your mind is there, lest you falter through passion. The whispering breeze does not toss steady minds, nor does it easily distract them through light fickleness. Thus glory accompanies a path so well set, (70) for a disciplined mind conducts itself with maturity. Watchfully you re-examine policies from the very roots and matters which are closed to others are open to you. If public concern stirs all the nobles and brings them together, their hope is to follow with you guiding their counsel. (75) Thus as often as an embassy then proceeds in success, it proceeds shrewdly, for your eloquence guides it. Since your forebearance abounds with such wonderful care, you show in your life the clemency of David[61]. The master of justice, lover of revered law, (80) in wisdom you draw your judgements from Solomon, though you are superior through the merit of your faith; for as far as sense of duty is concerned, you restore the spirit of the great Emperor Trajan. Why should I speak again of your mature character, since you delight our age with the weightiness of Fabius of old. (85) If certain disputes come with various mutterings, soon the weight of the laws flows from the king's lips. However confused the voices disputes send forth, you are able to tease out the threads of knotty legal litigation. The man who approaches seeking what is right, receives reward; (90) he whose cause sustains him, takes the prize as victor. As for him whose bright faith is held fast by strong roots, the mountain moves before your words fail. Hope, once offered, stands, unshakeable by any event; your word, once given, remains firm for ever. (95) That house is held firm from its own weight, which stands well grounded in its foundations[62].

Though you are a Sigamber[63], progeny of noble race, yet the Latin tongue flourishes in your eloquence. How great you must be in

---

[61] Rhetorical comparisons strengthen the tributes; first to the biblical kings, David and his son, Solomon; then to the Roman emperor, Trajan, and to the great general of the Roman Republic, who gained the name *Cunctator* (Delayer) for his patient, defensive strategy against Hannibal in the Second Punic War (218-202 B.C.) For Trajan, see R. Syme, "The fame of Trajan", in *Emperors and biography* (Oxford, 1971), pp. 89-112. For this section of a panegyric, see Struthers, op. cit, pp. 83 - 85.
[62] Cf. the New Testament image of the securely founded house; see Matth. 7.24-7.
[63] "Sigamber" recalls the legendary origins of the Franks (see Wood, p. 34) and links the two races in dignified tribute. The words may also have been a pointed reminder to Fortunatus' audience, and to Charibert in particular, of the words of Bishop Remigius, when

learned speech in your own language, (100) when you overcome us Romans in eloquence[64]? The bright light of day shines in your countenance from your clear brow; no cloud oppresses your candid spirit. Charming grace encircles your fair countenance, the people take joy in the appearance of the king. (105) Your graciousness fills all with the abundance of your gifts; the people are here as a witness for me, so that you can prove my words. O unmeasurable goodness of God, which considers that to be His which with rich generosity He gives to his servants. You raise those who are cast down, you protect by the law those who are raised up, (110) for all you are entirely all goodness. May the Almighty protect the king with His gift of goodness and may He preserve him as lord whom He gave as father. May the citizens wish you well, may you give joy to the citizens; may the people please in their service, may the king rule in virtue.

Poem 6.3: on Queen Theudechild[65]

Noble offspring, resplendent in your regal lineage, whose origins granted a lofty name from her forefathers; the fresh glory of your family[66] flies speedily through the worlds and at once your brother[67] is bruited aloud on this side, on the other your father[68]. (5) Yet though the noble stock of your parents is resplendent[69], the glory is doubled by your own virtue. We see in you all that is praiseworthy in them; you have added lustre to an ancient line, Theudechild. Your disposition is worthy of veneration, seemly, intelligent, devout, loving

---

he accepted the conversion of Clovis to Christianity, and baptised him: "Bow your head in meekness, Sigamber; worship what you burn, and burn what you worship" (Gregory, *HF*, 2.31).
64 See note 51 above for attitudes to the two races and to their languages.
65 This is most probably the same Theudechild as the queen whose epitaph Fortunatus wrote as *Poem* 4.25; see Biographical Notes.
66 His identity is not known.
67 I.e. Theudebert. See *Poem* 4.25.9. The tenses here, and in reference to Theuderic, must be read as vivid present tenses, referring to past deeds, if this Theudechild is indeed to be identified thus.
68 I.e. Theuderic 1. See *Poem* 4.25.9.
69 The structure of this eulogy echoes that of the formal royal panegyric; praise of lineage and family, followed by a catalogue of the typical Christian female virtues of pleasing character and charity. See note 46 above.

and affectionate[70]; (10) since you are powerful through your offspring, all the greater grace is with you. Avoiding what causes hatred, your abundant power is resplendent; you come all the more in love, the less you come in terror. The gentle sound from your lips echoes the most pleasing speeches, and the words of your discourse are like the comb's honey. (15) By as much as you surpass the female sex in honour, so too you outdo other women in your rich devoutness. If a stranger arrives, you welcome him with friendly spirit, as if he had already found favour with your forefathers through his services[71]. Your right hand produces the food for weary poor, (20) that you reap a harvest all the richer in its fruit[72]. You will always remain well provided with that from which you may sustain the needy, and that food is yours which the destitute receives. Whatsoever you bestow upon the needy comes to Christ; though none see, it remains without end. (25) When the final day comes to end the world, whilst all perish, you attain better things. Through your stewardship, holy churches are made new[73]; you establish Christ's house and he does yours. You give him dwelling places on earth, he will give you them in the world above; (30) you exchange for the better, thus in going to inhabit the heavens. The talent of yours which you lay by in the stars remains incorrupted[74]; the treasure which you generously disperse, this is treasure you lay up for yourself[75]. You who live for the Lord do not lose high honour; you hold a royal position on earth, you will hold one in heaven. (35) Now may you long flourish on this earth for your generosity to the people, you who, blessed through her merits, will dwell forever in light.

---

70 Cf. Gregory's catalogue of Brunhild's virtues; see Biographical Notes.
71 For the tradition of hospitality, see W. Goffart, *Barbarians and Romans A.D. 418-584: the techniques of accommodation* (Princeton, 1980), pp. 162-175.
72 For this thoughts, see *Poem* 3.13, note 7.
73 For other female church builders and restorers, see, for example, the other Theudechild (*Poem* 4.25.17), Placidina (*Poems* 1.6.21-2, 1.12.13-4, 1.15.109-10), Beretrud (*Poem* 2.8.25-34), and Berthoara (*Poem* 2.11.9-12).
74 For the New Testament parable of the talent, see Matth. 18.24-35.
75 For the New Testament imagery of laying up treasure, see Luke 12.16-21.

Poem 6.5: on Galsuinth[76]

The fortunes of life turn with unforeseen chances and uncertain life does not set down firm steps.[77] The hazardous wheel forever rolls life onwards in uncertainty and the track is trodden with falls on the brittle ice. (5) The day has certainty for none, for none is his hour more certain; thus we are in a more fragile state than glass. As deceptive unawareness leads us with wavering track, here lurks an ingenious pitfall where there appears to be a path[78]. Man's thought cannot tell which it is, death or safety; (10) will the daystar or the evening star be the death of his life? We are overwhelmed by this darkness, not knowing what comes by fate, and this uncertain life's span is so fleeting.

Toledo has sent you two towers[79], Gaul; as the first still stands, the second lies broken. (15) Raised high above the hills, splendid with its fine pinnacle, it has fallen in ruins, its crown toppled with hostile blasts. Leaving behind its foundations in its native abode,

---

76 In an attempt to rival his brother's dynastic alliance with the Visigothic royal family of Athanagild, Chilperic married Brunhild's sister, Galswinth. Her refusal to accept Fredegund's rival presence, however, so enraged the king that he had her garrotted a few weeks after the ceremony; see Gregory,*HF*, 4.28. Chilperic had given Galswinth an unusually generous *morgengabe* (the gift traditionally given to a queen by a king the morning after their first night together). A quarrel about the right of inheritance of the five cities in question exaccerbated the bitterness between Sigibert and Brunhild, and Chilperic and Fredegund; the issue was finally resolved explicitly in the Treaty of Andelot in 587; see Gregory, *HF*, 9. 11 and 20, and see Wood, pp. 122, 127, 170.
This poem is a lamentation and consolation on the princess' death, written by Fortunatus possibly in an attempt to avoid the bitter family feud which in fact arose from this event. For the rhetorical precepts for reaction to such tragic circumstances, see F. Cumont,*Afterlife in Roman Paganism* (Harvard, 1962), pp.128-47; for the genre in general, see*Poem* 4.26, note 22. For detailed analysis of this poem see G. Davis, "*Ad sidera notus*: strategies of lament and consolation in Fortunatus' *De Gelesuintha*", *Agon* 1 (1967), pp. 118-34; George, pp. 96-101; K. Steinmann, *Die Gelsuintha-Elegie des Venantius Fortunatus (Carm. VI.5): Text, Übersetzung, Interpretationen* (Zurich, 1975). For the intensity of the classical echoes, especially those of Vergil's*Aeneid*, see the verbal echoes noted in Blomgren (1944); also the similarity of the nurse's role to that of Dido's nurse in the Aeneid, and that of Rumour carrying the tragic news to Brunhild, as she bore that of Dido's death.
77 The brief introductory passage of *consolatio*, lines 1-22, echoes familiar motifs of life's uncertainty (see von Moos, *Testimonien*, T625).
78 The text is problematic here. The translation supposes a reading of *patet* instead of *putat*.
79 I.e. the two princesses, Brunhild and Galswinth.

having moved from its pivot, it did not stand long on its own; taken from its own soil, unfamiliar, it sank in sand, (20) it lies an exile, and, alas, a stranger in these lands[80].

Who can begin weaving the web of the presages of such great grief?[81] With what thread can sorrow begin to weave what is to be mourned? When first royal Galswinth was sought in marriage for a regal bed in the chill North (25) (when, transfixed by the fires of Cupid, she here desired the cold and lived well warmed in an icy realm), when the maiden, beside herself with fear and with what she heard, realised this, she fled to your embrace, Goiswinth[82]; then, with mind disturbed, lying enfolded in her mother's embrace, (30) she clung with nail, with hand, so that she would not be dragged away. Bringing her arms together she wove a chain without a rope and bound her mother in her embrace with her own limbs, demanding as a daughter to be kept still by that flesh from which earlier the beginnings of her life had been; (35) entrusting herself in confidence to be cared for by her royal power, in whose womb she had been safe and secure.

Then the house was afflicted with lamentations, the palace resounded with the clamour, and every noble wept for the sorrow of the queen. Rivers of tears disfigure the faces of the people, (40) and the very infant who did not know the cause, wails in sorrow. The envoys urge that they should set out for the German kingdom, recounting the long span of the lengthy journey. But, moved by the mother's grief, they soften their hearts, and those who are the driving force are willing to disguise their wishes. (45) As the mother is held entwined in her daughter's embrace, two days went past, a third, and a fourth. The envoys insist that they return from that familiar land; Goiswinth thus addresses them in lamentation[83]: "If I were brought low as a captive by the ferocity of a savage Gelonian, (50) it could be that you would be a respectful enemy in face of these tears; and if there were no respectful

---

[80] Such circumstances were considered cause for particular lamentation; see Cumont, op. cit, pp. 128-147.
[81] The *lamentatio* which takes up the major part of the poem, starts here with an account of how the tragedy happened. Throughout, Fortunatus stresses the ill-omened and sinister aspects of events.
[82] Goiswinth, mother of Galswinth, and wife of Athanagild.
[83] This is the first of a series of six plaints (*querelae*); three by Goiswinth (lines 49-82, 139-68, 321-46), one by Galswinth (lines 97-122), one by her nurse (lines 259-70), and one by Brunhild (lines 283-98). The first three *querelae* mourn different aspects of the cruelty of separation, this first the separation of mother and daughter.

heart, a greedy enemy would yield to my wishes and barbarian booty would give me my daughter back for a price; if he were unwilling even thus to change his bloodthirsty mind, it would be possible for the mother to take the same journey. (55) As it is, no delay is granted nor can we divert you at any price; he who makes no concessions, wounds more cruelly than an enemy. After the pain of the womb, after the many dangers of childbirth, and after the grievous toil of labour which I endured in delivery, am I as a mother not to be a mother to the child I bore, (60) has that very law of nature utterly vanished as far as I am concerned? Am I driven away weeping, fasting in my grief? Does respect not allow me to approach, does her origin not give me a place? Why hurry her away? Postpone the day, whilst I accustom myself to sorrow, and let the delay alone be the solace for my woes. (65) When may I see her again, when may my eyes again bring me joy, when may I fall again upon my daughter's dear neck? Where, pray, shall I again watch the steps of my gentle girl, and where will her laughter delight her mother's spirit? After the cares which the kingdom brings, where shall I rest, in sorrow? (70) Who will tend me with care, who will caress my head with her lips? Who will run with outstretched arms for a kiss, whose arms will wrap themselves round my neck? Whom shall I hold to my heart, bending beneath the dear burden, or be cuffed myself in jest with a light hand? (75) I would not be burdened by carrying you in my arms, though you are full grown, you who were so sweet and light a weight for me. Why should you seek a new country where I, your mother, will not be? Or perhaps one place cannot hold us both? So may the flesh which bore you be torn by lamentation; (80) when joy has vanished for her, it will be time for weeping. I shall destroy my sight by crying; take my sight with you; if all of me is forbidden to go, a part of me follows you."

Then the nobles and servants, house and city, the king himself echoed the cries, and a single bitter voice lamented wheresoever she sought to go. (85) At last they set forth, but the dismal crowd, as it hastens to let her leave, in its hurry ties itself up. As they went, emotion holds fast on this side, the bustle tugged from the other; so through both in turn, the wretched business is in turmoil. One urges departure, another beseeches them in love to turn back; (90) thus with differing allegiances, this one drags away, the other holds back. An ancient people are divided between new kingdoms; the father stays, the son goes; the father-in-law stays, the son-in-law goes. Anyone seeing the confusion would think that the nation was emigrating, and would believe that it was going alone virtually as a captive.

(95) They advance from the gates; as the carriage was checked on the bridge, Galswinth delivered these words in lamentation[84]: "Did you nourish me in your bosom, Toledo, that I, your fosterling, should be thrust from your gates, suffering and sorrowful? Giving my wounds over to lamentation, that I am tormented all the more; (100) the country is still prosperous, why am I dragged away as booty? Before I was confined, now I look upon you in your entirety; now you are known to me for the first time, as I leave, o harsh one. From here I make a reckoning of you, running my eyes over your eminences; but, lo, I alone am not among your number. (105) O cruel gates, who have released me on my way with keys set in place, and have not forbidden my journey! Would that a single adamantine boulder had locked you two together, before the wide open door had offered a way from here. O city, you had been more kindly, had you been all wall, (110) or if a high crag encircled you so that you should not allow me to go. I go, unknown in the land, fearful of what I should learn first; the people, dispositions, customs, cities, country, forest? Whom I pray, shall I find as a stranger in a foreign land, whither none of you come, fellow countrymen, friend, parent? (115) Tell me, whether an alien nurse can be kind and pleasing, to wash my face with her hand or to adorn my head with hairpins? Let no maid nor foster-sister delight in the dance; here you lie, my pleasure, here you lie, my care. If no other way, even an unmarked tomb would hold me; (120) cannot I live here? - then it is my pleasure to die here. I do not enjoy your embrace, nor do I depart sated with sight of you; farewell, cruel Toledo, you who banish me."

The floods of tears from a spirit thus inflamed burst forth, and the steadfast flame creates the moistening waters. (125) Then mother, daughter, the columns of weeping people take up the journey, nor is the mother, breathless through age, slow to follow. She leads her sweet daughter through the bitterness of the journey, the valleys are filled with weeping, the heights tremble, even the thick cloud is broken

---

[84] The second *querela*, by Galswinth, mourns her separation from her native city, emphasising her status as a foreigner.

up by vain cries, (130) and the very forest groans with the echoing murmur.

Her mother gives the long distance as the reason for coming further, but the time and the journey are short for her wishes. The mother reaches the point from which she said that she would return; but what was willingness first, then becomes unwillingness. (135) She wishes to advance again, the path by which she goes cannot be trodden by the mother; the leaders hold her back from pursuing her journey. They cling to each other in embrace, both equally turning back; Goiswinth begins in wild grief[85]: "Spain, wide spreading for your people, confined for a mother, (140) a region so swiftly closed for me alone. You may run from the west to the warm east, and stretch from the Tuscan Sea to the Ocean; though sufficient for the peoples with broad-spreading regions, the land where my daughter is absent, for me is straitened. (145) Likewise, wandering here without you, I seem a foreigner, and in my own land I am both native and exile. What, I ask, should my eyes behold, daughter, whom should they seek out? You who now take those eyes with you, love, you will be my sole sorrow; whatever child plays with me, (150) you will be the burden for me in another's arms. Let another run, stand, sit, weep, come in and go out, your gentle image alone comes before my eyes. As you flee, I will speed, lost amongst strange embraces, and I will press my dried breasts, lamenting over their mouths. (155) I shall bathe my weeping eyes with the faces of infants, and drink insatiably their tender tears. If only I might be refreshed by such a draft or by any part, or that the flood, wept vastly, might quench my thirst! Whatever will be, I am in torment; here no medicine avails, (160) which I drop on to the wound you have made, Galswinth. By what hand, I ask, will my dear daughter's hair be combed and shine? Without me, who will caress her gentle cheeks with a kiss? who will cherish her in her bosom, carry her on her knees, what arm will encircle her? But there will be no mother there for you without me. (165) As for the rest, fearful love bids you thus as you go; may you prosper, I pray, but beware - go, fare well. Send greetings to your eagerly awaiting mother even on the wandering breezes; if it comes, may the wind itself tell me good news!".

---

[85] The third of the *querelae* on the cruelty of separation; this, by Goiswinth, in ever-widening perspective, on Galswinth's separation from her homeland.

Then the daughter, burdened by her mother's forceful plaints, (170) mournful, bereft of thought, unable to speak, her voice for long choked, her throat scarce relaxing in speech, uttered a few words (her speech heavy with her heart's wound): "If God in His lofty majesty wished me now to grant me further days of life, He would not have granted them on this path. (175) But since irrevocable fate presses upon me[86], if none bar me, I will follow where passion leads. But I will speak these last words, to be remembered in sorrow; hence what is yours is not yours. Goiswinth, farewell.'"

Thus they break off their embraces, and hold away lip which was touched to lip; (180) love caresses the air, since they cannot caress each other. Galswinth, seeking the Gallic lands from there by carriage, stood, in misery, with fixed gaze, as the wheels turned. Lo, on the other hand, her mother, straining her eyes after her child, standing on one spot, yet travelled with her herself. (185) In complete distraction, lest the mule draw away the speedy chariot, or the impatient horse turn the wheels on their axle, her anxious gaze hovered round her loving daughter, following her in imagination where the road wound its path. She often spoke as though her daughter were seated at her side, (190) and was seen to clasp the absent girl to her bosom[87]. Convinced she will hold her, she throws her arms into the air; she does not clasp her child, but beats against the wandering breezes. She watched one making her way, amongst so many companions, alone she observed the path along which her love was going. (195) The mother was borne further by her imagination than her daughter was by the carriage; she travelled, shaken by her wishes, the other by the wheels. Until she disappeared far from sight and at a great distance and was out of sight, whilst shadows cloaked the day, she thought she could see the indistinct features of her daughter, (200) and, as the shape vanished, the sweet image came back. O name, warm with devoted love, o faithful care, what were you if not a mother, although to an absent child? Moistening your cheeks with tears, striking against the stars with your lamentation, recalling every happening - sweet, harsh, caring, (205) a mother easily moved, impatient, fearful, weeping, anxious, what do you seek with

---

86 For this familiar motif in consolation, see von Moos, *Testimonien* T527-51.
87 Cf. *Poem* 7.12.89-100, for a similar picture of fantasy about an absent loved one.

your tears? What does this deep love foretell? Yet she goes where the worn track cuts a way; each fills the empty fields with her tears.

Then she speeds over the Pyrenaean mountain range through the clouds, (210) where July is freezing with frosty rains, where the mountains, white with snow, disappear into the stars and their sharp peaks emerge above the rains. From here Narbonne welcomes her, where the gentle Aude, nibbling away at the flat coast, softly enters the waters of the Rhone. (215) After various other cities, she reaches the citadel of Poitiers[88], passing by in royal procession the area where that great and renowned Hilary[89] was born and bred, eloquent with thundering speech. Thracian, Italian, Scythian, Persian, Indian, Goth, Dacian and Briton (220) drank in hope from his eloquence, and took up arms. The sun spreads light over all by his rays, Hilary by his words[90]; the one brings daylight to the mountains, the other faith to minds.

Indeed, I, newly arrived, watched her passing by, the carriage gently bowling along with silver top. (225) With motherly love, gentle Radegund desired eagerly to see her, in case any could be of help to her. After close exchanges, the sweet princess came to her sweet presence, and spent time with her in peace; this Radegund now mourns bitterly. Thence she sought the lands of Tours, of Martin famed to the skies[91], (230) her slow progress continuing. The channel of the Vienne is crossed by an alder craft; the accompanying throng emerges briskly from the fast-flowing waters. From there the slow-moving Loire receives her with its bright and chilly stream, where the smooth sand gives cover not even to a fish. (235) She reaches the place where the Seine with fishy wave makes for the sea, near the curved bend by Rouen.

---

88 The warm welcome from Sigibert's kingdom is in strong contrast to her treatment by Chilperic.
89 Hilary, Bishop of Poitiers and theologian, was born about 315 and died about 367. A vigorous opponent of Arianism, he was banished to Phrygia in 356 by the Arian emperor, Constantinus ll, but sent back in 360 for being equally turbulent in the East. He wrote extensively, mainly in defence of Catholic orthodoxy, but did not neglect the needs of his people in Poitiers. Among those who came under his influence was St. Martin of Tours. See van Dam, (1993), pp. 28-41, for his cult.
90 For this light imagery, see *Poem* 5.2, note 3
91 For Martin of Tours, see Biographical Notes.

The maiden is then joined in wedlock to the most lofty king, and earned the great love and respect of the poeple[92]. Charming some by gifts, others by her words, (240) she thus makes even strangers her own. The armed ranks swear an oath on their weapons in their own right[93], that they would be loyal to her, and bind themselves by law. Getting her life in order on a peaceful track, she reigned; the stranger, by her generosity to the poor, was a mother to them. (245) That she might all the more live on in the eternal kingdom, she gained acceptance by being won over to the Catholic faith[94].

O infamous sorrow, why do you put off the time of weeping and by speaking more remain silent about man's harrowing doom? O harsh lot of mankind, lurking in unforeseen disaster, (250) which overwhelms so many good things with death hastening so swiftly! For, enjoying for a short time the binding relationship with her husband, she was snatched away by death at the start of her life. Caught up prematurely by swift misfortune she dies under the precipitate blow, and the light of her life dies as light is quenched[95].

(255) The wretched nurse[96], hearing of the death of her charge, with failing heart flies to the lifeless body. She first, leaning over in the midst of the faithful maidservants, choked with grief, was at last able to speak thus: "Did I, worst of nurses, thus promise your gentle mother, Galswinth, (260) that you would be safe and sound for many a long day? Do my eyes' light, thus extinguished, behold the light of my life? Is your face thus pale, which once was rosy? Have pity and say something, speak to me in my misery! What shall I tell your mother, if I am allowed to return? (265) Is this what I have achieved as a stranger, for all my labours? In return do you give me a gift like this, my child? You used to wish that we should be together in life and in death; you let me live by your side, but you died without me. If only the pattern of life for young and old had held - (270) that I would die first, with you remaining safe and sound." Scarcely has she

---

92 Lines 237-46 are a brief *laudatio* of the princess, emphasising her eminent suitability as a Catholic queen.
93 For oaths of loyalty, see James, pp. 142-143; this is unusual in being to a queen.
94 As Brunhild had been; *Poem* 6.1a. 31-35.
95 Note that no mention is made of the violence of her death, nor of its author, only of its prematurity.
96 The fourth *querela* is made by the nurse, acting as a mother substitute, and performing the role which is properly that of nearest of kin. The tone of epic tragedy is heightened by echoes of Vergil's account of the death of Dido; see note 76 above.

uttered her lamentation, another snatches the words from her lips, for one alone is not enough to tell the grief which the palace witnesses.

Meanwhile the princess is mourned and carried on her sad bier, and faithful love performs her last rites. (275) She is conducted in procession, adorned, set down, mourned on all sides, and thus, a foreigner in her own tomb, buried.

Here suddenly happens a miraculous sign of things[97]; as the hanging lamp casts light in service, it falls on the stone flags; it does not topple over but burns unharmed; the glass does not break on the stone, (280) nor is the flame quenched by the water.

Fresh Rumour struck the ear of her remaining sister, and the sister thus spoke with loving feeling[98]: "Was this the greeting which you bestowed upon your sister, my dearest? Is this what the letter, written in your hand, brings me? (285) With anxious eyes, I awaited your coming; you have not made the sort of journey I prayed for. I wished in Gaul that Spain would bring you here; a dear sister does not have you here, nor a mother there. I, Brunhild, did not come here in final service; (290) I would have paid you tribute in death, if I gave you none in life. Why, as a foreigner, did I not close your sweet eyes or drink in your last words with eager ears? I myself performed no sorrowful duty for my sister, this hand did not cover your limbs, hands, face. (295) I was not allowed to pour forth my tears nor swallow them back from my face, nor do I wash your chill flesh with warm tears. Why, o deepest sorrow, have you divided us on death's path who were reared together, who were joined by these lands?"

Thus the sister, abandoned, is torn by the misfortune befallen her lost one; (300) she calls, the other lies and does not return, even when she is sought. Germany hears the sister's loud lamentations, and beats against the stars with wailing, wheresoever the path runs. Oft calling you by name as sister, Galswinth, the springs, woods, rivers and countryside give utterance thus: (305) "Galswinth, are you silent? Reply, that the silent may reply to your sister; stones, mountain, grove, water and sky." Distraught, in agitation she questions the very breezes; but all hold silence about her sister's welfare.

---

97 For this miracle, see Gregory, *HF*, 4.28.
98 Brunhild, her sister, utters the fifth *querela*, symmetrically balanced against that of Goiswinth in lines 321-346, expatiating on Galswinth's death in a foreign land and the absence of family.

A messenger here straightway crosses over rivers and over the Alps, (310) and the flight of heavy grief speeds thus rapidly. It had been desirable that, after it reached all places, this sorrow would make its way more slowly to her mother. But the person who loves more, hears sooner what rumour brings, and believes what is not certain, fear lending credence. (315) Thus grief soon assails and reaches her mother's ears, she collapses in distress, her knees giving way. A second death threatens once the first one is announced, and the mourning rites almost happen with her scarce still alive.

Then ashen Goiswinth, suffused with red, (320) her spirit hardly returned, spoke thus in a whisper[99]: "Was it thus that I was warmed by gentle love of a daughter, that now an even more savage wound tears my flesh? If now the light of our life is dead, if my daughter is gone, why do you hold me, hateful life, to these tears? (325) Harsh death, you have erred badly; when you should have taken the mother in death, the daughter was allotted to you. O, if only the rivers had swollen to flood their banks, and the drowned earth had floated in overwhelming waters, if only the Pyrenees' lofty peaks had touched the skies or (330) the path frozen solid with glassy ice, when I released you, Galswinth, to the North, so that the carriage could not travel on its wheels, nor the boat on the waters. So was this what my mind foresaw in fear[100] when, parting from you, I gave you the last familiar things, and when the dread power of fate seemed unable to wrest you from my embrace[101], child? (335) We obeyed the commands of others, following orders; promised, you went away, not to return to me. Was this deep love, that with tranquil sweetness I gave my breast to be grasped by the soft lips of my daughter? Why did the nipple's channel produce sustaining milk from here? (340) Why did I give nourishment and yet I was not to receive it? Often I nuzzled my sleepy child with stolen kisses, and put my body under you so that you could sleep easily. What did it avail to have hoped for this final gift from you, that a baby granddaughter should play on her grandmother's

---

99 The mother's *querela*, the sixth, echoes Brunhild's, moving in a widening circle to cry in outrage against the cruelty of life and nature itself.
100 This phrase echoes Mezentius' presentiment of Lausus' death in Vergil's Aeneid (*Aen.* 10.843), lending epic dignity to the scene; see note 76 above.
101 There seems to be a break in sense in the text as it stands. Leo suggests that a pentameter and a hexameter have dropped out between lines 333 and 334; the translation follows his suggested supplementation.

knee? (345) I was not blessed in seeing my wish fulfilled; nor, accursed, did I see your death; alas, great travail has lost the latter, love the former."

Here the sister, there the distraught mother, with shared tears, one lashes the Rhine with her tears, the other the Tejo; the Batavians shared in the grief of one, the land of Andalusia mourns here; (350) the Waal's waters roared here, and there the Ebro's stream.

It is enough to have shed so many tears, but the drops from the shower of moisture do not offer succour in assuaging thirst[102]. If it is possible for feelings to calm, I will say: "She does not lie, to be mourned, who dwells in blessed places. (355) Tell me what harm was done to her, whom death's passage carried away with the lapse of time, but whom life everlasting nourishes? She who now dwells with Stephen[103], heaven's consul, who shines in glory with Peter, the leader of the apostles[104]? Applauding the Lord's glorious mother, Mary, (360) she serves under God, the everlasting King. Won over[105], she finds favour, she is resplendent in her precious death, and, her old one set aside, a beautiful robe now covers her. And if only God will grant in His love that we across the sea, through swords, may draw near to that countenance! (365) She holds the symbol of life[106]; as the glass vessel fell, the water did not quench the flame, nor did the stony ground break it. You also, mother, through the Thunderer's will have thought for your daughter and your son-in-law, for your granddaughter, grandson, and husband. Be assured that she is alive, Christians, because she believed; it is not right to weep for her who dwells in paradise."

---

[102] The final passage of consolation spells out the implications of the miracle Fortunatus has already mentioned (lines 277-80); that Galswinth is assured of eternal life as one of the "Very Special Dead"; see P. R. L. Brown, *The cult of saints; its rise and function in Latin Christianity* (Chicago, 1981), ch. 4, esp. pp.73 ff.. For the various consolatory motifs, see von Moos as follows; for the motif that the dead still live, *Testimonien* T1507-10; for the vision of Paradise, *Anmerkungen* A219; for grief being inappropriate for the blessed dead, *Testimonien* T910, *Anmerkungen* A405; for the comfort of children, *Testimonien* T1409.
[103] Stephen was the first of the Christian martyrs; see Acts of the Apostles, 6.8-7.60.
[104] See *Poem* 4.26, note 36.
[105] A reference to her conversion; see line 276 above.
[106] The lamp not only recalls the miracle at her tomb, but is also the symbol for eternal life derived from the New Testament parable of the wise and foolish virgins; Matth. 25.1-13.

Poem 6.6: on Ultrogotha's[107] garden[108]

Here spring's splendour[109] creates the verdant sward and sprinkles the heavenly roses with scent; here the soft vine leaves preserve the summer shade, and offer bosky cover with their grape-bearing tresses; (5) and flowers colour the place with their diverse buds, and white and here red clothe the apples[110]. Summer heat is gentler here, where a light breeze, caressing with its soft murmur, constantly stirs the dangling apples.

This was planted by King Childebert, in great love; (10) these give all the more delight which his hand bestowed; the shoot takes a honey sweet savour from its grower, and he too, it may be, intermingled the silent honeycombs. Through the king's merit, the virtue of the new apples is twofold, the scent is pleasing to the nose, the flavour is sweet to the mouth. (15) How much could he avail for

---

107 For Ultrogotha and her husband, Childebert I, see *Poem* 6.2, notes 53-54, and the Biographical Notes. It is likely that this poem was written at the same period, as a form of consolation for the widowed queen. For further comment, see George, pp.101-5.

108 The garden lay beside the church of St. Vincent, which Childebert had built in Paris to contain the ecclesiastical treasures he had brought back from Spain some ten years earlier (see Gregory, *HF*, 3.10; *Liber Historiae Francorum*, 26, p.284; *Vita Droctovei Abbatis Parisiensis*, 12-13, ed. B. Krusch, MGH SRM 3 (Hanover, 1896), pp.540-1). For the various names by which the church was known, see Meyer, p.57. For a description of the church, see Fortunatus, *Poem* 2.10. Meyer, pp. 56-9, with J. Derens and M. Fleury, "La construction de la cathédrale de Paris par Childebert I d'après le *De ecclesia Parisiaca* de Fortunat", *Journal des Savants* (1977), pp. 177-253, suggest that *Poem* 2.10 refers to the cathedral, and not to the church of St. Vincent. For discussion, see George, p.102, note 85. Childebert was buried in the church (Gregory, *HF*, 4.20; Gislemar, *Vita Droctovei* 15, p.541; see George, p. 102, note 56 for the suspect chronology here).

109 The first eight lines create the atmosphere of a classical *locus amoenus*, a pleasance, with Vergilian overtones; for line 1, cf. Vergil,*Ecl.* 9.40, Pseudo-Vergil, *Culex*, 50. There are also appropriate Christian resonances; the deep glossy colour visualised in line 1 recalls the deep purple associated with a queen and a widow in Christian imagery (e.g. Jerome, *Ep.* 54.14), whilst roses evoke the vision of Paradise (see C. Joret, *La rose dans l'antiquité et au moyen âge* (Statkine Reprints, Geneva, 1970) pp. 232 ff).

110 Apples not only instance Childebert's practical fruitfulness and goodness; they metaphorically recall the savour and scent of his virtues (lines 11-16; for the odour of virtue, see, e.g., Tertullian,*Mart.* 2.4; Lactantius, *Inst.* 6.22; Paulinus of Nola, *Ep.* 26.1). The fruitful tree (line 17) is also the Christian tree of redemption, the Cross, from the exile of sin caused in the first place by an apple (Genesis, 3.1-6). The reference to the Cross is particularly appropriate, given that one of the treasures Childebert enshrined in the church was a precious cross, brought from Spain (see note 108 above).

men's salvation, whose touch brings pleasure even in apples? May the fruit grow in blessedness from the everlasting tree, that all men be mindful of the good king. From here he made his way, when he sought the holy portals, (20) where he now dwells indeed for his merits. For previously he visited the holy places from time to time, but now he dwells constantly[111] in the blessed temples.

May you remain in blessed possession of this through the ages, Ultrogotha, a mother joyful as a third with her two daughters.

Poem 6.7: at the villa Cantusblandus[112], on the subject of apples

We came by happy path to Cantusblandus, where I rejoice to have found Father Aregius[113]. Since our appetites, stirring us on, hunt in the great troughs, the golden apples[114] capture my eyes. (5) Apples of all colours come piling in from all sides, so you would think I had earned a painted feast. Scarcely had I touched them with my fingers, put them into my mouth, rolled them between my teeth, and the booty, set in motion from that spot, sped down into my belly. For the flavour delighted before it attracted the nose's scent; (10) so the gullet won, whilst the nose lost its glory.

---

111 The church became the burial place of many of the royal family; Childebert himself (Gregory, *HF*, 6.46), Clovis and Merovech (ibid. 8.10), Fredegund (*Liber Historiae Francorum*, 37, p.306), Lothar II (Fredegar, 4.56). It is likely that Ultrogotha and her daughters were buried there; see R. Poupardin,*Recueil des Chartes de l'abbaye de S. Germain-des-Prés* 1 (Paris, 1909), pp. 5 ff.
112 The name means 'sweet song'.
113 Aregius was Abbot of Limoges. Fortunatus, with Agnes and Radegund, sends him greetings in *Poem* 5.19. Attached to the court of Theudebert as a well-born youth, he came under the influence of Bishop Nicetius of Trier. Thereafter he led a life of saintly devotion, becoming a "special foster-son" of St. Martin, performing many miracles, and building many churches, including the monastery of S. Yrieix (= Aregius) in the Limousin, where he installed relics of St. Martin. He died in 591. He was a close friend of Gregory of Tours. See Gregory,*HF*, 7.15, 10.29; van Dam (1993), pp. 81, 119, 182, 189-191, 248, 269-270, 286-287.
114 The sheer exuberant delight in colour, taste and texture perhaps also has behind it the imagery of the apple as the tree of the Cross and the means of man's redemption. See note 110 above.

Poem 6.8: about the cook who took the poet's boat[115]

Why do you ensnare me, o Care, in such troublesome plaints?[116] Alas, now at last depart my soul, o Grief. Why do you recall my misfortunes? My weight of baggage already weights me down. Why is the burden doubled, which I thought to toss aside? (5) I wander even more miserably as an errant exile, all too far from my native shores, than shipwrecked Apollonius[117], a stranger on the waters. When we reached Metz, that royal cook, importunate, stole from me in my absence ship and crew. Did he who snatches food from the flames with fiery hand, (10) not know to keep faith on the waters, and to keep his hands off a boat? Black hearted, smoke-fed, soot-dyed; his face is another cooking pot which his own implements have painted a filthy colour - frying pans, pots, bowls, plates, trivets; (15) unworthy of being marked by verse rather than by soot, may his foul image reflect the pitch-black man. The incident was most shameful, the wrong committed is heinous; a cook's broth carried more weight than my rights; a book is not as grand as a bowl, (20) so that I had no part in my own boat.

But nonetheless, Vilicus[118] who nourishes and sustains the Lord's flock, offered help with his usual loving care. He took it upon himself, and I skimmed along, quaking, in a slender skiff, soaked by rain, wind and wave. (25) I threw out everyone else, to follow on foot, for if no-one was outside, no-one was inside either. Soon it had in mind sinking everyone, danger seizing us; no-one remained to bear

---

115 Fortunatus is in Sigibert's entourage on this occasion - but only just, as the poem makes clear. So the poem is to be dated to the early days of his arrival at the court. For river travel, see Salin, 1, pp. 129-130. For the kitchen humour of this poem, see Curtius, pp. 431-432.
116 This first line closely recalls Horace's cry to his patron, Maecenas, in *Carm.* 2.17.1, and emphatically pitches this poem, however lighthearted and rueful the story, as a claim to be a court poet with powerful patronage, in the highest classical tradition. For analysis and comparison with *Poem* 10. 8, see George, pp.180-1.
117 The *Historia Apollonii Regis Tyrii*, a romantic adventure novel, probably written originally in Greek in the 3rd. century A.D. and the ultimate source of Shakespeare's *Pericles*, was circulated in a Latin version in the fifth and sixth centuries, and could well have been familiar to Fortunatus; see R. Helm,*Die antike Roman* (Berlin, 1948), pp. 47ff.. This sets the tone; but the poem is also well laced with allusions, in mock-heroic vein, to Statius' *Thebaid;* see Blomgren (1950).
118 See *Poem* 3.13, also addressed to Vilicus, Bishop of Metz, an early patron.

witness to the shipwreck. I was so close, after I threw everyone out, (30) that the water lapped my feet, buffeting them again and again. "Away with your services", I said, "I don't care to be washed just now." But all the same the water insistently went on soaking my feet.

Coming to Nauriacum, I tell the king my woes; he laughs, and with kindly voice orders a ship to be made available. (35) They hunt for one, but cannot find a single vessel, for the king's whole assembly was afloat on the waters. Only Gogo[119] now pressed on to afford me comfort; he does not deprive his own people of what he gives to all. He spoke more persuasively to Count Papulus[120] who was there, (40) to urge him to give me any boat whatsoever; surveying all, he saw a skiff on the shore; but my baggage would not fit in. He made me stay at Nauriacum for a short while, and arranged the provisions which the place itself afforded. (45) However little it produced, the will alone was enough for me; the help which a loving friend gives is no small matter indeed. My welcome friend gave me drink as well as food, insofar as he could obtain wine in the country. Thus you steered a ship which brought me pleasure, Papulus; (50) live happily, farewell, sweet friend, count and companion[121].

---

119 Gogo was also one of Fortunatus early patrons; for details of his life, see Biographical Notes.
120 Papulus is not otherwise known. He may have been one of Sigibert's counts. The *comes* was either the king's representative in a city, administering justice and commanding the troops levied there; or he remained at court to assist the king in administrative and judicial tasks; see D. Claude, *Untersuchungen zum frühfränkischen Comitat*, Zeitschrift der Savigny-Stiftung für Rechsgeschichte, germanische Abteilung 81 (1964), pp. 1-79; James (1982), pp. 58-60; -, (1988), pp. 184-188; Wood, pp. 61, 64-65.
121 The one word *comes* can mean both "count" and "companion", or both, as here.

Poem 6.9: to Dynamius of Marseilles[122]

I await you, my love, revered Dynamius, whom my affection sees even though you are absent. I ask the breezes[123], as they come, what lands harbour you; if you elude my sight, you do not on that account escape my thoughts. (5) The kingdom of Marseilles finds your approval, Germany mine; torn from my sight, you are with me, bound to my heart. Why has a part of you[124] been so forgotten and stayed behind without you, and why do you not call back the abandoned presence with your will? If sleep comes over me, let even dreams tell you of me, (10) for dreams are wont to behold those truly of one spirit[125]. If you lie awake, I say, the charge will deny you an excuse; in your laziness, you have no excuse. A second circuit of the year, bearing the constellations as the months come round, wearies the Sun's panting steeds, (15) since you departed and took away with you my source of light, and now without you I can see nothing, though the daylight is clear. I pray that you would pour words forth for me from that eloquent source, so that the page you send would make me talk with you. But all the same I entreat you with even more affection to

---

122 Dynamius, a Provençal noble (see Biographical Notes) was one of a group who travelled to Metz from the south for Sigibert's wedding. Fortunatus also writes or sends greetings to Iovinus (*Poems* 7.11 and 12), to Bishop Theodore of Marseilles, Sapaudus, Albinus and Helias (*Poem* 6.10.67-70), who may be identified as members of a Provençal literary circle (see Riché, pp. 31-36, 184-9). At this time, Marseilles was part of Sigibert's kingdom, and administered by a *rector provinciae* (R. Buchner, *Die Provence im merowingischer Zeit: Verfassung -Wirtschaft - Kultur* (Stuttgart, 1933), pp. 6-29). Iovinus held this post at the time Fortunatus was writing these Provençal letters (title to *Poem* 7.11: Gregory, *HF*, 4.43), but was succeeded by Dynamius (Gregory, *HF*, 6.11). For further comment on this poem, see George, pp. 141-3.
123 A classical motif (e.g. Ovid, *Her.* 2.25-6, and 15.209) which Fortunatus also uses in writing to Gogo (*Poem* 7.4.1-4).
124 This Horatian echo (cf. Horace, *Carm.* 1.3.8, 2.17.5) gives an Augustan ring, but also recalls originals addressed to a friend or patron who was themselves a poet - a twofold compliment. The phrase is also used in early Christian consolations, emphasising the poet's protestation of grief; see von Moos, *Testimonien* T 131-135.
125 For classical examples of lovers thus haunted, see, e.g., Vergil, *Aen.* 4.465-6: Ovid, *Her.* 7.25-6, 12.109-10. For this language of ascetic love, see P. Fabre, *Saint Paulin de Nole et l'amitié chrétienne* (Paris, 1949), pp.137-54: C. White, *Christian friendship in the fourth century* (Cambridge, 1992).

come here after all this time, (20) and bring back the light to my eyes, my friend.

Book Seven

Poem 7.1: to Gogo[1]

When Orpheus[2] began to stir the strings with his thumb, and the cords gave forth their song, as the lyre was struck, then with the resounding instrument he caressed the woods with sweetness, and drew the wild beasts in love to his lute's song. (5) From all sides lairs are emptied and send forth the deer; the tiger itself comes, laying aside its fury. At the seductive strain, the nightingale speeds with rapid flight, the weary bird reckoning little for her brood[3]; but though she has tired her wings over the long distance, (10) the bird is revived, reaching her heart's desire.

Enchanted thus by your stirring sweetness, Gogo, the foreign traveller draws near the distant realm. Your eloquence, like Orpheus with his lyre, summons all to hasten here with greater speed from all quarters[4]. (15) When the weary exile himself has arrived here, he sheds through your healing whatever ailed him before. You banish lamentation from the afflicted and instill joy; lest they should be parched, you nurture them with the dew from your lips. You build combs with your speech, supplying new honey; (20) and with the nectar of your sweet eloquence you surpass the bees[5]. The great charm

---

[1] For Gogo's career, see Biographical Notes. For further analysis of this poem and others to Gogo, see George, pp. 136-40; Godman, pp. 15-21.

[2] This first line echoes Ovid's depiction of Orpheus (*Met.* 10.145) to praise Gogo's *dulcedo*, his sweet charm and generosity. For this quality, especially in reference to this poem, see Godman pp.14-21.

[3] The nightingale's action is all the more telling in that her song is often represented as a lament for the loss of her young; e.g. Vergil,*Georg.* 4.511-515.

[4] This is a reference not only to Gogo's welcome of the poet himself, but to the safe arrival of other travellers - the magnates of the entire kingdom, invited to Sigibert's wedding (Gregory, *HF,* 4.27), and also Brunhild, escorted from Spain by Gogo (Fredegar, *Chron.* 3.59, p.109). See the explicit reference to this in lines 41-2 below. Given the difficulty of organising this event, comparison with the magical powers of Orpheus is not inappropriate.

[5] The honey of eloquence is a familiar phrase; see Godman, pp. 16-21. But Gogo's knowledge of Vergil would enable to him to remember the Vergilian connection between

of your lips, from whose sanctuary flows the feast of your voice, revives with its rich fountain. Rich wisdom rules with ever watchful understanding, with which the flow of wit, with its hidden spark, overflows; (25) you hurl the rays from your heart with the splendour of your mind, and your brilliance, challenging the light of day, is radiant within; at times the earth is covered now by sun, now by cloud - but your fair heart always keeps the day's light; esteemed as a temple of piety, your inmost heart ready, (30) you are become a dwelling place wrought of holy offerings. Your noble appearance is resplendent with its own glory, so that your aspect in itself confirms the cast of your character. You draw together all manner of praise into one kind, and there is nothing more than what your nature creates.

(35) You are considered great in the judgement of the prince, Sigibert; no-one can deceive the judgement of the king. The sagacious man has chosen a sage, one who loves a lover, just as the wise bee singles out the flowers. From his virtue you learnt to be reckoned as such, (40) and you reflect back the ways of your master, gentle servant. Just now you bring the greatest joy for the noble king from the lands of Spain, through a myriad dangers[6]. You love him so much that you have won better fortune for him; no-one has been able to give him by force of arms what your tongue has bestowed[7]. (45) If I am silent about these blessings, my silence applauds you; you who dwell in my heart, do not expect my voice[8]. I sing the truth by my silence, and deceit does not condemn me, I speak with the people as my witness; I will go free of any charge of wrongdoing. May this passionate praise rise to you over the long years, (50) may this life long keep you safe and that life bless you.

---

bees and Orpheus, and be prepared for the more abstruse compliment of lines 37-8 below. In *Georgics* 4.453 ff. Vergil tells the story of Orpheus and praises the wise bee, connected with the Muses and possessing the power of reason. The bee is also a Christian symbol of wisdom and virtue (e.g. Basil the Great, *Address to young men*, 7.8.4; Athanasius, *Vita Anth.*, 3-4; cf. Fortunatus, *Poems* 4.11.9-10, 8.3.83-4, for further use of the image); see also T. Janson, *Latin prose prefaces* (Stockholm, 1964), pp. 152-153. The compliment in the later couplet is twofold; to Sigibert for his wisdom, and to Gogo as the worthy object of his discrimination.
6 The arrival of Brunhild; see note 3 above.
7 Fortunatus' praise of peaceable achievement is typical; see, for example, *Poem* 6.1, note 8.
8 A conventional modesty *topos*; see Curtius, pp. 83-5.

Poem 7.7: on Duke Lupus[9]

    Let great men of old and the lofty names of olden times give way one and all, vanquished by the achievement of Duke Lupus. You alone possess all the traits which were exercised by Scipio the wise[10], by Cato the venerable[11] and by Pompey the fortunate[12]. (5) With these men as consuls[13], Rome's might shone in splendour; but with you as Duke, Rome has now here returned for us. As you grant access to all, confidence has risen, a free tongue has given the succour of freedom. If anyone bore grief in his troubled breast, (10) after seeing you he abides with better hope. Firm fast with your weighty spirit, with a profound heart you pour from your lips the salt[14] of a tranquil sea; but your gifts of eloquence are of greater benefit to the people; you season our understanding, as the salt water seasons our food. (15) The source of counsel, a rich vein of good sense, a lively spirit, eloquent with rounded discourse, you who are glorious in two matters, well grounded in both, your tongue can give forth whatever you conceive in your

---

9 Lupus, Duke of Champagne, had his main residence at Reims, but served Sigibert widely in military and diplomatic matters. Fortunatus mentions a victory over the Saxons and the Danes (lines 49-60), and he took part in an embassy to Marseilles (Gregory, *HF*, 4.46). He befriended the poet on his arrival (*Poem* 7.8.49-50), and this poem was probably written shortly afterwards. The poem congratules Lupus on his appointment as *dux* (line 6), presumably for his military successes, and for the judicial and diplomatic skills the poet praises in lines 11-44. For an account of this post, see *Poem* 6.1, note 6.
Though this is not a full royal panegyric, it has many of the features of that genre, in tribute to Lupus' distinction; the sequence of topics - Lupus' achievements in peace and in war - , the use of classical examples, and the light imagery of panegyric; for the latter, see *Poems* 5.2, note 3; 6. 1, notes 10, 30; 6. 1a, note 37. For discussion of this poem, see George, pp. 79-82
10 P. Cornelius Scipio Africanus Maior, 237-183 B.C., the great Roman general of the Punic wars.
11 P. Cato, the Censor, 234-149 B.C., who served with military distinction, and then campaigned indefatigably at Rome against luxury and extravagance. He was the first major Latin prose writer.
12 Cn. Pompeius Magnus, 106-48 B.C., a general of great distinction and success; a member of the triumvirate which heralded the end of the Roman Republic, together with M. Crassus and Julius Caesar, marrying Caesar's daughter, Julia. Defeated at the battle of Pharsalus in 48 B.C., he was murdered shortly afterwards in Egypt.
13 These three Republican heroes evoke all the might and splendour of Rome; lines 7-19 list the Roman virtues which have contributed to Lupus' success - *gravitas*, eloquence and wisdom.
14 Salt is synonymous with wit, good sense and wisdom.

heart. The authority of the king is strengthened in your heart, (20) the cares of the state are fortified by your aid. With fresh love you submit your limbs to a multitude of tasks; the burden is considered sweet, for the sake of the king's peace. O blessed spirit which deliberates on the affairs of our country, o noble mind which lives for all men. (25) Ambassadors arrive[15]; they are bound by your response and soon lie prone with the javelin of your words. Your speech was a lance, your voice as you speak was armoured, and Sigibert holds you as a token of victory. The response of the nation is articulated by that understanding, (30) and a single voice suffices to speak the will of the people. Because of his ability the cause won a triumph, through the support of this advocate that cause was more just. For none would be able to expound thus their own cause as well as your noble tongue can thunder forth on behalf of all. (35) As the Nile revives Egypt when it inundates it with its flood[16], so you nourish all with the stream of your eloquence. With you as judge, the laws favour the flourishing of justice, and you are the scales for deciding cases, weighted justly. They flee to you, the noble belts[17] seek you, (40) nor do you look for your own advantage; all honour seeks you out; in your breast power is won and nurtured, the pinnacle of honour, granted to you as governor, knows how to grow in strength. How justly does he hold the honours constantly awarded, through whom the august, all the more worthily, win their highest ornament.

(45) Gaining your venerable traits from your Roman stock, you wage war with force of arms, you govern the sway of law in tranquillity. Supported by both virtues - by arms on the one hand, by the law on the other - how splendidly he becomes foremost upon whom all glory smiles! (50) The race of the Saxons and the Danes, speedily conquered[18], show what virtue is yours with blessing from above. Where the river Borda runs with winding stream, there the battle line confronting you as Duke was slaughtered and perished. Then a half of the forces were under your command; how deservedly did he win who carried out your orders! (55) As victor you sweated under the weight

---

15 This is possibly the occasion referred to by Gregory, *HF*, 4.46.
16 A traditional rhetorical comparison, which strengthens the panegyric overtones.
17 The Merovingian kings gave, as a sign of their favour, belts distinguished by the splendid and complex design of their buckles; see E. James,*The Merovingian Archaeology of South West Gaul*, British Archaeological Reports, Suppl. Ser. 2/5, i and ii (Oxford, 1980), p. 100.
18 This battle is otherwise unrecorded.

of your iron-clad tunic[19] and were resplendent under the cloud of dust, long fighting on, pursuing as the line of battle fled, until the end was reached at the Lahn with its glassy waters. That river gave burial to all who had fled without resistance; (60) the waters waged war for the lucky general. Gaul has won you as a beacon among your fellow countrymen, you who shine forth everywhere in splendour through the lustre of your spirit. There are those who are singled out by their powerful physique, others by their wisdom; others have single virtues, you have many. (65) In joining the lords, you add perfection to the noble palace, and glory, accompanying you as you enter, is multiplied. With your coming, the bountiful dwelling is lustrous with new tranquillity and the royal abode recovers its presiding spirit. Assuredly the court recovers its chief ornament when it sees you return, (70) whom the glorious leaders hold as their common glory; a succour to your prince, an adornment to your country, a bulwark for your parents, a source of wisdom for others, a unique love to all. What could I say of your admirable graciousness, you who, full of nectar, build honeycombs with your speech[20]. (75) Delightful grace[21] accompanies your bright aspect, and clear light, always renewed, glows even deep within[22]. You satisfy with your food, you refresh with your blessed speech; your words are a feast, food is put to one side. Who could speak of you in worthy fashion[23], (80) you whom the gracious king with powerful voice declares as his adornment. May the highest pinnacle be yours as he reigns throughout the age, and may life be propitious and bless you in times to come.

---

19 See Salin, 1, pp. 98-117, especially Plates 3-6; P. Lasko, *The kingdom of the Franks: northwest Europe before Charlemagne* (London, 1971), pp. 46-55.
20 For the classical and Christian overtones of honey, see note 5 above.
21 For this quality, see Godman, pp. 15-21.
22 The light imagery of royal panegyric (see *Poem* 5.2, note 3) compliments Lupus.
23 For this *topos* of inexpressibility, see Curtius, pp. 159-162.

Poem 7.8: to Duke Lupus[24]

When scorching July burns the fiery sands and the thirsty earth is parched on the dusty banks; when the vine tendrils, ennervated, scarce spread their gentle shade, the limp grass curls up its bright blades, and the grove, (5) its leaves drooping before the overpowering heat of Phoebus, hardly preserves the coolness of its own abode; when the heifer, unable to tolerate the heat, flees the pasture, and even vetch is not cropped by the suffering horses; in distress, the dog's tongue quivers, thrust far out of its mouth; (10) when the wretched sheep pants as it drags its weary flanks; then the traveller, happening to be treading his path at this scorching hour, is burned as the sun beats down with blazing rays. In distress he looks urgently for moistening water in the parched landscape, to revive himself with a modest draught, or that (15) the shade spilling from the verdant top of a quivering tree, its leafy branches set over him, may soften his thirst.

If, by change of luck, a grove near at hand now offers him shade, and if suddenly the waters of a limpid spring babble, in joy the man hastens there and stretches himself on the soft turf, (20) tumbling his limbs onto the grassy couch. Enjoying the granting of his wish, he is refreshed by two delights; the shade softens the light, and the stream banishes his thirst. If he knows any verses, he has recourse to them with measured song, and the gentler breeze summons forth also the gentle strains; (25) if he chances to be very familiar with Homer in Athens, or Vergil recited in Trajan's forum[25] in the city; or, if he has

---

24 This poem, looking back to Lupus' early support and friendship for the poet (lines 49-50), may well date nearer to *Poem* 7.9, written about 576 (lines 7-8), than to *Poem* 7.7. The later poems suggest regular, if not frequent, contact between the poet and his friend and patron; and Fortunatus also addresses Lupus' brother, Magnulf, in *Poem* 7.10. This poem, like 7.7, is classical in style and reference.
25 Trajan, Roman emperor 98-117 A.D., devoted large sums to building projects in Rome, including his Forum, where the Column of Trajan celebrated his campaigns, and the Bibliotheca Ulpia housed two great collections, one of Greek, and one of Latin writings. The forum was a centre for education and schooling; see Riché, p.30.

learned the teachings hallowed by David's lyre[26], he gives voice to the noble songs of the psalms with rounded lips. Or his fingers touch the lyre, flute, whistle or pipe; (30) each charms the birds in song with his own Muse.

In the same way I[27], exhausted by the fierce turbulence of anxiety, knowing that you are safe, am refreshed by spring waters. Lupus, name sweet to me, always on my tongue, inscribed on the page of my heart; the man whom, (35) once preserved within on tablets of sweetness[28], the indestructible ark[29] of my heart guards; possessing a wealth of love[30], a rich affection creating unalloyed talents[31] by its own feelings! A mind of gold surpasses the riches of the earth[32], (40) and brings the splendour of jewels[33] with its radiant heart. A fragrant disposition spreads forth sweet scents[34], bestowing for the spirit what incense is nobly wont to give. Honeyed[35] words spill over from your heart, and from your lips you render well-salted wisdom[36]. (45) Vanquishing the bright stars after night's darkness, for me your mind is as glorious as the rays of the morning star[37]. As the light coming from the rising sun revives the world, so your words illumine my mind.

When Germania, a strange land, filled my gaze, (50) you were like a father, and were there to take thought for my homeland[38]. When in joy I merited that you turn your tranquil countenance upon

---

26 I.e. the Old Testament psalms. For David, see *Poem* 9.2, note 54; also see Riché, pp. 282-283 for the teaching of the psalms in the episcopal schools of Gaul.
27 Fortunatus now explains the relevance of the vivid simile in lines 1-22 in terms of his own relief at good news about Lupus - we do not know what the nature of the crisis was. Like his traveller, he expresses his delight both in classical terms (lines 1-22 echo classical nature descriptions closely) and in biblical terms (lines 33-44).
28 Cf. Proverbs, 3.3.
29 Cf. Deuteronomy, 10.3.
30 Cf. Proverbs, 10.2.
31 Cf. Matth., 18, 23-5; 25, 14-30.
32 Cf. Proverbs., 16.16.
33 Cf. Proverbs, 20.15.
34 See *Poem* 6.6, note 110.
35 See note 4 above.
36 Cf. Matth. 5.13; salt is also the frequent classical synonym for wit or wisdom.
37 The light imagery in this and following lines perhaps echoes in compliment the light imagery of royal panegyric; see *Poem* 5.2, note 3.
38 This final passage is almost a mini-panegyric; introduction with conventional self-deprecation by the poet, Lupus' virtues in war and peace, and exordium, together with light imagery.

me, straightway the daylight blazed with double its radiance on this earth. Whenever I exchanged words with you, I felt that I lay down in heavenly roses. (55) Your kindness, remaining the same for everyone, has been even greater for me, it has bound me with urgent affection. And now, who could offer repayment worthy of such honour, for such great gifts[39]? I am overcome by the subject, my eloquence is unworthy. Thus an eminence towers over with its lofty peak; (60) my love urges me on, but your qualities stand in my way. But let the rest on my behalf compete to exalt you, and let each in the song he best can sing your praise; let the Roman applaud you with the lute, the barbarian with the harp[40], the Greek with epic lyre, the Briton with the crowd[41]. (65) Let these tell of you as brave, those of you as mighty in justice, let the one declare you fleetfooted in fight, the other as swift in learning. And because you duly administer what peace and war demand, let one sing your glory as a judge, the other as a general. Let me offer you my humble versicles, let the barbarian song offer its German lays[42]; (70) thus may one single paean resound to the man in differing modes. Let the latter record you as famous, the former as wise in law; but I will always hold you dear and gracious, Lupus.

---

39 For the *topos* of inexpressibility, see Curtius, pp. 159-162.
40 For reference to these songs, see Pseudo-Fred.*Chron.*, 4.1 (SRM, 2, p.124) in honour of Guntram; Paul the Deacon, *HL,* 1.27 (MGH SRL, 1.4) in honour of Alboin. Nothing survives, however, and we only know that they were accompanied by harp or cithara.
41 Or crwth, an early stringed instrument.
42 Lit. *leudos*, a Frankish term. By summoning both Roman and Frankish tributes, Fortunatus marks the importance of Lupus' acceptability to both cultures and ethnic groups, as he did to Charibert (*Poem* 6.2.7-8, note 51) and to Chilperic (*Poem* 9.1.93-4).

Poem 7.16: on Conda, the *domesticus*[43]

For long years rich splendour has been glorious in the king's court through your merits, Conda. For once it spied you as a young man with alert heart, it chose to have you always with itself even as an old man. (5) What intellect was it and what maturity of feeling, when you were thus the single love of such great kings? Your noble mind is glorious with splendid light, which magnified your forebears with its very merits. The succeeding generation, through which its own origin is dignified, flourishes (10) and causes your forefathers of old to rise in praise. For if he who maintains the family's honour is esteemed, how much more praiseworthy is it to ennoble a family? So he who wishes to exalt his name by his deeds, let him speedily think upon your achievement. (15) Starting from humble beginnings, you have always advanced to the heights and through all stages held to the lofty pinnacles. Theuderic[44], rejoicing, adorned you with the office of tribune[45]; from that point you already had the mark of successful advance. For Theudebert[46] granted you the prize of being a count[47],

---

43 Conda's position at Sigibert's court suggests that this poem was written in the first year or so of Fortunatus' life in Gaul; the *domesticus* is not otherwise known. The poem offers him the tribute of the full sequence of panegyric topics; introductory address (lines 1-6), family and parents (lines 7-14), virtues in peace and war, though these latter are the vicarious ones of the loss of two sons fighting for their country (lines 15-52), and exordium, with the usual light imagery of the genre. The reversal of the usual second section to pay tribute to Conda as the founder, rather than the product, of a noble line, is a neat reversal of that topic in presumably apposite compliment to a self-made man. For further discussion, see George, pp. 82-3.

The *domesticus* had the main responsibility for running the palace and the royal estates. On the duties and position, see A. H. M. Jones, *The Later Roman Empire* (London, 1967), pp.602-3; for the Merovingian development of the post, see A. Carlot, *Étude sur le domesticus franc*, Bibliothèque de la Faculté de Philosophie et Lettres de l'Université de Liège 13 (Liège, 1903).

44 For Theuderic, see Biographical Note on Theudechild, and *Poem 4.25.9*.

45 The duties of a tribune seem to have been mainly related to tax gathering; e.g. Gregory, *GC* 40, and for comment, see W. Goffart, *Romans and Barbarians A.D. 418 - 584* (Princeton, 1980), p. 85, note 53; p. 223, note 34.

46 For Theudebert, Theuderic's son, see Biographical Note on Theudechild, and *Poem* 4.25.9.

47 For the position of *comes*, see *Poem* 6.8, note 120.

(20) and added a belt[48] in recognition of your services. He saw that excellent characters deserve better, and was soon willing to raise the rank you had earned. He saw to it urgently that you then became *domesticus*[49]; you rose suddenly, and the court rose with you. (25) The revered palace flourished together with you, and the household applauded its vigilant marshal. Then, whilst Theudebald's young child was yet alive, your great care was for his nurture[50]. Thus by distinguished action you fostered the public order, (30) that you could bring the young king to mature age. You governed yourself, as though you were there as guardian, and the business entrusted to you flourished. Again, you held sway in Lothar's[51] great court, who ordered the household to be ruled with the same love.

(35) Kings changed, but you did not change your offices, and as your own successor you were worthy of yourself. So great was the people's love of you, so great was your expertise in management, that no-one would willingly have taken the task away from you. For now through the love of gentle King Sigibert, (40) gifts are lavishly given to reward your services. He has commanded you to establish yourself amongst the noble magnates, appointing you his table companion[52], a promoted post. The king, more powerful than the rest, has provided rightly better rewards, and your case demonstrates what he values more highly.

(45) Thus your condition has always been to deserve better, and your honours have grown as your life has progressed. Saxony in mourning proclaims the valour you had; it is praise to a valiant old man that he did not fear arms, for the prayers of his country and the great love of his king, (50) for which two dear sons lie dead. May you

---

48 For the significance of this belt, see *Poem* 7.7, note 17.
49 For the *domesticus*, see note 42 above.
50 For the role and influence of a royal tutor, see J. Nelson, "Queens as Jezebels: the careers of Brunhild and Balthild in Merovingian history", in D. Baker (ed.), *Medieval Women*, Studies in Church History, subsidia 1 (Oxford, 1978), pp. 41-42; also Biographical Note on Gogo.
51 Lothar, Sigibert's father, ruled the kingdom of Soissons from 511-61; see Gregory, *HF*, 3.1, 7, 11, 18, 23, 28-9: 4.1-3, 9-12, 14-21: Wood, pp. 50, 58-60, 111-2, 114.
52 The honour of being formally included amongst those who eat at the king's table, of being a *conviva regis*, is mentioned in Salic and Burgundian codes of law. See *Leges Burgundionum, lib. constit.*, 38.2, ed. L. R. de Salis, MGH *Legum Sect.* 1, 2/1 (Hanover, 1892), p.70; *Lex Salica*, 41.8, ed. K. A. Eckhardt, MGH *Legum Sect.* 1, 4/2 (Hanover, 1969), p.156. For a general account, see F. Lot, *La naissance de la France* (Paris, 1948), pp. 203-11.

not mourn grievously that both died manfully, for to die with praise will be to live for ever. Your countenance radiates joy from your happy expression, and bears sure rejoicing without any cloud of mind. (55) In generosity and kindness you bestow gifts in plenty on all, and bind men to you by your gifts. May long-lived wellbeing be with you, with ever more blessing through serene years, may glorious children restore their father.

Poem 7.24: verses for a salver and festive occasions[53]

(*a*)   You who read the words inscribed round the beautiful metal, if you come pure in heart, you imitate this piece of work. For, as silver is proved in the hot furnace, so man improves himself by cleansing his heart[54].

(*b*)   You who come as a loyal companion to feast with your dear friends, you take more in love that which is lesser at feasts. A foreign guest did not bear these over the sea; take happily what the homestead gods[55] have produced.

(*c*)   Though grave care with learned speech oppresses you, come here and join in as a poet with your festive merriment[56]. But in such a way that an honourable man keeps his proper reason, for unguarded speech tends to create strife.

(*d*)   Man's life is short, present moments flee away; devote yourself rather to what will remain undying. Establish justice, spread

---

53 The title refers to verses engraved on a kind of elaborate metal platter. This clearly derives from the content of (a), but the rest of the verses may well be the short epigrams for declamation at a feast, of which we have other examples; see *Poem* 3.13, note 9. Here, as elsewhere, the title is a later addition, and not always even derived accurately from the sense of the poem; see Koebner, p. 123; Meyer, pp. 72, 87-88.
54 For this idea, see Malachi, 3.2; 1 Peter, 1.7.
55 Lit. the Lares, the Roman household gods; i.e. a domestic wine.
56 For an example of the continuation of the classical practice of literary entertainment at the dinner table, Fortunatus praises Radegund for such verses in *Appendix* 31.1-2. *Poems* 11.23 and 23a are also examples of Fortunatus' own contributions.

peace abroad, love Christ, seek the delights which you will enjoy for ever.

(*e*)   After the weight of business, throw off the palace squabbles; a hospitable table bids us enjoy life. Let quarrels, anger and tumult fall silent, the courts, disputes and laws; here let the tranquillity rule which a welcome day brings.

(*f*)   I'm asking you, bring a peaceable spirit to table; seek an enemy elsewhere, if a fight is what you want. Refuse to pursue a quarrel in the midst of pleasures; let the field furnish you with arms, the table with vegetables.

(*g*)   If you are to be considered a greathearted man of steely virtue, tell of fierce war to the wine cups without threat. He who comes here to acknowledge the festivities of our table, let grace alone commend the food set in front of him.

Book Eight

Poem 8.2: on the subject of his journey, when he should have journeyed to Lord Germanus[1], and was held back by Lady Radegund

Behold the day shines glorious, our journey awaits our going, and, fulfilling its obligations, behold the day shines glorious. There my father summons me, Germanus splendid on this earth, here my mother holds me back; there my father summons me. (5) Each dear to me, tied to me with a binding promise, filled with God's love, each dear to me. She is dearer than my soul, though he may be more renowned with holy rank, she is dearer than my soul. A single intent holds both, as they travel with equal step, (10) striving for what is righteous, a single intent holds both. Each is benefited by whatever good the other has done, by every good deed of the one the other is benefited. Because they are equally dear, I do not refuse to go when I am ordered; I will obey them both, because they are equally dear. (15) Yet I do not depart from here, though I will see new abodes; I leave in body, but yet I do not depart from here. I will be here completely, and not removed in heart nor in mind; thus whilst I am returning, I will be here completely. May my mother hold out blessed protection for me as I go; (20) that she may have all the more for herself, may she hold out blessed protection.

---

[1] For Germanus and Radegund, see Biographical Notes. This poem gives insight into the relationships between the poet, Germanus and Radegund, both powerful characters, by its sentiments and also by its pattern - each couplet seesawing between two phrases identical in weight and force (cf. *Poem* 3.30, for the same technique).

Poem 8.6: to Lady Radegund about violets[2]

If the season bore me the customary white lilies, or the rose were brilliant with dazzling scarlet, I would pick these in the countryside or from the bed in my poor garden, and send them gladly as a humble gift to the great. (5) But since I have not got the former, at least I will perform the latter; he who offers vetch, in loving intent, would bear roses. Yet amongst the sweet smelling plants I send, the purple violet has a noble flower. Dyed with regal purple[3], they exhale a regal scent, (10) and with their leaves pervade all with their scent and with their beauty. May you both have equally both of these things which they bear, and may the scent of your merits[4] be a glory everlasting in flower.

Poem 8.7: to Lady Radegund and Agnes about the flowers upon the altar[5]

With the ice of winter's chill the earth is fettered[6] and all the fields' brightness dies with the flowers' absence. In the season of spring, when the Lord conquered Tartarus, the grass comes forth and opens out, more joyous with its greenery. (5) There the men deck the

---

2 This poem is very much in the classical tradition of only giving what you have been able to pick yourself; cf. Martial, *Epp.* 7.31, 7.91; Pliny, *Ep.* 5.2; Ausonius, *Epp.* 18.7-9, 25, 33, 34.
3 The symbolism in the purple flowers of Radegund's regal status and her honourable widowhood (see Jerome, *Ep.* 54.14) is underlined by the classical dignity of a strong echo of Horace in this phrase (cf. Horace, *Carm.*, 2.16.35-36). The reference, to a poem in which the poet rejects the worldy paraphernalia of wealth and success, also pays tribute to Radegund's life of abstinence. Fortunatus emphasises Radegund's royal status, making it, as he does in his prose hagiographies, a quality from which spiritual power derives; for this change in tradition, see R. Collins, "Observations on the form, language and public of the prose biographies of Venantius Fortunatus in the hagiography of Merovingian Gaul", in H. B. Clarke and M. Brennan (eds.), *Columbanus and Merovingian mentality* (Oxford, 1981), pp. 105-131.
4 For the odour of virtues, see *Poem* 6.6, note 110.
5 The title, as given, mentions only Radegund, though the poem clearly addresses both of the nuns. For the occasional inaccuracy of the titles, see *Poem* 7.24, note 53.
6 The first line echoes the classical nature writing of Claudian (cf. Claudian, *Bell. Poll.* 60), though line 3 puts the poem firmly in the Christian tradition.

doors and platforms with flowers, here the women fill their bosoms with the scent of roses. But you bring sweet scent not for yourselves, but for Christ you make these first offerings to the holy temples. You interweave the festive altars with garlands of various hue, (10) and the altar is painted with fresh flowers, like coloured threads. On this side the golden rank comes forth from saffron, and here the purple from violets, here the scarlet glows red, and there the milky white is like snow. The Blue takes his stand against the Green[7]; the colours compete even in flowers, and in a place of peace, you would imagine a battle of plants. (15) This delights with its glossy whiteness, that glows with ruddy beauty; this has a more delightful scent, that is a more exquisite crimson. Thus the flower buds rival each other with their varied beauty, so that the colour here outstrips jewels, here the scent rivals incense. You too, who have arranged these, Agnes and Radegund, may your odour breathe with the scent of eternal flowers[8].

Poem 8.18: to Bishop Gregory in greeting

If a tongue directed its flow of eloquence like a whirlpool, or was snatched along in the rush of a raging torrent, in response to these lofty proclamations of yours, Gregory, I would become a mere drop, so long as I could not discharge my response in a stream. Not even Vergil's muse would compare in the generosity of her patron: tell me, good friend, how much can anyone say on my behalf? With this brief note, holy man, I commend myself, Fortunatus, your servant, to your attention; have mercy upon me, I pray.

---

7 This sophisticated metaphor from the circus factions of Byzantium conveys the vivid demand for attention. For these colours, see Alan Cameron, *Circus Factions; Blues and Greens at Rome and Byzantium* (Oxford, 1976), pp. 45-73. The Byzantine reference may be prompted by Radegund's contact with the court there in search of relics; Baudonivia, *VR*, 2.16; see also *Appendix* 2, note 1.
8 See note 4 above.

Poem 8.19: to Bishop Gregory for the offer of a villa[9]

    The page which your love produced with sweet-running verse[10] celebrated its passage in generous manner, in which the offer of the gift was made, where the bold Vienne dashes its waters against the bank, (5) and the sailor, as he is carried in his boat on his rolling passage, sees the ploughed acres as he sings the time out to the rowers[11]. I thank you, dear friend, who are amply provided with the fruits of goodness, you who see to it that a goodly total is multiplied. And apart from these, mine are whatever I hold from you: (10) the whole flock has in the fields what you, good shepherd, have[12].

Poem 8.21: to Bishop Gregory for the skins he sent

    The page, put together in excellent fashion[13], ornamented around, and stiffened by Sophoclean wisdom, richly waters my aridity with your bedewing, and makes what I say due to your eloquence. (5) Kind, dear, good, eloquent and bountiful Gregory, father of his country, both holy and wise, of equal gifts, virtues, intellect and character, in all matters being such that you are cherished; I throw my humble self, Fortunatus, before your loftiness, (10) and with my prayer and entreaty duly commend myself to you; to me you grant that the sandals you sent are strapped up and that the soles of my feet are covered with white skins. For these, may a white robe be granted you by the Lord[14]; may you who give this to the lowliest one, from that gain reward.

---

9 This gift is represented in terms of the generosity of an Augustan patron such as Maecenas, who gave a similar gift to the poet Horace. For the literary relationship of Gregory and Fortunatus, see *Poem* 9.7, note 99.

10 This and the following poem make it clear that Gregory and the poet were in the habit of exchanging poems - as does *Poem* 9.7 below.

11 For river traffic in Gaul, see L. Bonnard, *La navigation intérieure de la Gaule à l'époque gallo-romaine* (Paris, 1913).

12 For this sentiment, see *Poem* 3.13, note 7.

13 Fortunatus' thanks are expressed in a humorous high-flown, mock tragic style.

14 I.e. in heaven

Book Nine

Poem 9.1: to *King Chilperic on the occasion of the Synod at Berny-Rivière*[1]

O company of priests[2], Christ's revered champions, you whom bountiful faith has made our fathers in our religion, I humbly beg to

---

1 In 580 Chilperic summoned Gregory of Tours to a synod of the bishops of his kingdom at his villa at Berny-Rivière. Gregory was accused by Leudast, count of Tours, of spreading the malicious slander that Fredegund was committing adultery with Bertram, Bishop of Bordeaux. Bertram was present at the synod to lay the charge and interrogate Gregory, whilst, according to Gregory, public feeling ran high in his favour (Gregory, *HF*, 5.49). The context of this trial is complex, but may be roughly outlined as follows: on Sigibert's death, Brunhild married Merovech, Chilperic's rebellious son. Bertram, previously friendly to Gregory and Fortunatus during Sigibert's lifetime (see *Poem* 3.17.18), presided over a court in 577 which charged Bishop Praetextatus of Rouen, who had married Brunhild and Merovech, of corruption in buying support for Merovech. Chilperic and Fredegund had Praetextatus removed from his see through bribery and trickery, and in the process attempted to bribe Gregory, to his well-publicised outrage (Gregory, *HF*, 5.18). Leudast, a long standing enemy of Gregory (*HF*, 5.47-9), exploited these divisions in an attempt to gain revenge for past humiliations; his accusation was perhaps particularly threatening to Chilperic, since Bertram was half-cousin to the king (see Meyer, p. 83 and the genealogical table). Moreover, if Gregory were cleared, the king and queen ran the risk of being excommunicated for bringing such a charge (Gregory, *HF*, 5.49). The synod looked likely to be a re-run of the mock trial of Praetextatus, with a similar outcome threatening the bishop. But in the event, Gregory was cleared, and Leudast and others involved in the plot were killed or fled.

Fortunatus addressed the synod with this panegyric of Chilperic. Some have interpreted it as opportunistic betrayal of his friend (see S. Dill, *Roman Society in Gaul in the Merowingian Age* ((London, 1926), p. 333; Koebner, p. 95, attacks Meyer's earlier apologia for the poet (pp.115-26)). For the view that the poem is a skilful use of the genre to defend Gregory and prevent future tensions, see George, pp. 48-57; Godman, pp. 28-37). See also James (1988), pp. 165-169; Wood, pp. 86-7; van Dam (1985) pp. 185, 213-214 (especially useful on Gregory's vulnerable tenure of the bishopric).

The poem has the usual order of panegyric topics: introduction, early years and family, virtues in war and peace, and exordium. A short eulogy of Fredegund (lines 115-26) is included; cf. the address to Brunhild in *Poem* 6.1a.29-40, and note 46.

2 In traditional fashion, the poet acknowledges the audience to his address to the king. Given the context, and the support Gregory reports for himself, this appeal is particularly significant. Cf. *Poem* 6.2, note 48, for a similar context.

speak forth the praises of our noble king. May your love compensate for my lowly verses[3].

(5) O king, renowned in war and sprung from a noble line of kings[4], foremost of those of old, commanding the foremost heights, as leader you inherited honour by birth, but increased it by your wise rule. Sprung as a vigorous shoot from your father's line, in turn you each have ennobled the other; (10) you have been an ornament to your forefathers' line, as they likewise are to you. You have received glory from your lineage, but through you lustrous distinction has been added to your ancestors. When you were born to your father, another light was created for the world[5]; you cast the new rays of your fame in every direction; (15) the East, the South, the West, and the North exalt you[6]; by your honour and renown you reach even places where your foot does not tread. Through your fame, o king, you have traversed every sector of the world, you speed on the track the sun's wheel traces; you are known even by the Red Sea and the Indian Sea, (20) your dazzling reputation for wisdom has crossed even the Ocean. Neither wind nor wave prevent your name from being proclaimed abroad; thus do all things, heaven and earth, favour you. O king, of admirable virtue, of lofty fame and noble ancestry, in whom so many exalted leaders find their leader; (25) defender of our country[7], our hope and protection in time of war, of steadfast courage for your people, of renowned vigour, o powerful Chilperic; if a barbarian interpreter were at hand, your name would be rendered also as "valiant defender"[8]. It was not for nothing that your parents named you thus; (30) this indeed was a

---

3 A conventional self-deprecation; see Curtius, pp. 83-5.
4 The Horatian flourish of this phrase (an echo of Horace, *Carm.* 1.1.1) pays an imperial classical compliment to a king who not only had strong views on theology and education, but was also a poet, albeit a poor one in Gregory's view (*HF,* 5.44).
5 Note the light imagery of regal splendour in lines 11-19, and 102 (for this imagery, see Poem 5.2, note 3).
6 The panegyric motif of universal consensus is used here on a grandiose scale; see Poem 6.2, note 50.
7 For the poet's constant emphasis on peace, see *Poem* 6.1, note 8. The architectural symbolism here and in lines 79 - 84 is suitably defensive, rather than offensive. For such symbolism in panegyric, see E. Baldwin-Smith, *Architectural symbolism of imperial Rome and the middle ages* (New York, 1978): MacCormack (1981), pp. 1-4.
8 The element "Chilpe-" means "help"; "-ric" means powerful. Cf. *Poem* 6.1a.1, for similar play on the derivation of Sigibert's name.

complete presage[9], an omen of your repute. Even then, events gave a sign for the newborn, yet later blessings bring to fruition earlier promises. On you, dear one, rested all your father's hopes[10], among so many brothers you alone thus were his love. (35) For he realised even then that you were worthy of greater things; just as your father nurtured you more, so he gave you preference; the sire set on high the child he loved best; no one can set aside the king's judgement.

You grew up under auspicious signs, greatest prince, (40) abiding in the love of both the people and your father. But suddenly life's fortune, jealous of such qualities, seeking to disrupt the peace of your reign[11], and disturbing the disposition of the people and the agreements of your brothers[12], favoured you with success in its attempt to bring you down. But then, (45) as danger menaced your valiant head[13], the hour which could have struck you down instead drove death

---

9 The childhood portents of future greatness are a commonplace in this section of a panegyric; see L. B. Struthers, "The rhetorical structure of the encomia of Claudius Claudian", *Harvard Studies in Classical Philology* 30 (1919), pp. 67-70.

10 At the time of Lothar's death, only four of his seven sons were still alive: Charibert, Guntram and Sigibert, his sons by Ingund, and Chilperic, his son by Ingund's sister and successor in the king's favour, Aregund (Gregory, *HF*, 4.3 and 22). The two elder sons of Ingund, Gunthar and Childeric, were dead; Chramm, his son by Chunsina, together with his wife and daughters, had rebelled unsuccessfully against his father and been killed (Gregory, *HF*, 4.20). On the succession, see Wood, pp. 58-60. But Fortunatus' reference to Lothar's favour for Chilperic need not be taken so literally, as Wood does, given the literary and political context. Panegyric is a genre for negotiation and diplomacy. Given a context in which the charge against Gregory stemmed largely from Chilperic's insecurity, the poet's concern may well be to defuse the situation by sending all possible messages to the king that there is no challenge, from these notables at least, in what was formerly Sigibert's kingdom. Chilperic's pre-emptive seizure on Lothar's death of the royal villa and treasure - at Berny - may suggest a lack of certainty about his standing and rights, rather than the reverse (Gregory, *HF*, 4.22). And the location of this trial would aid the judicious re-interpretation of the past. For a similarly pointed comment on the relationship between Lothar and one of his sons, see *Poem* 6.2.49 - 62, and notes 54 and 59.

11 Peace was never a feature of Chilperic's rule. But if we see the purpose of the poem as reconciling Chilperic and Gregory and bringing a period of potentially disastrous tension to an end, we may also see here the poet beginning to build up the persuasive portrait of the king as a peace-loving Christian ruler in an exhortatory "mirror of princes" approach (see also the panegyric to Charibert, *Poem* 6.2, note 53).

12 This must refer to Chilperic's attempt to steal a march on his brothers (Gregory, *HF*, 4.22), which, with a talent for the politic reconstruction of events such as we see in the account (or non-account) of Galswinth's murder in *Poem* 6.5, Fortunatus here presents as fate's failed attempt to break the brothers' unity.

13 The reference of lines 45-54 is unclear. It may be to otherwise unrecorded events during the redistribution of Lothar's kingdom. It may be the desperate plight of Chilperic and Fredegund at the siege of Tournai in 575, when they were only saved by the murder of

away from you. When you were held encompassed around by the weapons of destruction, fate rescued you from the sword by God's intervention. Brought to life's extremity, you returned from the point of destruction; (50) the day which had been your last became your first. When enemies were seeking to raise destructive war against you, faith, strong against arms[14], fought for you. Your cause successfully reached a judgement without you, and the lofty seat returned to its rightful place[15].

(55) Good king, do not weep. The fate which wearied you with troubles, now for the same reason has given you better fortune. Through your enduring such hardship for so long, happier times have now come, and you reap the joy which is sown of such sorrow. Having endured many threats, you take up your royal power again; (60) for it is by great labours that great achievements usually grow. Harsh fortune has not harmed you; in its harshness it has proved you; you emerge the more exalted from what bore you down. You rise all the higher with constant trials of arms. You are not broken by them; the effort itself makes you a master of war-craft. (65) Through the multitude of your dangers, you become a stronger ruler; through your sweated toil you gain the benefits of peace[16]. Whilst you live on as king, the world does not grieve for any loss; the lands due to you have stood firm. The Creator decreed that for the sake of your house, your country, and your people, (70) you live, a hero, whom the nations fear.

Sigibert (Gregory, *HF*, 4.51); though the context and the claim that the murder was due to "God's intervention" might make this reference inappropriate here. Or, perhaps more plausibly, it may be the siege of Soissons the following year, and the pattern of insurrection which the king attributed to Merovech (Gregory, *HF*, 5.3), all of which he may have seen as an early stage of the plot which now seemed to involve Gregory himself.

14 This phrase reminds Chilperic of the loyalty of the audience of bishops, and perhaps also mirrors to Chilperic the loyalty he should have to them in return.

15 If this passage is taken as referring to the trial of Praetextatus, the only bishop whose loyalty was overtly in doubt during the troubles with Merovech, *cathedra* can be taken in its common meaning, as referring to an ecclesiastical seat, and primarily to an episcopal see (see Thesaurus s.v.). "Its rightful place" can then be understood as "in loyalty to Chilperic". Tardi, p. 106, argues that *cathedra* refers to the king's own restoration to his royal seat, i.e. Paris (for this usage of the word, cf. Gregory, *HF*, 2.7, 2.38 etc.). Reydellet (1981), p. 319, convincingly argues for Soissons, rather than Paris. But even so, given that the issue here is the loyalty of the bishops, the more common meaning of the term seems preferable. The message to the king is that the banishment of Praetextatus is accepted, and that the king is mistaken in looking for treachery in the present company.

16 Fortunatus now develops the earlier comment in line 43 on the essentially peace-loving nature of the king.

You are here hailed as victor and give protection far and wide, to prevent the armed rebel rampaging through the countryside of Gaul. You inspire fear in the Goths[17], the Basques[18], the Danes, the Jutes[19], the Saxons[20] and the Britons[21]. With your father, as men know, you vanquished them in battle[22]. (75) You are a terror to the furthest Frisians and the Suebi[23], who seek your rule rather than prepare to fight you. To all these peoples you were given as a terror on the battlefield through His judgement; by this new threat you have been transformed into an object of deep love. In you, our governor, the land has a wall of defence cast around it[24], (80) and an iron portal raises its lofty head. You shine forth, an adamantine tower for your country from the south, and you shelter the people's hopes under a steadfast shield. Lest any should oppress these, you set out your protective defences and cherish the wealth of the land with your strong boundaries.

(85) What shall I say of your adminstration of justice, o prince?[25] No-one fares badly with you if he truly seeks justice, for in your honest speech are held the scales of just measure and the course of justice runs straight. Truth is not hindered, falsehood and error settle nothing, deceit flees before your judgement, and order returns. (90) What more? By your superior learning and eloquence you master even those you hold sway over already by the authority of your power[26],

---

17 For the Goths, see M. Todd, *The early Germans* (Oxford, 1992), pp. 149-176.
18 For the Basques, see James (1982), pp. 20-21, 150.
19 For the Jutes, see J. C. Zeuss,*Die Deutschen und die Nachbarstämme* (München, 1837), pp.500-501: M. Todd, op.cit., p. 223.
20 For the Saxons and Frisians (line 75), see M. Todd, op. cit., pp. 216-224.
21 This claim, in the absence of any notable foreign campaigns, seems as much a rhetorical flourish as the earlier claim of *consensus universorum* (lines 13-22). Chilperic's presence on his father's campaigns is not recorded.
22 For Lothar's campaigns, see Gregory, *HF*, 3.7 (Thuringians), 11 (Burgundy), 29 (Spain); 4.10 (Saxons), 14 and 16 (Ripuarian Franks and Saxons), 20 (Chramm in Britanny).
23 I.e. the Suebi in Spain; see M. Todd, op. cit., pp. 184-188.
24 See note 7 above for this defensive architectural symbolism.
25 An ironic question, in the circumstances. Justice is an essential attribute of the Christian king (see *Poem* 6.1a, note 43); but the reference here may have more of commendation about it than accurate description, especially in the light of Gregory's account of the king's behaviour at both synods (Gregory, *HF*, 5.18 and 49).
26 For the emphasis on the literary accomplishments of the *rex doctus* in classical panegyric, see *Poem* 6.1a, note 44.

understanding different languages without the aid of an interpreter[27]; a single tongue echoes back the languages of the nations. (95) Your generosity raises up all the needy; you consider to be yours what you give your servant[28]. Thus your praises spread forth, and this wave of approbation strikes the heavens with its clamour.

At one and the same time war looks upon you with favour, and learning grants you her abiding affection; (100) you delight by your valiant courage in the former, by your learning in the latter. In both spheres you are wise; tested in arms and in law, you are glorious as a warrior and resplendent in your law-giving. Your courage recalls your father[29], your eloquence your uncle[30]; but you surpass your whole family in your enthusiasm for learning. (105) Amongst the kings, your equals, you are given higher esteem for your verse[31], no forefather was your equal in learning. Warlike qualities make you like your family, but your literary pursuits single you out as exceptional. Thus you are at once the equal and the superior of the kings of old. O king, whom I greatly admire, (110) your strength wages war nobly, your polishing perfects your verses. You rule warfare by law, and enforce law by strength of arms; so the paths of the different arts converge. If everyone, my lord, could learn of each and every virtue of yours, more would praise the good which you alone do.

(115) Yet may your good fortune remain and increase, and may it be granted that you enjoy your spreading dominion with your

---

27 For Fortunatus' emphasis on this bond between the two racial groups, see also *Poem* 6.2, note 50:, 6.2 7-8, 97-100, and note 50. For comment, see Brennan (1984); Godman, pp. 24-6; M. H. Hoeflich, "Between Gothia and Romania; the image of the king in the poetry of Venantius Fortunatus", *Res publica litterarum* 5 (1982), p. 127.
28 For this sentiment, see *Poem* 3.13, note 7.
29 See note 10 above.
30 For the same attribution on Charibert's behalf, see *Poem* 6.2.13-26 and note 54.
31 Gregory, *HF*, 5.44, has a more jaundiced view of the king's literary abilities. For Chilperic's *Hymnus in solemnitate Sancti Medardi Episcopi* see *Poetae Latini Aevi Carolini*, ed. K. Streker, MGH Poetarum Latinorum, vol. 4, fasc. ii (Berlin, 1923), pp.455-7; D. Norberg, *La poésie latine rhythmique de haut moyen âge* (Stockholm, 1954), pp.31-41; Riché, pp. 224-225. Gregory also records the king as having a lively interest in theology, and as attempting to reform the alphabet; for this latter activity, see W. Sanders, "Die Buchstaben des Konigs Chiperichs", *Zeitschrift für Deutsches Altertum* (1972), pp. 54-84. For his innovations in legislation, see F. Beyerle, "Das legislative Werk Chilperichs I", *Zeitschrift Savigny-Stiftung für Rechtsgeschichte*, Germanische Abteilung 78 (1961), pp.1-38.

rightful consort[32]. She adorns the king's domains with her virtues, and shares the rule on high; wise in counsel, clever, shrewd, a good mistress of your palace, (120) intelligent, of pleasing generosity. The noble Fredegund excels in all virtues, the glorious light of day shines forth from her countenance[33]; she carries the oppressive weight of the cares of state, she cherishes you with her goodness, she helps you by her service. (125) With her guidance at your side, your palace grows, by her help your house gains greater honour. Seeking to double the prayers for the safety of her husband, she seeks benefit from Radegund[34] for you. She shines resplendent through her own merits, a glory to a king, and, (130) made queen, a crowning glory for her own husband. In the fullness of time, may she honour you with offspring, so that a grandson will be born to make you a grandfather, giving you fresh life. Therefore[35] may thanks duly be given to the Creator. Worship, o king, the King who gives you His aid, (135) so that He may preserve and increase your good fortune. For the Prince on high Who alone possesses all is He Who has given you so much.

Forgive me, victorious lord, that your praises have overwhelmed me; the very fact that I am so overcome is to your greater honour. Humble though I am[36], yet I wish that these hopes may be realised, (140) and that those blessed gifts are given from heaven to earth. May the skies prosper you with gentle breezes, may the seasons bless you with peace, may the fields glow with harvests, and may treaties hold the kingdoms fast. May you vanquish your enemies, may you protect the faithful with love, may you be the pinnacle of faith for

---

[32] A brief eulogy of Fredegund recognises her power and influence, as Brunhild's was acknowledged in *Poem* 6.1a. 29-40 and note 46.
[33] The conventional light imagery of royal panegyric is used here to praise the queen; cf. *Poems* 5.2, note 3, 6.1a.1, 6.2.1-6.
[34] An attractive, though by no means certain, emendation is from *Radegunde* to *Rigunthe*, in reference to the princess whose strong support for Gregory is mentioned in *HF,* 5.49. This reading would make better sense of the following two couplets, which are difficult to interpret if the reference is to Radegund. The picture is of the two royal women seeking the king's salvation by the vindication of Gregory, the attack on the latter being a threat also to Chilperic. Cf. the mention of the princess in the following consolation,*Poem* 9.2.96.
[35] This strong conjunction perhaps suggests strongly to Chilperic that family prosperity is closely linked with a pious and orthodox rule, with due respect to the Church; a train of thought which would make sense to a king and queen who, a few months later, remitted vast amounts of tax in an attempt to save the lives of their two sons (Gregory, *HF,* 5.34; cf. 10.11).
[36] A conventional modesty *topos*; see Curtius, pp. 83-85.

all true Christians, (145) most noble king, through whom honour is given, with whom may long life and bountiful faith abide.

Let others bring their rulers gold and gifts of jewels; from Fortunatus, a poor man, accept these words.

Poem 9.2: to Chilperic and Queen Fredegund[37]

O harsh condition and irreversible destiny of time[38]! which its tragic origin bequeathed to humankind, when the seductive serpent spat poison from its fang, and when baneful Eve through the snake's

---

37 This poem was written in consolation to Chilperic and Fredegund for the death of their two young sons, Chlodobert and Dagobert, in the dysentery epidemic in the late summer of 580 (Gregory, *HF,* 5.34), twenty days after the end of the synod at Berny-Rivière (Gregory, *HF,* 5.50). Chilperic himself was affected, but recovered. Dagobert succumbed, and was immediately baptised; the queen offered prayers and remitted taxes, but the prince died and was buried at St. Denis in Paris. Chlodobert was taken to the shrine of St. Medard in Soissons, where his parents prayed for his recovery, but he also died. In terms of the succession, this was a bitter blow to Chilperic and Fredegund. Theudebert, son of Chilperic and Audovera, had been killed in 575 (Gregory, *HF,* 4.50). Gregory claimed to have foreseen the deaths of all the four remaining sons in a vision of 577 (*HF,* 5.14) - rightly, as it transpired. Merovech committed suicide in 578 (*HF,* 5.18); Clovis was still alive at the time of the dysentery outbreak, but alienated from the king - he and his mother were killed by Chilperic shortly afterwards (*HF,* 5.39).

For the genre of consolation, see *Poem* 4.26, note 22. In considering *Poems* 9.2 and 3, as well as the other consolations of Fortunatus, Davis' thesis is fruitful; that the formula for prose consolation is relatively static and inflexible, but that verse consolation may be best considered as dialectic, as the use of traditional themes to react relevantly to the emotions triggered by the particular situation. Thus, the balance between *laudatio* (eulogy), *lamentatio* (lamentation) and *consolatio* (consolation), firmly maintained in prose consolation, becomes more fluid and responsive in verse to the mood the poet is seeking to create. This poem and its successor, *Poem* 9.3, have been seen as conventional elaborations of stock motifs; see von Moos, *Darstellung,* C 216 and 221. But, analysed in their political context, and in view of the character and interests of the two bereaved parents, a good case can be made that, far from being trite or fawning compositions, they represent constructive advice and Christian consolation, sensitively attuned to different stages of mourning, the poet seeking to guide Chilperic from the great grief which Gregory records (*HF,* 5.34) towards his duties as a Christian king ; see George, pp. 88-91.

38 The poem begins with a short passage of *lamentatio*; the harsh fate of man, condemned by the Fall (lines 1-12), and a catalogue of the great men of the Old Testament who have succumbed to death (lines 13-40). There is no *laudatio* for the princes; cf. the lack of personal commendation in their epitaphs, *Poems* 9.4 and 5, their age possibly making this inappropriate (see note 93). The main focus of the poem is on *consolatio*.

For the motif of the inevitability of death as the condition of fallen man, see von Moos, *Testimonien* T 526-51, 597-614.

bite was death[39]. (5) From that moment the earth inherited grief from father Adam himself, and the world, bewailing, received a bitter gift from its mother. Both by their transgressions are sentenced to bitter disgrace; he is afflicted with toil, she groans in childbearing. Hence comes rapacious death, handed down to their descendants; (10) their sinful origin carries off their heirs. Lo, this grievous wrong our parents begot for us: the whole race comes to ruin because of its first beginnings. First fell Abel[40], slaughtered with that wretched wound, and his brother's hoe dug into his limbs. (15) Later Seth too died[41], he who was given to them in place of Abel, and, though he came instead, his life was not without end. What should I say of Noah[42], praised by the voice of the Thunderer[43]? The heavy earth now weighs down on him whom the light ark bore up. Thus too Shem and Japheth, and then the most righteous offspring (20) and holy scion[44] journeyed on that same path. What of the patriarch Abraham[45] or Isaac[46], and worthy Jacob[47], when none are exempt from the law of death? Even Melchisedech[48], priest holy through the voice of the Lord, and Job[49]

---

39 For the story of the Fall and Eve's part in it, see Genesis, ch. 3.
40 For the murder of Abel by his brother, Cain, see Genesis 4.1-15.
41 For Seth, see Genesis 5.3-8.
42 See Genesis 6-9, for Noah and his sons, Ham, Shem, and Japheth. Noah was the one righteous man God was willing to save from the Flood he sent to cleanse the earth of the wickedness of mankind.
43 This epithet, traditionally given to Jupiter in classical literature, is commonly transferred to the Christian God in early Church writings, particularly in verse.
44 Possibly Nimrod, the great hunter, descendant of Ham; Genesis, 10.8-9.
45 Abraham was the great patriarch of the Old Testament, father of the nation of Israel; for his story, see Genesis 12-25.10.
46 Isaac was the son of Abraham, leading the nation of Israel in his stead; Genesis, 17.15-18.15; 21.1-9; 22.1-19; 24.1-67; 25.20-28.5; 36.27-29.
47 For Jacob, see *Poem* 5.2, note 14.
48 Melchisedech, king of Salem, (Genesis 14.18-20) was seen as the exemplar of royal priesthood, in the Old and New Testaments (e.g. Psalm 110.4, Hebrews 5.6, 10) and in the writings of the early Church. Fortunatus would have known the famous mosaic of Melchisedech in the church of San Vitale in Ravenna, in which the king offers bread and wine in a prefiguration of the Eucharist; the poet uses this image of Childebert I, in his poem on the king's church to St. Vincent in Paris (*Poem* 2.10.17-24).
49 The question, "Why do the righteous suffer?" may be said to be the theme of the Book of Job, which moves from the idea prevalent at the time that suffering was a sign of sin, to the idea that God used suffering as a way of strengthening and refining human virtue. Job emerges after terrible tribulations which lead him to complete humility, to be rewarded with redoubled wealth, a new family and years of prosperous life.

also and his sons departed thus. (25) The lawbearer Moses[50] himself and Aaron[51] the priest lie low, and the friend worthy of talking to God[52], died. His successor, the famous leader of the people, Joshua[53], the fathers whom you read of in the books have lain in rest. What of Gideon[54], Samson[55], or any of the Judges[56] in their ranks? (30) None escapes from death under the judgement of the Lord. David[57], mighty king of Israel and prophet, is laid in his grave with Solomon[58], his son. Isaiah[59], Daniel[60], Samuel[61] and blessed Jonah[62], alive below the sea,

---

50 Moses was the great leader who brought the people of Israel out of their captivity in Egypt, and led them towards the new land of Canaan; who promoted the people's faith in the God of the Old Testament, and was the great moral teacher who brought the Ten Commandments of God down from Mount Sinai. His story and teachings are found in the Books of Exodus, Leviticus, Numbers, and Deuteronomy.
51 Aaron, the brother of Moses, was the first High Priest of Israel; Exodus 4.14-16, 27-31: 5.1-4: 7.1-12.51: 28: 32: Deut. 9.20, etc.
52 Moses spoke directly with God on Mount Sinai: Exodus 19 and 34.
53 Joshua was appointed successor to Moses, and led the people of Israel to conquer the promised land of Canaan; see the Book of Joshua, passim.
54 Gideon led the struggle for the Israelites to free themselves from the power of the Midianites: see Judges 6-8.
55 Samson was famous for his strength and valour as one of the champions of Israel against the Philistines: see Judges 13-16.
56 "Judges" is the title given the succession of leaders of Israel during the years after they settled in Canaan; see the Book of Judges.
57 David was first king of the Israelites, forefather of Jesus Christ, notable for his military successes and for his composition of (some of) the psalms; see 1 and 2 Books of Samuel, 1 Book of Chronicles, and 1 Book of Kings.
58 For Solomon, king of Israel and successor to David, famed for his wisdom, see 2 Book of Samuel, 1 and 2 Book of Kings, 1 and 2 Books of Chronicles, passim; also attributed to him in ancient times were the Book of Proverbs (see Proverbs 1.1), Ecclesiastes, and the Song of Solomon.
59 Isaiah was the greatest of the prophets of Israel, pronouncing on the political and moral issues of some forty years from 760-698 B.C., and foretelling the coming of the Christ; see the Book of Isaiah.
60 Daniel, one of the captives of Israel taken to Babylon in 605 B.C., was one of the major prophets of Israel; he interpreted the dreams of King Nebuchadnezzar and also declared his own apocalyptic visions; see the Book of Daniel.
61 Samuel, also one of the great prophets, was called as a child to serve God; he anointed Saul king of Israel, but, when Saul failed in obedience to God, anointed David to be king in his place; see 1 Samuel.
62 Jonah, shipwrecked because of his refusal of God's command to pronounce God's word to the people of Nineveh, was swallowed by a great fish and lived in its belly for three days and nights. He was saved and carried out the command, thus saving the city and being brought to realise the pettiness of his narrow nationalism and the infinity of God's love through a further miracle; see the Book of Jonah.

now remain weighed down by the earth. (35) Peter[63], the foremost with the key, and Paul first with his doctrine[64], though their spirits are on high, earth covers their bodies. He who is surpassed by no-one of human seed, the Baptist, the mighty John himself[65], is dead. Enoch[66] and Elijah[67] still look on; (40) he who is begotten of man, must also come to death. The Creator Himself, Christ, rising fast in triumph from the shades, because He was born here a man, was buried in earth in the flesh.

Who, I ask, does not die, his welfare tasting death?[68] though He, my life, was willing to die for me? (45) Tell me, what power have the Augusti[69] or the lofty kings, when the limbs of the Creator lay in the rock? Neither their brawn nor their purple restores valiant kings, every man comes from dust and will be dust. Alike we all are born, and alike we die[70]; (50) there is one death from Adam, and one salvation in Christ. Our fortunes are different, but there is one end for all; thus babes, young, and old die.

So what are we to make of this, I ask you now, your lofty excellency, when we guilty ones can avail nothing? (55) We weep, we groan, but we are not able to avail anything; grief fills our eyes, but there is no benefit of succour. Our hearts are torn with the shock, our stomachs turned: our dear ones are dead, our eyes fail with weeping. Lo, love is called upon, but a lover is not now recalled, (60) and he whom the deep-planted stone covers does not now come back to us.

---

63 For Peter, see *Poem* 4.26, note 36.
64 For Paul, see *Poem* 5.2, note 8.
65 For John the Baptist, see *Poem* 5.2, note 15.
66 Enoch was the son of Cain, and, for his goodness, was "translated" (i.e. removed from this life without suffering death); see Genesis 5.21-24, Hebrews 11.5. This intermediate state of Enoch, and of Elijah (see note 64) was the subject of continuing theological debate.
67 For Elijah, see *Poem* 4.26, note 34.
68 The tone of the poem changes here, posing questions, to become gradually more challenging to the king to rouse himself from his state of stricken grief. For the motif that all must die, see von Moos, *Testimonien* T633.
69 *Augustus* was the title held exclusively by all the Roman emperors with the exception of Vitellius. In 293 A.D. the emperor Diocletian divided the empire amongst four rulers, thus creating a tetrarchy. He established two nominally joint emperors who shared the title of *Augustus*, to rule the eastern and western halves of the empire, each with a subordinate ruler, designated a *Caesar*, who might be expected to succeed to the higher rank. Although this system failed as a means of establishing the succession, the titles and their general application survived. For the motif that even the great must die, see von Moos, *Testimonien* T561, 655, 808, 1501.
70 For this motif, see note 68.

Death is deaf and takes no heed, not hearing, whatever the cries, and, stony-hearted, knows not how to turn again to godly affection. But I will travel there with everyone else, whether I like it or not; we will all leave this earth, and no-one returns from there; (65) until dead flesh takes on life at the coming of the Lord, and man rises again from his own dust, when the moist skin begins to cover the dry ashes and the living embers leap from the tombs. Thus will we all go to take our place in another realm, (70) we, whom a foreign land holds, will go to our home.

So do not be tormented, good king, most valiant leader, that your sons go where every man makes his way. The vessel of clay is made as the potter sees fit; when the potter sees fit, the vessels are broken and come to nothing[71]. (75) We are not able to fight against the will of the Almighty, in whose sight the stars and the earth tremble. He Himself creates man; what can we say? the same who gave also takes away; He does not incur any blame. Behold we are formed by Him and our life is from Him; (80) when He commands, we who are His work go hence. If He wishes, He whose works please Him, He changes in an hour the mountains, oceans and stars; what can man, mere smoke, do?

So I pray, mighty king, do what may be best for you, great lord, what benefits your soul with the help of God; (85) be dignified and manful, bear your suffering patiently; let the burden be borne which cannot be avoided. What we acquire by being born, no man goes without through life; let him bear with wisdom what no-one changes.

May you take thought for the lady queen, the beloved of a lover, (90) who receives all good things by association with you; urge her as she mourns[72] to quiet her maternal feelings, do not yourself weep nor allow her to cry[73]. With you, her husband, as king, it is not right that she should be desolate, but rather she should rejoice on high from your couch. (95) I make this prayer, hoping for a long life for

---

[71] Fortunatus uses the imagery of Isaiah 64.8, of God as a potter, to stress that our lives and fate are, literally, in God's hands, and that we must accept His will. For this image in consolation, see von Moos, *Testimonien* T704 ff.

[72] Gregory records Fredegund's great distress before the children's death (*HF*, 5.34), and her grief and violent reaction to the death of Theuderic (*HF*, 6.34-50).

[73] For the motif of the inappropriateness of grief, see von Moos, *Anmerkungen* A405, *Testimonien* T910.

your wife, that you should take thought for your daughter[74], and for your country. The people will be as they all see you are, the populace will set its expectations by your aspect.

Finally, Job, losing seven sons in one bitter blow[75], (100) offered up praise to God. David, the psalmist, when he lost his beloved son[76], gave a feast of celebration as soon as he had laid him in the grave. The godly mother of the Maccabees[77], a woman twice blessed[78], bore the simultaneous death of seven sons with joy, (105) saying without hesitation to the Lord, "May glory always be with you, o Ruler, a mother keeps her children as you wish, o highest Father".

So you should instead offer thanks to our God, Who brings it about that those from your seed go to heaven, and Who choses the fine jewels out of the dung on earth, (110) and leads them from the mire to the stars by His throne. Your harvest pleased God, and He gathers it into His granaries, as He reaps the fine grains with the young ears of corn. You do not beget chaff[79], but father whole corn, which is not to be burnt in the fire but brought to new life in heaven; (115) they especially merited to be taken hence, thus purified by holy baptism, renewed in the cleansing stream. Standing before God like golden vessels of splendour[80], or like the beautiful shining lamp on a stand[81], unspotted souls, always resplendent with glory, (120) they retain a place in the dwelling of the living and flourish in light, set in place in the house of the Lord, like white lilies mingled with the crimson roses[82]. And when the Lord has commanded the buried bodies to come

---

74 I.e. Rigunth.
75 See Job, ch. 1. Fortunatus here lists *exempla* of those who have born the loss of children with fortitude and resignation.
76 For David's reaction to the death of his son Absalom, see 2 Samuel, 18 and 19.
77 Judas Maccabaeus and his four brothers, sons of the priest Mattathias, led the Jewish resistance movement against the rule of Antiochus Epiphanes, and then of his successors. This reference is to the death by torture of seven brothers and their mother, killed by Antiochus in an attempt to make them foreswear their Jewish faith; see 2 Maccabees, 7.
78 Once by the possession of seven faithful sons, secondly by her own faith.
79 A reference to the New Testament parable of the separation of the chaff from the grain; see Matth. 3.12.
80 See 2 Timothy 2.20 for man potentially as a valuable vessel of gold.
81 The lamp is associated with the New Testament parable of the wise and foolish virgins, and signifies those who serve Christ faithfully; see Matth. 25.1-13; see also Revelation 1.11-13 and 20, for the 7 candelabra and the 7 churches.
82 For the association of roses with Paradise, see C. Joret, *La rose dans l'antiquité et au moyen âge* (Statkine Reprints, Geneva, 1970), pp. 232 ff.

again[83], then a fair robe will clothe your sons (125) or a triumphal tunic woven with ruddy gold, and their brow will bear a crown of diverse jewels; as they wear a snowy white tunic[84] over their fair breasts, a brilliant belt encircles their purple toga[85]. Then you, father and mother, will rejoice in the midst of them, (130) when you see them amongst the men of heaven.

Yet He, who increased the seed of Abraham[86], is all powerful, and will give you what He gave Job in love, restoring the number of his sons with worthy stock[87], and He gives offspring again with ennobling faith. (135) He Who brought about the birth of Solomon for David's throne[88], when he himself returned to his father instead of his brother, He will be able to grant you a son by your wife[89]; may his father play with him, his mother feed him at her breast, and may he snuggle round his parents' necks, between you, (140) and long bring happiness to rulers and country.

---

83 For the Christian belief in the resurrection of the body, see e.g. Matth. 22.23-33; Luke 14.14. For this as a motif of consolation, see von Moos, *Anmerkungen* A219.
84 A snowy white tunic signifies purity, especially the purity of baptised souls; cf. Fortunatus' description of the white robed baptismal procession in Clermont-Ferrand in *Poem* 5.5.119-120.
85 A token of their royal birth.
86 As part of God's covenant between Himself and Abraham, Abraham's wife, Sarah, became pregnant, though she had been barren and Abraham was old. Her son was Isaac, forefather of the people of Israel. See Genesis 17. Given the deaths of all but one of their sons (see note 37 above), this was a particularly pertinent example for Chilperic and Fredegund.
87 See Book of Job, 42.13.
88 David's son by Bathsheba died because of David's sin in having Bathsheba's husband killed; David listened to his servants' advice to accept God's will, and his next child with Bathsheba was Solomon, who became one of the great kings of Israel (see note 58 above, and 1 Samuel, 12). This reference directly reinforces Fortunatus' advice to the royal couple, as well as underlining the rewards of obedience to God and his Church (it was the prophet Nathan who pointed out David's wrongdoing to him and its consequences).
89 A further son, Lothar, was born to Chilperic and Fredegund some two years later (Gregory, *HF,* 6.41) and survived infancy to rule as Lothar II. It was he who, by his gruesome execution of Brunhild, brought the divisions of the kingdom to an end and ruled over a united realm; see Wood, pp. 90-1, 96-100, 140-44. For this motif of consolation, see von Moos, *Testimonien* T1421, 1409.

Poem 9.3: to Chilperic and Fredegund[90]

After storms and cloud-swirling skies, when the earth is wont to be rigid with bitter ice, after the harsh winter[91] and the dreary chill of winter, or when the blast of the gusting South wind sweeps harshly over the countryside, (5) once more the season of spring returns to the earth and, after the ice, a pleasant breeze summons forth the light of day. Once again the meadows are enlivened with scented flowers, and every wood is verdant with leafy trees; the bough is bent with sweet tasting apples, (10) and the fields are joyous as the grass returns.

In the same way too, my lords, now, after mourning your tragic losses, rejoice with your spirits restored, I pray. Behold, the gentle season recalls the Eastertide of Christ, and the whole earth likewise murmurs with new hope. (15) May joy find more welcome throughout the high palaces of the king and, thanks to you, may your servants observe a blessed festival. May the Almighty grant us your salvation on earth and may your Highnesses long reign over this land.

---

90 The poem, the second consolation to Chilperic and Fredegund for the deaths of their two young sons, appears, from the reference to the season, to have been written about six months after the first. The emphasis is still on *consolatio*, but the mood of the poem is significantly different from that of the first. The bleakness of immediate loss has faded, and the king and queen are urged to take cheer from the joys of Easter to move beyond mere acceptance of fate to a readjustment of life, and to the resumption of ordinary cares and responsibilities. As in the first poem, Fortunatus appears to be taking a positive and interventionist role in advising and encouraging the king.
91 The tone given by the classical nature writing in this poem is enhanced by two close echoes; here, in line 3, cf. Ovid, *Trist.* 4.7.1, and line 8, cf. Vergil, *Ecl.* 7.59. These may be well judged to appeal to a king with literary tastes, and a composer of sub-Sedulian verse (Gregory, *HF,* 6.46).

Poem 9.4: epitaph on the tomb of Lord Chlodobert[92]

    The cruel deaths of kings urge the people to weep, when the sorrowful tomb covers with earth the head of the world. Thus Chlodobert is held lying in this tomb, he who was taken from the world as he completed his fifteenth year[93]; (5) this noble scion sprung from the line of Clovis his forefather[94], grandson of Lothar[95] and offspring of Chilperic; he received him from his wife, Queen Fredegund, and the boy by his birth had raised the hopes of the Franks. Whilst the high hopes of his father and his fatherland grew greater through him, (10) hostile fortune carried him off, as his final day hastened. But let no loving heart weep for him, for he is not harmed by any contact with the world's strife, and honour now wreathes him round. For a boy, living in innocence, dying without guilt, is priviledged to enjoy the citadel of the everlasting kingdom.

Poem 9.5: epitaph on Dagobert[96]

    Dear one, Dagobert, everlasting in the people's love, support of his country, a hope in childhood, you die; born nobly of royal stock, displayed to the lands as a babe, you who are snatched away soon to

---

92 For the death of Chlodobert, see note 37 above. For epitaphs in general and those of Fortunatus, see *Poem* 4.16, note 1. Though this is quite a wordy epitaph, there is no reason to suppose that it was not inscribed on or near by the prince's tomb in the Church of St. Crispin and St. Crispinian.
93 It is interesting that in neither poem is there a *laudatio* of the two princes. Yet Vilithuta, who was approximately the same age as Chlodobert (*Poem* 4.26.35), receives a *laudatio* (lines 13-28). Vilithuta may have been known personally, and the gender difference may be significant here in that Vilithuta, as a married woman, has entered the adult world. However, for Franks, a first majority took place at 12 years, perhaps even 7 for a king, a second at 14; see Riché, pp. 232-233.
94 Clovis, king of the Franks, 481-511, and great-grandfather of these two princes.
95 King of Franks, 511-561.
96 The younger of the two princes to die; see Gregory, *HF*, 5.34 and 50. This poem is an acrostic, the first letters of each line form the prince's name; this decorative feature and the length of the epitaph suggest that the poem was inscribed on or near by the prince's tomb in the church of St. Denis; see *Poem* 4.16, note 1. For this verse form, see D. Norberg, *Introduction à l'étude de la versification latine médiévale* (Stockholm, 1959), pp. 54-63.

the heavens, (5) arising from the powerful line of the warrior Clovis[97], offspring equal in honour to his resplendent ancestor, a noble infant in counterpart to the kings of old, child of his father Chilperic and Fredegund. Yet the holy waters of the font soon bathed you[98]; (10) thus, though you are snatched away, kindly light encompasses you by the throne. Thus you live in honour and, when the Judge of the world comes, you will rise and be resplendent with radiant countenance.

Poem 9.6: to Bishop Gregory for the Sapphic verses[99]

The letter came at a run, with powerful eloquence, but for my wishes it needed to come slowly. Yet, though it asks for what has been much delayed, it does not offend the man whom it holds, his mind binding him fast. (5) For I wish that you would restore with your teaching such a Gregory as was that of Nazianzus[100], as a father in his see. Behold I have sent you, father, the poems which you commanded, and they will profit me, dear friend, if they please you. You also

---

97 Clovis, king of the Franks, 481-511, and great-grandfather of these two princes.
98 Gregory notes the eleventh hour baptism of the prince (*HF*, 5.34), assuring him of a place in heaven for his youth and innocence.
99 This poem is the covering note for poems written for Gregory, apologising for the delay in writing the Sapphic stanzas also requested (i.e. *Poem 9.7*, sent later). These poems give insight into the serious literary dimension of the two men's friendship. Gregory, the prose historian who speaks of his own literary talents and of the failing literary tradition in his own country in deprecatory terms (see the *Preface* to *HF*), has great admiration for Fortunatus, the Italian educated in the best classical fashion, who can range successfully through the traditional genres of Latin literature for public or private occasions, the epitome of all that Gregory and his contemporaries hold in high esteem in the *Romanitas* they aspire to. In return, Fortunatus reflects back to Gregory the respect a classical poet would have for a worthy patron, who is himself a serious writer (see, e.g. *Poems* 5.8b, 13, 17 etc.). For Gregory as a writer, see Biographical Notes. The prompt for this request from Gregory is a book which he has acquired and sent to Fortunatus (*Poem 9.7.33-36*). This book is a handbook on metre, which catalogues the various metres, with examples and discussion of their use (lines 41-48). Meyer, p.127, suggests that the book is a copy of Terentianus Maurus' work, *De Metris*.
100 Gregory of Nazianzus, 329-389 A.D., was one of the four great Greek doctors of the Church, associated with St. Basil the Great and St. Gregory of Nyssa in the final defeat of the Arian heresy. Well educated, he was ordained a priest in c. 362, though against his will - he wanted to be a monk; and, again unwillingly, he was made a bishop in c. 372 by St. Basil, and eventually in 379 accepted charge of the orthodox community in Constantinople, where his eloquence contributed largely to the overthrow of Arianism in the general council there in 381. He withdrew soon afterwards, to end his days in quiet contemplation.

command that I should send you back Sapphic verses; (10) forgive me, while the crop from a modest field puts pressure on me. Give me time, whilst I reap; I will soon be ready to obey you; perhaps I will sing all the better, if I am glutted with fruits. If I am able to compose them, I will send you a small volume with the verse; may you receive them in the spirit in which love wrote them for you.

Poem 9.7: to Bishop Gregory[101]

With joyous heart and charming quill, you
send letters with an eager wish, composing pleasantnesses
in a set of greetings,
dear Gregory;

(5) urging me just now to stir afresh verses
such as Sappho[102] gracefully sang[103],

---

[101] These are the Sapphic stanzas promised to Gregory in the previous poem, and conform to the traditional format for the metre, three Sapphic hendecasyllables being followed by an adonic. This lyric metre was adapted into Latin verse by the Augustan poet Horace (65 - 8 B. C.) from the early Greek lyric poems of the two Greek poets, Sappho and Alcaeus, who lived and wrote as virtual contemporaries in the 7th century on the island of Lesbos. For an account of these metres in general, see *The Oxford Companion to Classical Literature* (2nd. ed. Oxford, 1989), under Metre, Greek (8) and Latin (3. iii); for more detailed discussion of Horace's adaption of the Greek metres, see R. G. M. Nisbet and M. Hubbard, *A commentary on Horace Odes, Book 1* (Oxford, 1970), pp. xi-xiv, xl-xlvi; see also p. xiii for discussion of the influence of Pindar and the choral ode tradition on Horace, of which Fortunatus is also aware (see line 9). Fortunatus would also have been familiar with later Latin examples of Sapphic stanzas; in Ausonius, for example, (*Ephemeris*, sect. 1; *Commem. Profess. Burdig.* nos. 7 and 8); in Sidonius, *Ep.* 9.16. 3. For this later versification, see D. Norberg,*Introduction à l'étude de la versification latine médiévale* (Stockholm, 1958), pp. 77-78. (The prose rendering of this poem in no way attempts to imitate the metre, but merely by its layout to signal its difference from Fortunatus' usual metre)

[102] Sappho, a Greek lyric poetess, was born in the late 7th century at Eresus in Lesbos. When still young, she went into exile in Sicily, presumably because of political troubles in Lesbos, later returning to spend the rest of her life in Mytilene. She had three brothers, was married to Cercylas, and had a daughter, Cleis. A famous story, perhaps originating from Greek comedy, told how she threw herself off the cliff of Leucas because of unrequited love. The date of her death is unknown. She wrote in the Lesbian vernacular, a branch of Aeolic Greek, and her works were divided into nine books according to metre. Of her poems, only the address to Aphrodite survives in complete version; we know the rest from quotations, or from papyrus fragments discovered in the twentieth century. Her subject matter seems to have been restricted to her world of family and female friends. She was a leading figure in a

thus recording Dionean[104] loves,
a clever girl[105].

Pindar the Greek[106], and then my Flaccus[107]
(10) with Sapphic metre, a player gently plucking
his cithara with measured plectrum,

---

circle of women and girls, bound in a common cult of Aphrodite and the Muses, writing in intimate and intense terms of individuals, both in hate and in love, but also composing more formal *Epithalamia*.

103 Though the love Fortunatus expresses is not Dionean, he is following the ascetic tradition of representing a more spiritual love in erotic terms; for this tradition, see P. Fabre, *Saint Paulin et l'amitié chrétienne* (Paris, 1949), ch. 3: C. White, *Christian friendship in the fourth century* (Cambridge, 1992).

104 Dione is the consort of Zeus at Dodona, the only seat of her cult, and by him the mother of Aphrodite. Her name is the feminine of Zeus.

105 Cf. Propertius, 2.11.6.

106 Pindar (518-after 446 B. C.), a Greek lyric poet, was born in Boeotia, near Thebes. Little is known about his life; but he is famous for the great choral odes he wrote in honour of victors in the four great panhellenic Games. These odes are grouped accordingly, as Olympian, Pythian, Nemean, and Isthmian. His devotion to the god Apollo was rewarded by special priviledges at Delphi; he travelled widely, writing, for example, for the Sicilian tyrants (to Hieron 1 of Syracuse in particular); he appears to have had a notable affection for Athens, but had a panhellenic, rather than narrowly national, view of events, seeing the Persian invasions and their defeat as a threat, and then a blessing, for Greece as a whole. His many poems, written in the literary Dorian dialect, were grouped by Alexandrian scholars into seventeen books according to their types; but of these, only the victory odes survive, the rest being known only by quotation and by papyrus fragments discovered in the late nineteenth and twentieth centuries.

107 Quintus Horatius Flaccus (65-8 B.C.), a Roman poet, was the son of a freedman from Venusia in Apulia. Educated at Rome and later in Athens, he was caught up in the civil war whilst he was still in Greece and fought on the losing side at Philippi. Returning to Italy and obtaining a pardon, he purchased the post of a secretary in the office of a quaestor, being driven by poverty to start writing poetry. About 38 B.C. he was introduced by Vergil and Varius Rufus to Maecenas, who took him under his protection and in about 33 B. C. gave him a villa in the Sabine Hills beyond Tivoli, a place which gave him great happiness. The emperor Augustus later offered him a post as private secretary, but this was politely refused. One of the greatest of the Roman poets, he set out to challenge the perfection of the Greek tradition by adapting their metres and subject matter to the Latin language. During the thirties, he wrote the *Epodes* and the *Satires*; the first three books of the *Odes* were probably published in 23; the *Carmen Saeculare*, a long ode commissioned by Augustus for the Secular Games of 17, was followed by the fourth book of *Odes* in perhaps 13 B.C. The final years of his life saw the publication of three literary essays. Horace died a few months after Maecenas, in 8 B.C In relation to Fortunatus' line, Horace, in the opening stanzas of *Odes* 4.2, praises Pindar's eloquence, his originality in metre and diction, and his wonderful use of myth, and despairs of reaching such heights of perfection. The phrase "my Flaccus" here has the touch of a Latin poet writing for a cultured patron, complimenting Gregory by that literary bond (cf. *Poem* 8.18.5)

played a sweet song.

Why do you urge lyric melodies upon me,
I who now scarce whisper in a cracked voice?
(15) my right hand knows not how to speak upon the strings
with sweet thumb[108].

And if once this skill had been known to me,
ready to learn from the compliant goddess,
I had long forgotten the kindly Muse
(20) over the years[109];

for it is difficult for the learned for the verses to embody
this technique, and no-one embarks hastily,
and their metres should sufficiently accord to echo
these few poets.

(25) It is no small matter for a sailor to cross the sea
or to conquer the ocean depths by swimming;
the canvas scarce regains port
in a stormy southerly wind[110].

---

108 Lyric poetry, meaning "poetry sung to the lyre", was traditionally performed in Greece either as choral lyric or as a monody. Choral lyric was sung (and often danced) by a chorus to a musical accompaniment usually played on the lyre, though some times on the flute; a monody was usually performed by an individual on private occasions. Latin lyric, however, though modelled on the Greek forms, was a literary product, intended to be read, not sung (with the notable exception of the maiden-song to Juno of Livius Andronicus, written in 207 B. C., and Horace's *Carmen Saeculare*, a choral ode to be sung by a chorus of youths and maidens; see note 96 above). Fortunatus is thus speaking somewhat metaphorically.
109 Cf. lines 49-52, which speak of it being twenty years or so since he last practised this metre, which might suggest a date of the early 580s for this poem, if the reference is to his training and work in Ravenna (cf. also the final incomplete prose sentence which speaks of his long sojourn in Gaul). He stresses the fact that writing in this metre is slow work (*Poem* 9.6.10), and difficult (*Poem* 9.7. 25-32); his insistence on this point, and the slight content of the poem itself, lend credence to his plea.
110 Sidonius uses the same image of a ship making its hazardous way through storm-tossed seas to a safe harbour (*Ep.* 9.16.3). The metre is the same as Fortunatus' here, and, though the image for Sidonius is of his career, and for Fortunatus of a difficult challenge, there may be a conscious echo in the later poet's mind of this earlier example of this unusual verse form - and another level of sharing the same literary culture with Gregory, who might also recognise the common image in the metrical context. For further comment on the ship metaphor, see T. Janson, *Latin prose prefaces* (Stockholm, 1964), pp.146-147.

The path goes to the heights and the depths,
(30) which you command me to tread; yet I will go at your command;
if I am little able to travel with feet,
I am guided by love.

Your will, shepherd, presented me
with a book crammed with elevated tragic style[111],
(35) one which my poor state is scarce able
to approach in sentiment.

It resists the lowly with regal words,
refusing rich verses to the needy,
loath to reveal to me, a Mopsus[112],
(40) the lore of the wise;

disputing greatly with various rubrics
which are appropriate to rhythms or metres,
and how much the sweet epode[113] adorns
the Sapphic or the trimeter.

(45) A great number of writers is included,
speaking volubly with harmonious measure;
wishing to recall them in that metre,
I break up the names[114].

---

111 See note 90 above.
112 Mopsus is the name of a shepherd in Vergil's fifth and eighth Eclogues, a bucolic and unlettered figure.
113 In Greek lyric poetry, the third of a group of stanzas is the epode. The first two, which are symmetrical, are the strophe and the antistrophe; the epode has a different though related metrical form. This form of composition, which broke the monotony of a long series of similar stanzas, was employed by Pindar, and is generally thought to be characteristic of choral odes, rather than monody. Such an epode might well use a verse form Fortunatus would describe as "Sapphic". The trimeter, i.e. the iambic trimeter, was the metre used for occasional poems, sometimes political, often scurrilous, and for inscriptions. Archilochus in the seventh century used iambic metres; the trimeter was the metre of the spoken parts of drama, of tragedy and of comedy. Perhaps the discussion in Gregory's book to which Fortunatus refers is whether "epode" is being used in reference to the Greek lyric metre and Pindaric odes - or to Horatian style iambics in that poet's *Epodes*, where the Augustan poet professedly imitates Archilochus to comment on personal and political themes.

I, whose skill is much enfeebled,
(50) sing this after twice ten years[115],
what she composed by plucking her cithara,
the famous maid of Lesbos.

He who wants to know this, let him first
strive to count the Libyan sands across the shore[116],
(55) before he with metre and prudent thought
encompass all in song.

For I held back, myself dallying
for many reasons, on that side or the other,
nor have I read attentively in tranquil peace
(60) that sweet learning[117].

So realise, shepherd, I have not yet sped
through the whole text of the book, perusing it;
yet it is enough, believe me, it is enough for one who loves
that it is your will.

(65) So, let loose in swift flight,
speed to the holy father with accompanying prayer,
renewing in him love of us,
little book[118].

As it happens, I am sluggish and unable to go
(70) where that countenance, beloved to me, summons:
in my stead, I beg you, little book,
give my greetings.

May the father be mindful of his son, with sweet words

---

114 Leo, ad loc., suggests that this refers to the names of metres derived from poets - e.g. Anacreontic, Sapphic, etc.
115 See note 108 above.
116 A classical metaphor; e.g. Catullus, *Carm.*7.3-4; 61.202-206.
117 Reading, with Leo, *sophisma* for *sophistae*.
118 The anthropomorphic despatch of the "little book" with messages is a common motif; see, for example, Catullus,*Carm.* 45.1-6; 42.1-4; Ausonius, *Ep.* 25 (*Carm.* 14 ff).

praying to Him Who made us, the sea and the stars,
(75) and may he hold in his heart his devoted servant
with godly prayers.

The dear women, bound in mind to him
whom they esteem, Agnes and Radegund[119],
like daughters, they make the same request,
(80) give their greetings.

Add the same prayer from Justina[120],
assuredly commending his kin and handmaid,
and tell him how much honour his dear niece
affords him.

(85) With prayer, voice and mind, I readily carry out your bidding,
fulfilling it with difficulty, I who am so bereft of skill,
yet overflowing with great love,
dear Gregory[121].

And sweet master, pray for me, and take thought, you who, after I have dwelt in Gaul for so many years[122] - - - - .

---

119 Fortunatus is clearly writing from Poitiers.
120 Justina, Gregory's niece, daughter of his sister and her husband, Justinus, became Mother Superior of the convent on Agnes' death, and had to cope with the troubles which beset the community after Radegund died; Gregory,*HF*, 10.15. For Justina, see Stroheker, no. 208.
121 The terms of affection throughout the poem (lines 4, 32, 63, 67, 87, 88) give a tone of intimate affection to the poem which is only found elsewhere in poems to Radegund and Agnes.
122 This underlines the fact that Fortunatus is still an Italian poet, linked closely by that to "his Flaccus" and the great literary tradition Gregory so much admires. Cf. for the same awareness of still being alien, *Poem* 7.9.7-8, to Lupus, "I pass my ninth year, I think, as an exile from Italy, where the salt water of the Ocean's shore laps". The final words are missing, but for the general sentiment, see the endings of *Poems* 8.18, 19, and 21. For such prose accompaniments to verse, see T. Janson, op. cit., especially pp. 106-112, and, for echoes in motifs, Part 2, pp. 113-161.

Book Ten

Poem 10.8: in praise of King Childebert and Queen Brunhild[1]

If it were my task to pronounce the eulogy of the royal pair[2], night and day would not suffice for me to tell how greatly this people

---

[1] For Childebert ll and Brunhild, see Biographical Notes. This poem is to be dated shortly after the Treaty of Andelot in November, 587 (see Biographical Notes on Childebert ll), which seemed to assure the position of Brunhild and the succession of her family. Moreover, about this time, Brunhild and Childebert had consented to the marriage of Chlodosind, Brunhild's daughter, to Reccared, son of Leuvigild, king of the Visigoths, subject to the approval of Guntram - broadening the basis of the family's power and influence, and offering Brunhild the prospect of more grandchildren; see Gregory, *HF*, 9.16: Wood, pp. 103-104, 130. *Poem* 10.8 may arguably be dated to shortly after this event; the details of family security and prospects of grandchildren in the poem echo the terms of the treaty closely; the tone of happy optimism is appropriate; the poem is associated in its place in the collection of poems and in its addressees with *Poem* 10.7 (a plea to the royal pair for the special case of the city of Tours), with *Poem* 10.9 (written on a royal progress down river from Metz), and also probably with *Appendix* 5 and 6, poems of exuberant praise of the royal pair. The sentiments of the poem also echo Guntram's prayer on the occasion of the treaty (Gregory, *HF*, 9.11). Meyer, p. 22, and Koebner, pp. 208-209, argue convincingly that Fortunatus accompanied Gregory to the court at Metz (Gregory, *HF*, 9.20), though Gregory was sidetracked to meet Guntram, and that this was the occasion of these compositions. In that case, though *Appendix* 5 and 6 were letters, send by the same messenger, Audulf (*Appendix* 5.13, 6.15), there is no reason to suppose that the other poems were not declaimed to the royal pair and the court. Reydellet, (1981), p. 301, argues that *Appendix* 6 and *Poem* 10.8 were both letters, written shortly after the death of Chilperic in 585 to establish contact between the two kingdoms, suggesting that the reference in *Appendix* 6.3-6 to a daughter ruling in Spain more easily applies to Ingund, Brunhild's daughter married to Hermangild (Gregory, *HF*, 5.38). But Ingund's marriage had been ended in effect even by that date by Leuvigild and his wife, who separated her from her imprisoned husband in about 581 (Gregory, *HF*, 5.38, 6.40). *Appendix* 6.7-10 wishes Brunhild happiness in her grandchildren, as do *Poems* 10.7.59-64 and 10.8.21-24. The two latter references are to Childebert's children; the former would apply better to Chlodosind's prospective marriage (the present tense and *puella regens* in line 3-4 being vivid present tenses) than to Ingund's failed one.

[2] The poem is not a formal panegyric, but delivers its message with a direct simplicity which gives a convincing impression of heartfelt thankfulness. Yet the formal introduction, the traditional self-deprecation (lines 1-2, 27-28), and the light imagery (5-6, 9-20) combine to produce a tone of dignified literary exhilaration. For the former, see Curtius, pp. 83-85; for the latter, *Poem* 5.2, note 3.

rest upon the love of their lords, and fix their gaze upon your eyes. (5) You are both a precious adornment[3] and a glory to those to whom you are always a mirror, a light, and a sweetness. Your special gift is a peaceful and peace-loving kingdom, and the height of devotion in the world rests in your being. Here family, country, and guardianship are resplendent, (10) here is dignity and rank, here are the works of piety, here is tranquil peace, here is the hope which delights the faithful; after God, the gift of their salvation abides in you.

Here I join my own prayers and joy with the people; may Christ in His goodness see that they multiply and grow. (15) May God's care grant that He protects you long on your throne, and that you hold your realm long through heaven's gift[4]. May you gain yet new lands and govern those you already possess, and, as you partake of them, may you devoutly nurture these riches, so that you, o mother resplendent with glory, (20) may see a rich harvest flourishing from your son and offspring; thus may further noble offspring be granted to a grandmother, from your son and from your splendid grandsons. From Childebert - sweetness, flower, salvation - may you, his mother, reap the fruits, and the people see their prayers answered. (25) From your daughter and daughter-in-law may the Creator heap gifts upon you, and with your devout merit, may you remain pleasing in God's sight. Returning here, may I be worthy of uttering words of greeting, myself, humble though I am, rejoicing with my worthy Lords; may royal affairs prosper, may the people's joys increase; (30) let the land rejoice, let this splendour stand fast for all ages.

---

3 There is none of the conventional panegyric catalogue of events and actions, which convey movement and change. Rather, these abstract nouns for moral and aesthetic qualities give the sense of a poised moment of happiness and stability. This visual, tableau effect is intensified by the opening vignette of the people gazing up at their rulers in respectful gratitude.

4 The following lines echo the terms of the Treaty of Andelot; see Gregory, *HF,* 9.20.

Poem 10.9: on his voyage[5]

Coming upon the royal pair[6] where Metz' walls stand strong, I am observed and held back from my horse by my lords. From here I am commanded to skim the Moselle by oar, a sailor, and to make my way, swiftly gliding over the trembling waters. (5) Boarding the vessel, I sped, a sailor in my slender craft; without being driven by the winds, the prow flew on through the waters. Meanwhile there is a passage through the hidden rocks on the riverside; as the banks narrow, the waves toss their heads higher; the swift current catches the boat up, snatches it, and drives it there, (10) for it has now nearly swallowed the swelling waters. I wanted to escape and see the broad spreading fields[7], and, fleeing the water, I make for the pleasant countryside. I am caught up from below by the waters of the River Orne also; the stream, doubled by this, favours my journey. (15) From there we make our way with cautious boat through enclosed waters, in fear that the fishing nets might take me like a fish.

Amongst the smoking villa roofs[8] on the bank, I reach the point where the Sauer has the strength to roll. From there, between the jutting hills and valley depths, (20) we glide on the river's swift-rolling waters to the Saar. I am carried to where the lofty walls of Trier stand clear[9], a noble city, likewise a capital of noble people.

---

5 For the date of this poem, see *Poem* 10.8, note 1. For more detailed discussion of this poem in relation to Ausonius' poem on the same river, the *Mosella*, see L. Navarra, "A proposito del De navigio suo di Venanzio Fortunatuo in rapporto alla Mosella de Ausonio e agli Itinerari di Ennodio", *Studi storico- religiosi* 3, part 1 (1979), pp. 79-131. See also the discussion of the poem and its relation to the poet's earlier autobiographical account in *Poem* 6.8 in George, ch. 8; also M Roberts, "The description of landscape in the poetry of Venantius Fortunatus: the Moselle poems" in *Traditio* 49 (1994), pp. 1-22, and D. Pearsall and E. Salter, *Landscapes and seasons in the medieval world* (London, 1973), pp. 3-24.
6 I.e. Childebert and Brunhild.
7 The land is rich and fertile, flourishing in peace, a relevant comment after the Treaty of Andelot; cf. also the picture of the smoke curling up from the villas (lines 17-18), the fertile vineyards (lines 29-42), well-tilled fields (lines 65-68), and plentiful fishing (lines 69-74).
8 For the villas of this period and of this area, see E. M. Wightman, *Roman Trier and the Treveri*, London, 1970), ch. 4; J. Percival, *The Roman villa* (London, 1976), ch. 8.
9 The second impression in the journey is of Childebert and Brunhild's realm, one of imposing, ancient Roman strength: the walls of Metz (lines 1) and of Trier, the Roman buildings of Trier, the "noble capital of ancient times" (line 45), and "the citadel of Andernach" (line 63). For the Roman city of Trier, see Wightman, op.cit., ch. 3.

From here we are carried by the river past the senate's lofty summits of old[10], where the very ruins give evidence of its power. (25) We look round on all sides at the crags with their threatening heights[11], where the sharp rocks rise to pierce the clouds, where the rugged crags stretch up their lofty peaks, and the rock, rough with outcrops, rises to the stars. But not even here are the unyielding stones free to be without fruit; (30) indeed the rocks are fruitful and flow with wine[12]. Here you see on all sides the hills clothed with vine shoots and the wandering breeze stirs their tendrils[13] ; the vines are clustered thickly in rows, planted on the crags, the painted line reaches the ridge; (35) the patches cultivated by the farmers shine amidst the savage rocks; the pleasant vine glows red[14] on the pale rock, where the rough stone produces honey-sweet clusters of grapes, and on the barren flint the fruitful grape delights on the ridge where vineyards grow luxurious tresses below the bald mountain, (40) and shady verdure clothes the dry quarries; from them the vine-dresser plucks the deep-hued grapes, and himself hangs from the overhanging rocks as he picks them.

I had a feast for my eyes and a feast of food having these delights; and following the royal boats, (45) I was led from hence on

---

10 This appears to be the small semi-fortified palace of Pfalzel, mistakenly thought by Fortunatus to have had some official function. See E. M. Wightman, *Roman Trier and the Treveri* (London, 1970), p. 169.

11 The impression of savage, though domesticated, Nature is intensified by the angle at which the poet and the travellers are craning up at these stupendous sights; see lines 25, 35, 37, 42.

12 As in the earlier villa poems of Statius, the owners' or rulers' achievement is all the greater for being a domestication of the savagery of nature; see Statius, *Silv.* 1.3, 2.2.

13 The classical atmosphere created in tribute to the *Romanitas* of his listeners and their fitting place as inheritors of this part of the Roman empire, is emphasised by the style of description in general, and in particular by echoes of Ovid; line 32, cf. *Amor.* 1.7.54; line 35, cf. *Met.* 4.778-779.

14 There is debate whether the Mosel wine of this time was white, as it is today, or red. Paint colour on frescoes and sculpture suggests white; but the adjective *coloratas* in line 41 might argue for red, though it has been suggested that this merely refers to the russet of the leaves; see E. M. Wightman, *Roman Trier and the Treveri* (London, 1970), p.192. The evidence of place names of the Mosel valley, deriving largely from Celtic and Latin roots, in contrast to the Germanic names in areas around Bitburg and Dalheim in Luzembourg, suggests that the Franks left the specialised work of viticulture in the hands of the previous inhabitants, however much they might engage in sampling the produce; see Wightman, op.cit, p. 252, and Plate 19. Fortunatus' description shows that the vineyards were still flourishing at this time.

the waters to where Contrua[15] is busy with boats, where was once the noble capital of olden times. Then I come to where the two rivers flow and join together, here the foaming Rhine, there the fertile Moselle. Throughout that entire journey the waters served the royal couple with fish[16], (50) and the waters teemed with abundant supplies for the lords.

Yet, lest I should lack any pleasure on my journey, I feasted upon the Muses, my ear drinking in their song; tongues struck the hills with their practised song, and the overhanging rocks gave back their own melodies. (55) Soon the burnished strings stirred gentle rustlings, and the bushes responded in turn with their reeds from the mountainside. Now with quivering murmur, now with clear song, the music echoes from the rock exactly as it passes from the air. The songs unite the sundered banks with their sweetness, (60) and there was a single voice of song in hill and river. The kings' grace demands this to refresh their people; he discovers always the means whereby his care gives pleasure[17].

Thence making for the towers of the citadel of Andernach, I press on my approach, the burden of the craft[18]. (65) Although there are vineyards here in broad stretches on the hills, another area is of level tilled land; but the abundance of that beautiful place is all the greater because there is a second harvest for the people in the waters[19].

Finally, whilst the royal couple preside on their thrones in the court (70) and enjoy a festive banquet as a formal occasion, the nets are inspected where the weighty salmon are lifted, and he counts the fish, as he sits on high; the king looks with favour upon the table, as the fish leaps up from the wave, and restores spirits because his catch has come. (75) Seeing prosperity there, and here restoring joy to the palace, he feasts his eyes first, and then nourishes himself with food. The stranger to the Rhine is welcomed to the feast as a citizen, and the people who live there enjoy themselves banqueting. May the Lord

---

15 Contrua is commonly identified as the modern Kobern-Gondorf; see E. M. Wightman, op.cit., p. 130.
16 Nature is not only domesticated, she serves the royal pair with her riches.
17 This proud declaration that Fortunatus' declamation is an essential part of a royal occasion, in true Roman tradition, is in stark contrast to the marginal part the poet played in his earlier trip down the same rivers, in Sigibert's entourage; see *Poem 6.8*.
18 *Per accedens* in line 64 is clearly corrupt; the translation takes the sense of Brower's suggested *prope*.
19 Again, the prosperity of their lands compliments Childebert and Brunhild.

long grant the lords such a sight, (80) and may you grant that the people have such pleasant days; with your peaceful countenance may you give joy to all, and may your eminences be made joyful by your people[20].

---

20 This ending reveals that Fortunatus is declaiming this poem, presumably to the assembled court, as the literary contribution without which the king realises a civilised progress is not complete (lines 61-62) - a contrast to the context of *Poem* 6.8.

Book Eleven

Poem 11.6: to Agnes[1]

Mother to me in honour, sister sweetly loved, whom I esteem with devotion, faith, heart and soul, with heavenly affection, and not with any bodily sin; I love, not in the flesh, but what the spirit yearns for. (5) Christ is my witness, with Peter[2] and Paul[3] by His side, and holy Mary[4] looking on with her godly host, that you were nothing other to me in sight and spirit than if you had been my sister by birth, Titiana[5], and as if our mother Radegund had given birth to both of us (10) in a single delivery from her chaste womb, as though the dear breasts of the blessed mother had nurtured the two of us with a single stream of milk. Alas, I bewail my danger, the fear lest by a slight whisper malicious words thwart my feelings; (15) but yet it is my intent to live with the same hopes, if you wish me to be cherished with sweet love.

---

1 Fortunatus writes with great affection to Agnes, affection which was obviously reciprocated, given the milk puddings, butter and general companionship she gave him. But this relationship had clearly given rise to scandal at some point, and the poet writes to rebut the accusation. This type of "passionate friendship" was not uncommon in the church; cf. that of Jerome with Marcella, Paula and Eustochium (see J. N. D. Kelly, *Jerome, his life, writings and controversies* (London, 1979), especially chs. 10-12). And such friendship in an ascetic context found expression in passionate, even, erotic verbal expression; see P. Fabre, *Saint Paulin de Nole et l'amitié chrétienne* (Paris, 1949): C. White, *Christian friendship in the fourth century* (Cambridge, 1992). Given this, there is no reason not to accept Fortunatus' protestation at its face value. The reference to Radegund as *beata* (line 11) suggests that this poem was written after her death, i.e. after 587.
2 For Peter, see *Poem* 4.6, note 36.
3 For Paul, see *Poem* 5.2, note 8.
4 Mary, the mother of Jesus Christ.
5 There is no other mention of his sister.

Poem 11.8: to Agnes[6]

The happiest of fortunes granted my wish, when my prayers deserved to receive a gift. The sisters' food has rather benefited me; you satisfy them with a feast, you cherish me with your goodness. (5) With what shining excellence do you combine the two aspects! as you fill them with food, you revive me in spirit. A meal feeds the body, love nourishes a soul; where the need is greater, there you come all the more sweetly as nourishment[7]. May the Almighty hear your holy prayers, (10) that he may pour everlasting sustenance into your mouth. May you flourish through the long ages with our mother still living, and may that choir through your guidance remain in the Lord.

---

6 For the title, see *Poem* 7.24, note 53.
7 A common metaphor, but one where Fortunatus perhaps intentionally echoes the thoughts of Caesarius, founder of the Rule which guided the community; see *Poem* 5.2, note 26. Instruction was an important part of each day's routine, and, at the end of each day, Caesarius would ask "what have you eaten today", in reference to their spiritual nourishment; see *Vita Caesarii* 2.31, *PL* 67, pp. 337-338.

Poem 11.11: a poem about flowers[8]

Behold the blessed delights, fortunate fellow banqueter, which scent makes attractive before taste declares their worth. The mass of rosy-glowing flowers give delightful pleasure; the meadow hardly has as many roses as does the table now, (5) where the milk-white lilies glow pale amonst the purple hyacinths, and the place is vibrantly full of fresh scents. The feast, piled upon the dewy buds, rises up; why do beautiful roses cover what a cloth usually drapes? The table gave all the greater pleasure without its woven cover, (10) and the sweet scent mantles it with a variety of gifts; the wall is resplendent with the verdant cluster hanging there; crushed roses glow red, where your heel treads. There is such exuberance that you would think that soft meadows were blooming indoors with bright flowers. (15) If transient delights, which fade and die so quickly, give pleasure, may your feasts summon us as guests, Paradise. Our sister's[9] tapestry was glorious

---

8 A poem written to be declaimed at some special festive meal, and in the presence of Radegund and Agnes (lines 15-16), the addressee "fellow feaster" probably being the rest of the company. The other guests may have been members of the community - for the kind of festivities referred to in e.g. *Appendix* 11, 18 and 19; or they may have included visitors - for example, Vilthuta and Dagaulf who appear to have been known to Radegund and Agnes (*Poem* 4.26.97: *Appendix* 9). The poem reveals the same vivid delight in flowers and vibrant colour as do *Poems* 8.7 and 8; for similar feasting, see *Poem* 11.23. The question may be asked whether there is a conflict between the picture presented here, and the life of an enclosed community. Radegund's biographers, Fortunatus and Baudonivia, both speak of Radegund's renunciation of worldly goods and status, and her ascetic life style; see *VR* 1, 3, 9, 17-24 (especially 21); *VR* 2.8-9.7. The Rule of Caesarius, adopted by Radegund (*Poem* 5.2, note 26), forbids the women to go outside the convent (ch. 1); only clergy are allowed inside, or workmen under strict supervision (ch. 33), but not lay men and women (ch. 3); hospitality may only be offered to holy women coming from far afield (ch. 36). Gregory's account of Radegund's adoption of the Rule of Caesarius implies that she acted thus only after long attempts to get the Bishop of Poitiers, Maroveus, to give them the needed pastoral advice and guidance; see *HF,* 9.40: *Poem* 5.2, note 26. We may either conclude that these poems are to be dated to the period before the adoption of the Rule, and that life was more relaxed and open at that stage - or that they made good use, as was often done, of a "parlour" to which the rules which governed life inside the convent did not strictly obtain. Meyer, pp. 25-29, 108, suggests that the last two books were put together by Fortunatus' friends after his death; Koebner, *Excursus* 2, pp. 125-128, proposes that Fortunatus composed the books in the 590s, after the deaths of Agnes and Radegund, of hitherto unpublished and more personal poems (for discussion of this question, see George, Appendix 2, pp. 208-211). In either case, the poems to the two women about such meals may well have been written in the early years of the poet's life in Poitiers, but only published much later.
9 Agnes.

through her skilful hands; our mother[10] was worthy of receiving such beauty.

Poem 11.13: to Lady Radegund and Agnes, for the chestnuts

That small basket was woven from osiers by my hands[11]; believe me, dear ones, mother and sweet sister[12]; and I give here rustic gifts, which the countryside produces, sweet chestnuts, which the tree gave to the fields.

Poem 11.14: to Agnes, for milk

I observed the fingermarks over the milky gifts, and your hand remained imprinted here where you pick up the butter pat. Tell me, please, who encouraged your gentle fingers to fashion in that way? Was Daedalus[13] your teacher in this art? (5) O revered love, whose image comes to me, though the mould has been stolen away. But my hope was in vain, for this image broke up in its flimsy covering. Thus not even a small part could be given to me. May you make these over the long years the Lord gives you, (10) with our mother abiding long with you in this life.

Poem 11.19: for other delicacies and for milk

In the midst of abundant feasting you send a fast, and consume my spirit by letting me see so much. My eyes see what the doctor[14] has forbidden me to touch, and that hand forbids what my

---

10 Radegund.
11 This gift is in the classical tradition, a humble present, but picked by the poet himself; see *Poem 8.6*, note 2.
12 Radegund and Agnes.
13 Daedalus was the legendary Athenian craftsman, who devised many ingenious contrivances, including the labyrinth of King Minos on Crete, where the Minotaur lived.
14 There is little evidence about the availability or the level of medical skill at this period, though kings, abbeys and hospitals all seem to have had physicians. See G. Baader, "Early medieval adaptations of Byzantine medicine in western Europe", *Dumbarton Oaks Papers* 34 (1985), pp. 25 -259: G. Clark, *Women in late antiquity; pagan and Christian lifestyles*

appetite demands. (5) Yet since above all else you serve me rich milky food, you surpass kingly gifts with your presents. Now, my sister, I pray you rejoice with our devout mother; for the happy feasts of joy possess us.

Poem 11.23: verses composed after a feast[15]

Whilst I was drowsing and feasting in the midst of various delights and mingled savours, (I was opening my mouth, and shutting my eyes again and was chewing away, seeing many a dream), (5) my wits were muddled, believe me, dear ones, and I was not easily able to utter freely the words I wished. I could not trace verses with my finger, or with a pen, my befuddled Muse had made my hands uncertain. For it seemed to me, and to everyone else drinking the free-flowing wine, (10) that the table itself was swimming with neat wine. Yet now, as best I could, I have addressed humble verses in sweet speech to my mother[16] and my sister besides. Though sleep assails me with its many bonds, love has driven me to write these lines with wavering hand.

(Oxford, 1993), pp. 63-93 (mainly on women's health, but useful overview): J. Duffy, "Byzantine medicine in the sixth and seventh centuries; aspects of teaching and practice", *Dumbarton Oaks Papers*, 34 (1985), pp. 21-27: R. Jackson, *Doctors and diseases in the Roman empire* (London, British Museum Publications, 1988): V. Nutton, "From Galen to Alexander: aspects of medicine and practice in late antiquity", *Dumbarton Oaks Papers* 34 (1985), pp. 1-14: Riché, pp. 69-71, 204-205: J. Scarborough, *Roman medicine* (London, 1969).
15 See note 1 above on feasting. This feast is more explicitly just that, even allowing for poetic licence. For a call to contribute such epigrams, see *Poem* 3.13, note 9. For the reason for the liberal translation of the title *item versus in convivio factus*, see *Poem* 7.24, note 53.
16 Radegund and Agnes.

(a) The charming mistress of the feast has refreshed her servant with her words and sustenance, and satisfies him with various delightful pleasanteries[17].

Poem 11.25: to Radegund and Agnes about his journey[18]

The changes of men's lives are set in motion by events without number, and life proceeds uncertainly with staggering steps[19]. Our minds, perplexed and anxious about the future, do not know what the coming day will bring forth. (5) For when I left you, Eomundus[20], your admirer, received me with his usual kindness. Hastening on swiftly from there, I travel to the abode at Cariacum[21]; from there, I go on to Tincillac[22]. The holy bishop Domitianus[23] caught me up from there, (10) taking me off to the joyous festival of St. Albinus. Released from there, I was then driven wearily by the waves and rain in a small craft[24] through many a danger, where the fierce driving North wind had turned the river upside down and the water raised billows which curled threateningly; (15) its banks were not holding the agitated floods; the waters poured forth and invaded fresh terrain. With angry strength a single foray takes possession of pastures, countryside, grove, crops, wayfaring trees, and willow thicket. As I was entrusted to the ragged roaring of the torrent here, (20) the unfettered storm raged with

---

17 This neat couplet, referring presumably to Radegund as mistress of the feast, is in answer to verse of hers (see *Appendix* 31, note 50, for her writing).

18 This poem reflects the network of contacts within Gaul for which Fortunatus acted as emissary for Radegund, as the nun furthered the interests of her community, and also, those of Sigibert and his kingdom, as Baudonivia observes (*VR* 2.10); see, for example, *Poems* 2.9 and 10 to Germanus in Paris: 3.26, to Rucco, a Parisian deacon: 9.11, to Droctoveus, abbot of St. Vincent in Paris: 9.10, 12 and 13 to Germanus' successor and clergy: 3.21 and 22, to Avitus of Clermont-Ferrand. For comment, see George, pp. 167-8: R. A. Meunier, "L'intérêt politique de la correspondance de Saint Fortunat", *Études mérovingiennes, Actes des journées de Poitiers* 1952 (Paris, 1953), pp. 239-248.

19 A commonplace, found often in consolation; see von Moos, *Testimonien*, T625.

20 Eomund is otherwise unknown.

21 Cariacum, mentioned also in *Poem* 5.7.8, is near Nantes.

22 The exact location of the monastery of Tincillac is not known.

23 Domitianus was Bishop of Angers; see Duchesne, 2, p. 358. Albinus had been abbot of the monastery of Tincillac from 504 to 529, and then Bishop of Angers. Fortunatus' visit to the monastery, to Domitianus and his subsequent writing of a *Vita Albini* for the bishop suggests Domitianus' development of the cult of the saint; see Brennan, (1983) pp. 156-180.

24 For river travel in this area, see *Poem* 6.8, note 115.

terrifying blasts, and the stern would rise up as the bow fell through the liquid peaks[25], climbing the watery paths as the mountain-mass shifted; when the boat was held atop a swirling eddy, the sailor occupied the clouds, and then, as the waters drew back, he returned to the fields. (25) As the storm boiled with hostile waves, the prow constantly drank in fast-flowing waters; waters lapped the hull with hostile peace, intent on more deadly harm to us in their embrace. But lack of time stops me mentioning my various troubles; (30) I conceal in my heart the plaints to be told later. But may God's power grant this especially to me, that I may speedily be able to see you, blessed friends, again.

Poem 11 26: to Lady Radegund[26]

Everywhere the ice lies stiffly locked, hardened with frost, and the pliant grass does not raise its prostrate blades. The earth lies encrusted with rime under its rigid casing; soft, deep snow laps the trees' foliage. (5) The flowing streams have built up an encrusted wall, and the thickened waters have donned a thick casing. The waters are reined in by their own mass, the current has constrained itself, and can scarce make a path for itself under the barrier it has created. In the midst of the river is formed a crystal bank; (10) we do not want to go under, and we cannot go over. The ice has swollen the more severely under the howling North wind; to whom will that water give passage, which fights against itself? But if now that breath of warmth is created, which then in the beginning was carried over the waters[27], (15) if you prevail upon the Almighty with constant prayers, you give

---

25 For this "world upside down" motif, see Curtius, pp. 94-98. The dramatic over-exaggeration turns the danger into a mock-epic episode, with the intention, perhaps, of taking the edge off Radegund and Agnes' fears for his safety.

26 This title is conjectural, since the text does not make clear to whom Fortunatus is writing; see *Poem* 8.7, note 5. The exact reference and significance of the poem is difficult to make out. But Fortunatus elsewhere translates a vivid nature description mid-poem into a simile or metaphor for his feelings, or a situation he is in; e.g. *Poem* 7.8. On that parallel, it would appear that there is tension and frustration here, probably between the poet and Radegund, which he wishes to resolve, but does not know how.

27 Possibly a reference to Genesis, 1.2, to the Spirit of God, moving upon the face of the waters; or to Genesis, 8.1, to the wind which God sent to assuage the waters of the Flood.

me too, as you wish, more happiness. For if only it were as possible for you to obey whatever is commanded, as I am eager to be willing.

Appendix

Appendix 2: to Justin and Sophia[1], the August[2]

May the highest glory be to the Father, Son and bountiful Spirit, a single God to be worshipped in this trinity[3], majesty, of three

---

1 For Justin and Sophia, see Biographical Notes. Radegund, chosing to put her community under the protection of the Holy Cross, wrote to Justin, with Sigibert's support, requesting a fragment of this most prestigious relic; see Gregory, *HF*, 5.40. For the significance of such relics, see P. R. L. Brown, *Relics and social status in the age of Gregory of Tours* (Stenton Lecture, Reading, 1976). This was a shrewd request, given that Byzantium by the mid-sixth century held a great number of important relics, and, under the patronage of Justin and Sophia, was an important artistic centre; see J. Herrin, *The formation of Christendom* (Oxford, 1987), pp. 84-5: MacCormack (1981), pp. 84-86. This request was reinforced by three poems from Fortunatus: *App.* 1 and 3, and *Poem* 8.1, which presented Radegund's credentials as a learned and devout nun. The embassy returned successfully with a fragment of the True Cross set in a splendid reliquary, together with other relics and a fine gospel book. Maroveus, Bishop of Poitiers, refused to celebrate their reception, and the ceremony was performed, at Sigibert's request, by Bishop Eufronius of Tours (Gregory,*HF*, 9.40; Baudonivia, *VR*, 2.16; for the reliquary, which still survives in Poitiers, see M. Conway, "St. Radegund's reliquary at Poitiers", *The Antiquaries' Journal* 3 (1923), pp.1-12; P. Lasko, *The kingdom of the Franks* (London, 1971), pp. 74-79, Plates 59, 60; E. Mâle, *La fin du paganisme en Gaule et les plus anciennes basiliques chrétiennes* (Paris, 1950), pp. 294-295. It was for this occasion that Fortunatus composed his great hymns to the Cross, *Poems* 2.2 and 6 (for these, see J. Szöverffy, *Venantius Fortunatus and the earliest hymns to the Holy Cross*,Classical Folia 20 (New York, 1966), pp. 107-22); and, on Radegund's behalf, he sent *Appendix* 2 in thanks to Justin and Sophia in Byzantium (probably the thanks mentioned by Baudonivia in *VR* 2.17). The poem is a *gratiarum actio*, a formal thanksgiving in the rhetorical tradition, using many of the motifs of panegyric; cf. Ausonius' *Gratiarum actio ad Gratianum imperatorem pro consulatu,* and see *Poem* 5.2, note 1. See George, pp. 62-67 for further discussion of this poem.
2 For this title, see *Poem* 9.2.45, note 69. Use of the title here stresses their supreme position, in a world which encompasses the Franks as well as the Byzantine court.
3 Fortunatus immediately sets the poem in the context of the long and bitter division of the Church over the question of the Three Chapters. This concerned three church writers of the fifth century, Theodore of Mopsuestia, Theodoret of Cyprus, and Ibas of Edessa. Despite their Nestorianism, the Council of Chalcedon had failed to condemn them as heretics, but the emperor Justinian had declared an edict of anathema against them in the 540s. This action roused fierce opposition, especially in the Western Church. Western bishops feared that the edict eroded the authority of the Council of Chalcedon, which had defined and established church orthodoxy on the question of the Persons of the Trinity; they doubted whether dead men could be anathematized, and they resented imperial interference in church matters. However, the Fifth Ecumenical Council, held in 553 without the pope, Vigilius, supported the emperor. The result was the exile of the pope and the disaffection of large areas of the

persons but one substance, equal, partaking equally and of equal age, (5) a single virtue abiding the same, a single power to the three (what the Father can do, so can the Son and the Spirit), distinct in persons indeed, united in strength, of a single nature, alike in might, light, and throne, existing ever as a Trinity amongst Themselves, ruling time without end, (10) lacking no function nor powerful by receiving power.

May the highest glory be to Thee, Creator and Redeemer of the world, Who in Your justice establish Justin as head over the world. He, who pleases the King of Heaven by his service, duly lays claim to the citadel which holds mastery over kings. (15) How rightly he rules over Rome and the Roman world who follows the docrine which Peter's throne proclaims[4], which Paul[5] sounded out everywhere, a single trumpet to thousands, who poured the salt of wisdom forth from his lips for the confused gentiles; the wheel of his eloquence circles the four corners of the earth, (20) and cold hearts warm in the faith of his eloquence.

May the highest glory be to You, Creator and Redeemer of the world, You who in Your justice establish Justin on high in the world. The faith of the church, once shaken, now made whole, is glorious again, and venerable law returns to its place of old[6]. (25) Offer your prayers to God, for the new purple[7] holds fast by what the Council of

---

Western Church. On his accession, Justin ll recalled exiled bishops and restored rights to the penalized partisans of the Three Chapters. See J. Herrin, *The formation of Christendom* (Oxford, 1987), pp. 119-25; E. Stein, *Histoire du Bas-Empire* 2, tr. J. R. Palanque (Paris - Brussels, 1949-59), pp. 671 ff. Against this background, Fortunatus hails the emperor and empress as champions of Chalcedon orthodoxy, indeed addressing himself to the three Persons of the Trinity, and in lines 1-10 paraphrasing the credal propositions of the Council. Each of the two sections of the poem, the one to Justin (lines 11-50), and that to Sophia (lines 51 ff.) are structured round the significant triple repetition of the couplet beginning "glory in the highest" and magnifying the Triune Deity (lines 1-2, 11-12, 21-2, 49-50, 61-2, 71-2).
4 "Peter's throne" is the papal throne in Rome. The suggestion here that the validity of Justin's rule derives from his obedience to the doctrines of Rome and the Pope reflects the church's earlier concern that Justinian's edict had overruled its dictates. For Peter, see *Poem* 4.26, note 36.
5 For Paul, see *Poem* 5.2, note 8.
6 See note 3 above for Justin's ending of the divisions of the Three Chapters.
7 I.e. the newly enthroned emperor. This phrase suggests a date near Justin's accession in 565. But Poitiers only came within Sigibert's kingdom in 568. Assuming that the envoys set off with the king's permission almost immediately, they were probably back in 569 (Sigibert's later embassy was away for about a year; see Gregory, *HF*, 4.40). The return journey, with the tribute of thanks, could then have been made in 569/70, when the

Chalcedon decreed[8]. Gaul[9] too sings this song to your merits, Augustus, the Rhone, the Rhine, the Danube and the Elbe proclaim this. Under the western heavens Galicia has heard this deed, the Cantabrian with the neighbouring Basque[10] relates this. The godly story of faith speeds to the farthest people, and, across the Ocean, the land of Britain looks with favour. How well do you love and share your cares with the Lord! He makes your concerns His, and you, behold, make His yours. (35) Christ affords you succour, you pay honour to Christ; He gave you preeminence, you give him faith in return. There has been nothing more in the world he could give you to rule over, nor could you give more in return than the power of nurturing faith. The fathers[11], set in exile in the name of Christ, (40) returned home when you received your crown. Released from prison, living in their former abodes, they declare you a single blessing to all alike. Having cured the ills of so many confessors, Augustus, you come as a unique panacea for people without number. (45) Thracian, Italian, Scythian, Phrygian, Dacian, Dalmatian, Thessalian and African[12] now offer prayers to you because they have won their homeland. These praises of you, emperor, have traversed the earth with the sun; wherever humankind exists, there your honour reaches.

---

accession could be termed "recent", if not "new". See R. Aigrain, *Sainte Radegonde vers 520 - 587* (3rd. ed., Paris, 1924) p. 102.

Justin's accession and entry upon his first consulship on 1 January, 566, were celebrated by Corippus' panegyric, *In laudem Iustini minoris*, probably written at the latest by 567; for the date, see Averil Cameron, "The early religious policies of Justin II", in *Continuity and change in sixth century Byzantium* (London, 1981), ch. 10; for text, ed. and tr. by Cameron (London, 1976). Corippus wrote in the panegyric tradition, and, like Fortunatus, celebrated Justin's orthodoxy. It is possible that Fortunatus wrote the trinitarian section of this poem with Corippus' credal paraphrase (4.290-311) before him. But the verbal parallels are not striking (see M. Manitius, "Zu spätlateinischen Dichtern", *Zeitschrift für österreichischen Gymnasien* (1886), p. 253), and the detailed structure of Fortunatus' poem so distinctive, that direct borrowing is implausible. There are, however, striking parallels between Corippus' lines to the Virgin Mary (2.52-69) and the poem *In laudem Mariae*. Attribution of this to Fortunatus was rejected by Leo in his edition, but persuasively argued for by Cameron in the article noted above, p. 61.

8 See note 3 above.

9 Fortunatus depicts the Western Church, disaffected from the East and the Eastern emperor by the dispute, being reunited. This picture of the acclaiming nations also serves as a typical *consensus universorum* in the panegyric tradition; see *Poem* 6.2, note 46..

10 For the Basques, see James, (1982), pp. 20-21, 150.

11 I.e. the recall of exiles and release of prisoners by Justin; see note 3 above.

12 This list rounds off the picture of universal acclaim, whilst leaving the emphasis naturally on the peoples of the Frankish and Western world.

May the highest glory be to You, Creator and Redeemer of the world, (50) who in your justice establish Justin on high in the world. Of equal merit to him, marrying him in blessed years, noble Sophia[13] gains august rank. The holy places she tends with devotion[14], she adorns with love, and by this offering she causes herself to draw near to heaven. (55) Her abundant faith, shining in splendour from the eastern skies, sent resplendent gifts to God as far as the setting of the sun; when Thuringian Queen Radegund asked, she bestowed the sacred gift of the cross she desired, on which Christ, thinking it worthy, hung in the flesh He had taken on (60) and bathed our wounds in His blood.

May the highest glory be to You, Creator and Redeemer of the world, because noble Sophia holds august rank. O loving care, flowing even this far from a bountiful source, whose love pours faith in Christ everywhere. (65) Behold, Augusti, you rival each other with like offerings; you enoble your sex, as he does his; the man brings back Constantine[15], the godly woman Helena; as the honour is alike, so is the very love of the Cross. She found the means, you scatter salvation everywhere, (70) and what was first the Rising fills the Setting[16] too.

May the highest glory be to You, Creator and Redeemer of the world, because noble Sophia holds august rank. Through you the Cross of the Lord claims power over the whole world; where it was unknown now it is manifest and offers protection. (75) Greater faith has reached Christ's people, when hope, with eyes to see, perceives the power of salvation, and faith is doubled through the senses, when, through your gifts, souls believe all the more in what they verify with the Cross as witness. The Augusta, nurturing this, as the apostle did[17], sets herself to the plough; (80) you make the field fertile by the wood, as he did by the word. This renown celebrates you where the North

---

13 For Sophia, see Biographical Note under "Justin", and note 1 above. For the panegyric tradition of praise of an empress or queen, see *Poem* 6.1a, note 45. For Sophia's public image, see MacCormack, (1981), pp. 79, 257, plate 58, 264.
14 For Sophia (and Justin's) patronage of art and architecture, see note 1 above.
15 The imperial couple are likened to the Emperor Constantine, who first established Christianity as the religion of his empire, and to his mother, Helena, who was said to have discovered the original Cross of Christ; a relevant reference given the relic in question, and one which recalls the relationship between church and state. See MacCormack, (1981) pp. 84-86, plate 24.
16 A variation of the light motif of panegyric; see *Poem* 5.2, note 3.
17 I.e. Paul; see note 5 above.

stretches forth, East and West enlist to serve you by the words of their mouths. There the Roman offers praise, here the barbarian himself, German, Batavian, Basque and Briton. (85) May your fortunes flourish through the ages with the Cross, Augusta, to which you have made prayers swell in distant lands. Radegund, prostrate on the ground in supplication, adores this, and prays for long years for your rule, and, joined with her sisters in outpourings of tears, wishes (90) that your faith will garner great joy from this. May you remain blessed as spouse of the Emperor Justin, Sophia, girt with the sacred patrician order[18]. Ruling the kingdom of Romulus[19], may you grant its rights to the senate, and may the equestrian order revere you as mistress. (95) May God add heavenly prayers to blessed ones, and may what Radegund loves not pass away from you; she prays, pouring dust over herself, with constant chanting, that the highest honour may remain yours through the long years. In prayer, mind, feeling and intent always pursuing good, (100) may you have care for her, may He be mindful of you[20].

---

18 This ancient title had been revived by Constantine and bestowed as a rare and personal honour.
19 The founder of the city of Rome.
20 For the possible significance of the number of 100 lines in this poem, see Curtius, "Excurcus XV: Numerical composition", pp. 501-509: C. Butler, "Numerological thought" in A. Fowler (ed.), *Silent Poetry* (London, 1970), pp. 1-31.

Appendix 3: to Artachis[21]

After the ashes of our homeland and the fallen roofs of our parents, which the land of Thuringia suffered in hostile war, if I tell of the battles fought in that doomed conflict, to what tears will I, a woman raped, first be drawn[22]? (5) What am I free to mourn? that this nation was overwhelmed by slaughter, or that this noble family was destroyed by various calamities? For my father[23], falling first, and my uncle[24] following him, both near kin, dealt me a bitter blow. My brother had remained as head[25], but by evil fate (10) the sand bows me over his grave too. You who alone survived when all were dead (alas, the agonised entrails of grief), Amalfrid, now lie dead. Am I, Radegund, sought out for this purpose after so long? Was it this news which your page brought me, to my distress? (15) Have I waited long for such a gift to come from my loving kin, and do you send me this

---

21 In *Appendix* 1, Fortunatus represents Radegund addressing her cousin, Amalfrid, son of Herminfred, who fled to Byzantium after the overthrow of Thuringia to serve the emperor (Procopius, *de bell. Goth.* 4.25). He draws a picture of tragic genocide, echoing the epic writing of Lucan and Claudian, reproaching Amalfrid for lack of care of his sole surviving relative. In the context of the embassy to Byzantium (see note 1 above), Amalfrid was probably the least of the audience this poem was intended for; Fortunatus was concerned to establish Radegund as the last survivor of a royal family, devout and civilised, and to demonstrate that such a relic would not be going to some heretical and barbaric backwater. Line 14 of this shorter poem suggests that there was a reply to *Appendix* 1, announcing the death of Amalfrid (lines 13-16), together with a gift of silk (line 17). This poem is a response, nominally from Radegund, to that missive. Meyer, pp. 136-137, suggests that Artachis was the son of Radegund's brother, killed in Gaul about 550 (Gregory, *HF*, 3.7), that he lived with his mother (line 39) and was a support for the community in Poitiers (lines 37-8). But the close parallels with *Appendix* 1 in content and style make it more likely that this poem too was addressed to Byzantium, and that Artachis was possibly Amalfrid's son (line 29). In that case, this letter can be dated to the period of 568 when Radegund was in contact with Byzantium to lay the groundwork for her request for relics for the community.
22 Nisard, p. 104, identifies Radegund herself as the writer of this poem and *Appendix* 1, on the ground of its feminine depth and sensitivit, a conclusion with which Dronke concurs, though without explanation: P. Dronke, *Women writers in the middle ages* (Cambridge, 1984), pp. 27 - 28. But Tardi's analysis, pp. 196-200, shows close parallels with Fortunatus' technique in other poems. The sentiments, too, are appropriate to the genre.
23 I.e. Berthar: see Gregory, *HF*, 3.4. Fortunatus omits to mention that it was Herminfred who killed him.
24 Herminfred, father of Amalfrid: see Gregory, *HF*, 3.7.
25 See Gregory, *HF*, 3.7.

succour from your military service? Do you now send these silken hanks[26] for me to spin, so that, as I draw out the threads, I, your sister, may be consoled by your love? Did your care take such thought for my bitter sorrow? (20) Would the first and the last messenger give these gifts? Could we in any other fashion have run through our prayers with flooding tears? The outcome[27] was that I who hoped for sweetness, was given bitterness. My anxious heart was tormented by feelings of disquiet; is so great a fever of the spirit refreshed by these waters? (25) I did not merit seeing him alive, nor being present at his grave, I endure a second loss through your burial[28]. But why should I recount these things to you, dear Artachis, fosterling, and by my tears, add to yours. I ought rather to have offered consolation to your parent[29], (30) but grief for the dead compels me to speak of what is bitter. He was not a relative from some distant branch of the family, but a very close kinsman, of my father's brother. For my father was Berthar and his Herminfred; we are born to brothers yet we are not in the same world. (35) But you, dear nephew[30], restore to me a relative in peace and be mine in love as he was before, and, I beg, often seek me out with things sent for the convent, and may that place stand firm in God by your help, that for you with your godly mother (40) this everlasting care may gain due reward on the starry throne. May the Lord now grant to you in blessing that at this time you may have salvation in abundance, and glory in times to come.

---

26 Byzantium had only just started producing silk. See Procopius, *De bell. Goth.* 4.17: A. Muthesius, "From seed to samite: aspects of Byzantine silk production" in L. Monnas and H. Granger-Taylor (edd.), *Ancient and medieval textiles: studies in honour of Donald King* (Textile history 20, Pasold research fund, 1989), pp. 135-149. For the availability of silk in Merovingian Gaul, see Salin, 1, pp. 101, 134-5, 165. If the reference is to silk thread (cf. Vergil, *Georg.* 2.121), this would be a splendid gift for nuns who devoted much time to spinning: see Gregory, *GC*, 104; *S. Caesarii Regulae* 14, PL 67, p. 109.
27 Reading, with Leo, *venerat* for *non erat*.
28 For these being considered particularly tragic circumstances, see F. Cumont, *Afterlife in Roman paganism* (Harvard, 1962), pp. 128-147.
29 Though this term strongly suggests that Amalfrid was Artachis' father, it could refer to any near relationship.
30 A general term for a close male relative, of a younger generation.

Appendix 5: on King Childebert[31]

O king, pinnacle of the realm and ruler over the kingdoms; you who are the head of heads, a man who is the chief good, an adornment of ornaments, adorning more ornately, you who are a glory and in your honour perform everything honourably, (5) the first, and born of the first[32], in the forefront even of the foremost, you who in your might are mighty, whom the Almighty succours, delighting the delightful, beloved sweet power, goodly hope and goodness, good from goodness. Worthily never displeased, dignity dignifying the worthy, (10) flowery flower of flowers, flowing flowerily with flowers, esteemed Childebert; I, Fortunatus, in love, humbly from humble understanding[33], offer you this. I commend as a servant Audulf with suppliant prayer, and myself also: may you thus rule over us in majesty.

Appendix 6: on Queen Brunhild[34]

Royal offspring, mother also of excellent honour, girt on all sides with the godly glory of rulers; Gaul has your progeny[35] and Spain your offspring[36], the son ruling here and the daughter there; (5) may the auspices be propitious for years yet more prosperous; may he protect the Allobroges[37], may she govern the Goths, may your offspring

---

31 For Childebert ll, see Biographical Notes. For the date of this poem, see *Poem* 10.8, note 1. The intense alliteration may reflect a youthful taste for such word play, as well as a general liking among the Franks for such writing; see Meyer, p. 138. For the even greater complexities of some of Fortunatas' acrostics, see M. Graver, "Quaelibet audendi: Fortunatus and the acrostic", *Transactions of the American Philological Association* 123 (1993), pp. 219-245: D. Norberg, *Introduction à l'étude de la versification latine médiévale* (Stockholm, 1958), pp.54-63. Both this and the following poem were sent by the same messenger, Audulf, presumably at the same time; so this was intended to be read, not declaimed.
32 His father, Sigibert, was the fifth of Lothar's sons (Gregory, *HF*, 4.3); so the term merely means "foremost' here.
33 For this self-deprecation, see Curtius, pp. 83-85.
34 For the date of this poem, see *Poem* 10.8, note 1.
35 I.e. Childebert ll.
36 For the likely reference of this to Brunhild's daughter Chlodosind and her marriage to Reccared, rather than to Ingund and her marriage to Hermangild, see *Poem* 10.8, note 1.
37 A people to the east of the Rhone, and north of the Isère.

rule alike with twin peoples, and may this place and that present you with fruit, whereby a splendid crown of grandchildren[38], good queen, may encircle you, (10) a grandmother doubly fruitful through your son and your daughter. Joyfully reviewing those by hearsay, these by sight, rejoicing here in person, but favouring these by ear, and as a mother seeing both lands under your family, as a grandmother may you rejoice with your people and your country. (15) I commend as a servant Audulf[39], and me with him; may your glory abide in splendour for all.

Appendix 10: to Lady Radegund and Agnes[40]

What story is carried to the ear[41] in sweet discourse? If the welcoming board now holds peaceful souls for me, mark the compliant minds as the tablet[42] is passes back, so that the letters drawn by hand record affection. (5) Mother and sister[43], alike sweet in godly love, celebrate together the joyous occasion with festive sound.

Appendix 11: another poem[44]

Today I celebrated the festive day, on which the holy birth of the Lord came upon this earth. First from all directions came cheese - then came rounded wooden salvers - (5) a dish adorned on all sides bore meat and fowl - who in a moment of time offer food for all on your lips, and from all - . A mistress over you and you always with her, you who day and night pour honeyed eloquence from your lips.

---

38 See *Poem* 10.8, note 1, for the particular implications of this in the light of the Treaty of Andelot.
39 See note 30 above.
40 For the title, strictly *item aliud*, see *Poem* 7.24, note 53. Like that, this was written as an offering for amusement at some festive meal. No date can be assigned to this poem.
41 Reading *in aurem* as better sense with *fertur*.
42 I. e. the wax tablet on which the poem is written; see Riché, pp. 228-229.
43 I.e. Radegund and Agnes.
44 For the title, again *item aliud*, see *Poem* 7.24, note 53. This text may represent the fragments of a poem; but more probably, since the phrases are rough and unfinished, it is the preliminary jottings for a poem. If so, this would suggest that this collection of poem was made after the poet's death, by his friends, rather than by the poet himself; for discussion of the dating of the various collections, see George, Appendix 2, pp. 208-211.

Appendix 15: to Radegund and Agnes[45]

     May my mother and sister rest safely through the healing night; may the gracious prayers of your son and brother bring you this; may the angelic host descend upon your minds and rule over your dear hearts with its encouraging words. (5) The night hours urge me to greet you thus briefly; please now reply to my six lines, I pray, with at least two.

Appendix 26: to Radegund and Agnes[46]

     A son to my mother[47], at the same time a brother to my sister[48], I offer humble gifts with a devoted heart[49]. One of a trinity, I carry three gifts to two; sweet apples[50] befit such sweet spirits. (5) But forgive me that it is enclosed in such a shrine; the paper will be a basket to carry the gifts.

Appendix 31: to Lady Radegund[51]

     You have given me great verse on small tablets, you can create honey in the empty wax; you bestow a feast of many courses in

---

45 For the title, again *item aliud*, see *Poem* 7.24, note 53. This poem cannot be dated closely.
46 Another poem for an occasion which cannot be dated. For the title, see *Poem* 7.24, note 53.
47 Radegund.
48 Agnes.
49 Like *Poems* 8.6 and 11.13, a poem accompanying a humble offering; see *Poem* 8.6, note 2 for the resonance of this.
50 Apples also have the religious connotation of salvation; see *Poem* 6.6, note 109.
51 This poem to Radegund thanks her for verses she has composed for festivities such as those which were the occasions of *Poems* 11.11, 23, 23a, and *Appendix* 10, the three latter also prompting verse from Radegund or Agnes. For the possible existence of such verse, see note 21 above. It therefore appears we have only references to their verse, and no actual examples.

the joyful festivities, but your words are sustenance to me for which I am even more eager; **(5)** you send little verses composed of charming speech, by whose words you bind our heart. All the delicacies you produce are sufficient for the others, but to me may your tongue grant pure honey. I pray that you remember me amongst the holy words of the sisters, **(10)** that prayers for me make you my mother all the more truly; through your commendation, may I be restored to all the others, that I am worthy to attain through you what my plea requests.

Biographical notes

Brief notes are given here of relevant biographical details of major characters in Fortunatus' poems. Reference to this section is made in the text as necessary. For further general prosopographical detail, see Stroheker: Wood, pp. 350-363.

Agnes was adopted by Radegund at an early age and brought up as her daughter (Gregory, *HF*, 9.42: Fortunatus, *Poem* 8.3.59). Consecrated by Bishop Germanus of Paris (Gregory, *HF*, 9.42), she became first Mother Superior of the convent of the Holy Cross in Poitiers, dying shortly after Radegund (Gregory, *HF*, 9.39 refers to Leubovera as Mother Superior in 589).

Brunhild, daughter of the Visigothic king and queen of Spain, Athanagild and Goiswinth, was married by Sigibert to strengthen his position by a dynastic alliance. (For the Visigoths, see M. Todd, *The early Germans* (Oxford, 1992), pp. 153-176: P. Heather, *Goths and Romans 332-489* (Oxford 1991), passim: on education at the Visigothic court, see Riché, pp. 246-265). She was escorted to Metz by Gogo, one of Sigibert's counsellors (see note under "Gogo" below: and Fortunatus, *Poem* 7.1.12-14, 41-2, and note 4: Fredegar, *Chron.*, 3.59, p. 109). She was speedily converted to Catholicism (Fortunatus, *Poems* 6.1a.29-34), and Gregory commended her as "gracious in all that she did, beautiful to look upon, chaste and modest in her behaviour, wise in her generation and of good address" (*HF*, 4.27), though the bishop's possible bias towards the royal patrons who supported his appointment must borne in mind here (Fortunatus, *Poems* 5.3.15-16). The queen proved a loyal and capable partner, winning the reputation even before Sigibert's assassination in 575 of having "held the realm under her husband" (Gregory, *HF*, 6.4). She not only survived the vicissitudes of Merovingian politics in the succeeding years, but successfully pursued strong and individual policies until her death at the hands of Chilperic's and Fredegund's sole surviving son, Lothar, in 613. For the queen, see James (1982), pp. 138-139; G. Kurth, *Études franques* 1 (Paris-Brussels, 1919), pp. 265-356; J. Nelson, "Queens as Jezebels: the careers of Brunhild and Balthild in Merovingian history". in D. Baker (ed.), *Medieval women*, Studies in Church History, subsidia 1 (Oxford, 1978); Wemple, passim; Wood, 126-136.

Charibert was one of the four sons of Lothar. His brother, Chilperic, seized Lothar's capital of Paris immediately after his father's death in 561; but the other three brothers, Sigibert, Guntram and Charibert, forced a more equable division of the kingdom, and Charibert was established in Paris (Gregory, *HF*, 4.22). He fell foul of Germanus, Bishop of Paris, the bishop excommunicating him for his bigamous marriages to Merofled and to Marcovefa, a runaway nun, and died shortly after Fortunatus' arrival in 567 (Gregory, *HF*, 4.26).

Childebert I, son of Clovis I, ruled Paris from 511 till his death in 558, leaving a widow, Ultrogotha, and two daughters. His reign was notable for the number of energetic and distinguished bishops in the cities of his kingdom, and for the extent of royal monastic foundations. For Childebert, see Wood, pp. 56-9, 111-12; for Childebert's work, see J. Laporte, "Le royaume de Paris dans l'œuvre hagiographique de Fortunat", *Études mérovingiennes, Actes des journées de Poitiers* 1952 (Paris, 1953), pp. 172 ff.: M. Vieillard-Troiekouroff, *Les monuments religieux de la Gaule d'après les oeuvres de Grégoire de Tours* (Paris, 1976), no. 200, pp. 211-14.

Childebert II was the son of Sigibert and Brunhild. Brunhild held his father's kingdom as queen regent whilst he was a minor, appointing Gogo *nutricius* (Gregory, *HF*, 5.46). When Childebert attained his majority in 585, the queen took over his guidance herself, being commended by Gregory the Great for "the government of the realm and the education of your son" shortly afterwards (Gregory the Great, *Ep.* 6.5, in MGH *Epp.* 1, p. 383). By the Treaty of Andelot, dated 28 November, 587 (Gregory, *HF*, 9.11), the distribution of Charibert's former kingdom and the cities which had formed Galswinth's *morgengabe* was agreed; Guntram guaranteed the protection and inheritance of Childebert's two sons, and the protection of the women and daughters of the royal family (text of the treaty in Gregory, *HF*,

9.20). On Guntram's death in 592, Childebert took over his kingdom (Fredegar, 4.14), but himself died in 596.

Chilperic I was one of the four sons of Lothar. He seized Lothar's capital of Paris and his treasure immediately after his father's death in 561, but was evicted by his brothers, and ruled from Soissons thereafter. He attempted to emulate Sigibert's dynastic marriage to Brunhild by marrying her sister, Galswinth; but the princess was murdered only a few weeks after the wedding (Gregory, *HF*, 4.28) and Fredegund established as Chilperic's queen. The violent feud arising from this incident between the two brothers and their families ran for the rest of the century; Sigibert was murdered, supposedly on Fredegund's orders, in 575 (Gregory, *HF*, 4.51), and Chilperic himself was assassinated in 584 (Gregory, *HF*, 6.46).

Dynamius, a Provençal noble (Stroheker, no. 108) was one of a group who travelled to Metz from the south for Sigibert's wedding. Dynamius was a learned man, who corresponded widely; there are letters between him and his first wife, Aurelia, and Gregory the Great (Gregorius I Papa, *Ep.* 3.33, 4.37, 6.6, 7.12, 7.33, *Registrum epistolarum* l, pp. 191, 272-4, 384-5, 454, 484). One verse of his poetry survives (*Grammatici Latini* 5, ed. H. Keil, (Leipzig, 1855-80) p. 579, lines 13-14), and two other letters (*Epistolae Austrasicae*, 12 and 17, pp. 127 and 130-1). He also composed a *Vita S. Maximi*. His second wife, Eucheria (Stroheker, no. 118; Riché, pp.186-7), was a poet ; see *Poetae Latini* 5, ed. E. Baehrens (Leipzig, 1883), pp. 361 ff., for her single extant poem.

Fredegund supplanted Galswinth as Chilperic's queen, in all probability being responsible for her murder (Gregory, *HF*, 4.28). Her considerable energies were constantly focused on the advancement of her husband and her children. She engaged actively in the struggle for military and political control with Sigibert and Brunhild, and was probably for having Sigibert assassinated at Tournai in 575 (Gregory, *HF*, 4.51) when he was on the point of defeating them. Her two younger sons died in the dysentery epidemic in 581 (Gregory, *HF*, 5.34), Chilperic was assassinated in 584, and she herself died in 596/7. See Wood, pp. 123-124.

Germanus of Paris, born near Autun about 496, was first abbot of St. Symphorian's in Autun, and then Bishop of Paris in around 556. He was untiring in his efforts to put an end to civil strife (e.g. Gregory, *HF* 4.51), and to reform the wayward habits of the Merovingian kings (see *Poem* 6.2, note 45, for his action against Charibert). His skilful diplomacy and strength ensured the success of Radegund's attempt to achieve independence of Lothar (Baudonivia, *Vita Radegundis*, c.7). Together with other leading bishops of the kingdom, he signed the letter of support for her foundation of the community of the Holy Cross in Poitiers (Gregory, *HF*, 9.39), and consecrated Agnes as the first Mother Superior (Gregory, *HF*, 9.42). He founded a monastery in Paris, in whose church he was buried in 576 (Gregory, *HF*, 5.6), the church which later became known as S. Germain-des-Prés. Fortunatus dedicated his *Vita Marcelli* to the bishop, painted a vivid picture of Germanus in procession with his clergy in *Poem* 2.9, and later celebrated the bishop's life in his *Vita Germani*.

Gogo was one of Fortunatus' earliest patrons. He was a poet, though none of his verse, only letters, survive: *Epist. Austras.* 13, 16, 22, and 48, MGH Ep. 3, pp. 127-128, 130, 134-135. He had a good knowledge of Vergil (see D. Norberg, "Ad epistolas varias mervingici aevi adnotationes", *Eranos* 35 (1937), p.111), and wrote in the florid prose style of the period. He was one of Sigibert's counsellors (Fortunatus, *Poems* 7. 1.35), and possibly *maior domus* (*Poems* 7.4.25-6); see Riché, p. 238 and note 414, for the difficulty of interpreting this passage; also for this post, see James (1988), pp. 230-234; Riché, pp. 238-239; Wood, pp. 153-154. He was the envoy who brought Brunhild from Spain (Fortunatus, *Poems* 7.1.41-2: Fredegar, *Chron.* 3.59, p.109), and was appointed by the queen *nutricius* to the young Childebert after her husband's death (Gregory, *HF*, 5.46). For the position and influence of a royal tutor, see J. Nelson. "Queens as Jezebels: the careers of Brunhild and Balthild in Merovingian history", in D. Baker (ed.), *Medieval Women*, Studies in Church History, subsidia 1 (Oxford, 1978), pp. 41-42; cf. Gregory, *HF*, 5.46. She probably brought him into her chancery (see Riché, op.cit. pp. 222, 239: and the four surviving letters written by him in this capacity, *Epistolae Austrasicae*, 13, 16, 22, 48, pp. 127-8, 130, 134-5, 152-3).

He died in 581 (Gregory, *HF,* 6.1: Fredegar, *Chron.* 3.59, p.109, erroneously has Gogo murdered by Sigibert soon after Brunhild's arrival).

Gregory of Tours came from a wealthy and distinguished Gallo-Roman family with a tradition of service to the Church, all but five of the preceding bishops of Tours having been blood relatives (*HF,* 5. 49). His father died when he was young, and he was brought up by Bishop Gallus in Clermont-Ferrand; he was ordained deacon in 563, at the age of 25, and elected bishop of Tours in 573. By that date, Fortunatus had already gained his patronage, and wrote an *adventus* panegyric for the new Bishop's arrival in the city (*Poem* 5.3). From that point, the two men developed a close friendship, fostered by their joint literary interests. Gregory was a vigorous and influential figure in political and ecclesiastical circles, and also the foremost historian of his day. He died in 594. For an excellent discussion of Gregory as bishop and writer, see van Dam (1985), pp. 177-300, and (1993), passim. See also E. Auerbach, *Mimesis: the representation of reality in western literature,* tr. W. R. Trask (Princeton, 1953), chs. 2 and 4: H. Beumann, "Gregor von Tours und der sermo rusticus", in *Spiegel der Geschichte: Festgabe für Max Braubach,* ed. K. Repken and S. Skalweit (Münster, 1964), pp. 69-98: M. Bonnet, *Le latin de Grégoire de Tours* (Paris, 1890): O. M. Dalton, *The history of the Franks by Gregory of Tours,* tr. with an introduction (repr. Oxford, 1971): W. Goffart, *The narrators of barbarian history (A.D. 500-800)* (Princeton, 1988), pp. 112-234: G. Kurth, "Grégoire de Tours et les études classiques au VIe siècle", Études franques 1 (Paris, 1919), pp. 1-29: W. Levison, *Deutschlands Geschichtsquellen im Mittelalter* 1 (Weimar, 1952), pp. 99-108: R. W. Mathisen, "The family of Georgius Florentius Gregorius and the bishops of Tours", *Medievalia et Humanistica, Studies in Medieval and Renaissance culture,* n.s. 12 (1984), pp. 83-95: R. Morghen, "Introduzione alla lettura di Gregorio de Tours", Convegni del Centro di studi sulla spiritualità medievale 12 (Todi, 1979), pp. 15-25: M. Oldoni, "Gregorio de Tours e i Libri Historiarum", *Studi medievali,* ser. 3, 13 (1972), pp. 563-700: M. Thurlemann, *Der historische Diskurs bei Gregor von Tours: Topos und Wirklichkeit* (Berne-Frankfurt, 1974), pp. 59 ff.: J. M. Wallace-Hadrill, *The Long-haired kings* (London, 1962), chs. 3 and 7.

Justin ll was emperor of Byzantium from 565-587, reigning for nearly a decade before attacks of insanity rendered him incapable. He and his wife, Sophia, had a great devotion to the Virgin Mary, whose cult grew steadily from this period on, and were great patrons of artists and architects; see Averil Cameron, "The artistic patronage of Justin ll", *Byzantion* 50 (1980), pp. 62-84. Justin's accession was celebrated by a lengthy Latin panegyric, recited in public by the orator Corippus; see Averil Cameron, ed., *Corippus, In laudem Iustini Augusti minoris* (London, 1976), and "Corippus' poem on Justin ll: a terminus of antique art?", *Continuity and change in sixth century Byzantium* (London, 1981), ch. 6; MacCormack, (1981), pp. 78 -81, 152-153, 249-250. Justin's interest in establishing links with the Franks coincided with Sigibert's wish to strengthen his position by diplomatic contact with Byzantium; see Averil Cameron, "The early religious policies of Justin ll", op.cit., ch. 10; and Gregory, *HF*, 4. 40 for Sibert's embassy. For the date of the latter, possibly 571, see W. Goffart, "Byzantine policy in the west under Tiberius ll and Maurice", *Traditio* 13 (1957), p.77; E. Stein, *Studien zur Geschichte des byzantischen Reiches, vornehmlich unter den Kaisern Justinus ll und Tiberius Constantinus* (Stuttgart, 1919), p. 34, note 18. For the possibility of Fortunatus' closer invovlement in Byzantine politics, see J. Sasel, "Il viaggio de Venanzio Fortunato e la sua attività in ordine alla politica byzantina", in *Aquileia e l'occidente mediterraneo*, Antichità altoadriatiche 19 (1981), pp. 359-375: B. Brennan, "Venantius Fortunatus: Byzantine agent?", *Byzantion* 65 (1995), pp. 7-16.

Martin of Braga was a Pannonian, born about 515, who ruled as archbishop of Braga from 556 until his death in 579. For his life, see *Martini Episcopi Bracarensis Opera omnia*, ed. C. W. Barlow (Yale, 1950), ch. 1, "Life of Martin", pp.1-8. On Martin's work of conversion, see E. A. Thompson, "The conversion of the Spanish Suevi to Catholicism" in E. James (ed.), *Visigothic Spain: New Approaches* (Oxford, 1980), pp. 77-92. Martin had close connections with Gaul, and with the diocese of Tours in particular; he was the author of the verses over the south portal of St. Martin's church in Tours, and gave support to Radegund (see Gregory, *HF*, 5.37: Fortunatus, *Poems*,

5.1.10, 5.2.63-70).

Martin of Tours was the great evangelizer of Gaul and founder of monasticism in that country, whose hagiography was written by Sulpicius Severus in the mid-390s. See the edition, translation and commentary of J. Fontaine for the *Vita Martini* and of the *Epistolae* of Sulpicius Severus in *SChr*. 133 -135 (Paris, 1967-1969). See also H. Delehaye, "Saint Martin et Sulpice Sévère", *Analecta Bollandiana* 38 (1920), pp. 5-136: J. Fontaine, "Verité et fiction dans la chronologie de la *Vita Martini*" in *Saint Martin et son temps. Studia Anselmiana* 46, pp. 189-236: - ,"Un clé littéraire de la *Vita Martini* de Sulpice Sévère: la typologie prophetique." in *Mélanges offerts à Mlle. Christine Mohrmann* (Utrecht and Anvers, 1963), pp. 84-95: - , "Sulpice Sévère a-t-il travesti Saint Martin de Tours en martyr militaire?", *Analecta Bollandiana* 81 (1963), pp. 31-58: "Hagiographie et politique, de Sulpice Sévère à Venance Fortunat", *Revue de l'histoire de l'église de France* 62 (1967), pp. 113 - 140: E. Griffe, "Saint Martin et le monachisme gaulois, in *Saint Martin et son temps, Studia Anselmiana* 46 (1961), pp. 3-24: C. Jullian, "Notes gallo-romaines, XLVII: La jeunesse de Saint Martin", *Revue des études anciennes* 12 (1910), pp. 260-280: - , "Notes gallo-romaines, XCIII-XCIV-XCV: Remarques critiques sur les sources de la Vie de Saint Martin"., *Revue des études anciennes* 24 (1922), pp. 37-47, 123-128, 229-235: - , "Notes gallo-romaines, XCVI-XCVII-XCVIII-XCIX: Remarques critiques sur la vie et l'œuvre de Saint Martin", *Revue des études anciennes* 24 (1922), pp. 306-312, and 24 (1923), pp. 49-55, 139-143, 234-250: C. Stancliffe, *St. Martin and his hagiographer: history and miracle in Sulpicius Severus* (Oxford, 1983): van Dam (1993), pp. 11-28: - (1985), pp. 119-140.

Radegund, daughter of Berthar, was captured by Lothar during his conquest of Thuringia in 530; educated to be his wife, she fled her husband after his murder of her brother. Consecrated a deaconess by St. Medard at Noyons, she founded a community in Poitiers under the protection of the bishop, Pientius, and of many of the other bishops of the kingdom. She instituted Agnes as Mother Superior, and, after unavailing attempts to gain the advice and support of the succeeding bishop, Maroveus, adopted the Rule of Caesarius of Arles for the discipline of the community. She obtained a relic of the Holy Cross from Byzantium (see *Appendix* 2 and 3), and throughout her life constantly endeavoured to mediate in the tensions of the kingdoms, dying in 587. For the two main Merovingian accounts of her life, that by Fortunatus and that by the nun Baudonivia, see *VR* 1 and 2. For Gregory's references to her, see *HF,* 3.4, 3.7, 6.29, 6.34, 7.36, 9.2, 9.38-43, 10.15-16. For modern biographical works, see R. Aigrain, *Sainte Radegonde vers 522-587* (3rd.ed. Paris, 1924): E. Delaruelle, "Sainte Radegonde, son type de sainteté et la chrétienté de son temps" *Études mérovingiennes, Actes des journées de Poitiers* 1952 (Paris, 1953), pp. 65-74: S. Gabe, "Radegundis: sancta, regina, ancilla. Zum Heiligkeitsideal der Radegundisviten von Fortunat und Baudonivia", *Francia* 16 (1989), pp. 1-30: G. Marie, "Sainte Radegonde et le milieu monastique contemporaine", *Études mérovingiennes, Actes des journées de Poitiers* 1952 (Paris, 1953), pp. 219-225: F. Prinz, *Frühes Mönchtum im Frankenreich* (Munich, 1965), pp. 157 ff.: G. Scheibelreiter, "Königstochter im Kloster. Radegund (d.587) und der Nonnonaufstand von Poitiers (589)", *Mitteilungen des Instituts für österreichische Geschichtsforschung* 87 (1979), pp. 1-37: Wemple, passim.

Sigibert l, together with his brother, Charibert, Guntram, and Chilperic, succeeded Lothar on his death in 561. Chilperic tried to steal a march on his brothers, but they combined forces to effect a more acceptable division of the kingdom; see Gregory, *HF* 4.22; James (1988), pp 169-177. In this, Sigibert's lands were widely dispersed; a northern area of Austrasia, the Auvergne and part of Provence, his two capitals being Reims and Metz. The king's intention was clearly to consolidate his kingdom. Gregory records that he deliberately shunned the casual liaisons of his brothers, and sought a dynastic alliance with the Visigothic royal family of Spain to strengthen his position (*HF,* 4.27; for Merovingian dynastic marriages, see E. Ewig, "Studien zur Merowingischen Dynastie", *Frühmittelalterliche Studien* 8 (1974), pp. 38 ff.). The wedding was held in Metz in the spring of 566, and was celebrated in grand style, with the invitation of the great and good of the kingdom to the celebrations (Gregory, *HF,* 4.27) and with the declamation of a resplendent Latin epithalamium in true classical tradition by Fortunatus, fortuitously arrived in Metz. The king was murdered, probably by agents of Fredegund, in 575 (Gregory, *HF*, 4.51). See Wood, pp. 89-90.

Sophia was wife of Justin ll, empress of Byzantium, greatly devoted to the cult of the Virgin Mary, and a lavish patron of the arts. See Averil Cameron, "The empress Sophia", *Byzantion* 45 (1976), pp. 5-21: also note under "Justin ll" above.

Theudebert l was Sigibert's half cousin, strictly speaking; son of Theuderic, who was half-brother to Lothar through an early liaison of Clovis with a concubine. He died in 548. He "respected his bishops, was liberal to the churches, relieved the wants of the poor and distributed many benefits with piety and friendly goodwill (Gregory, *HF*, 3.25). He also remitted the taxes of the church in Clermont-Ferrand (*HF*, 3.25) and restored the city of Verdun to financial stability by refusing repayment of a loan he had made to their Bishop (*HF*, 3.35) - a king of distinctive and memorable generosity. See Gregory, *HF*, 3. 3, 23-28, 32-36: R. Collins, "Theodebert l, Rex Magnus Francorum" in P. Wormald (ed.), *Ideal and reality in the Frankish and Anglo-Saxon World* (Oxford, 1983), pp. 7-33: Wood, pp. 56-57, 66-67.

Theudechild was most probably the daughter of Theuderic 1 (511-534) and Suavegotta, granddaughter of Clovis, mentioned by Gregory, *GC*, 40 (see Krush's note ad loc.); see Wood, p. 361. Theudechild's brother was Theudebert l. She married Hermegesicles (Procopius, *De Bello Goth.* 4.20), returning home after his death. See E. Ewig, "Studien zur Merowingischen Dynastie", *Fruhmittelalterliche Studien* 8 (1974), pp. 47-49, and note 179: Reydellet, (1981), p. 315; P. Wareman, "Theudechildis Regina", *Classica et Mediaevalia* 37 (1986), pp.199-201.

Theuderic l, son of Clovis and uncle of Sigibert, ruled an eastern kingdom based on Reims (see Gregory, *HF*, 3.1-15, 20-23: Wood, pp. 51-54). It was during his campaign against the Thuringians, aided by his half-brother, Lothar, that Radegund was captured (Gregory, *HF*, 3.7). His son was Theudebert l, and his daughter, Theudechild.

Ultrogotha was the wife of Childebert 1. Driven into exile with her daughters by Lothar on his accession in 561, she was restored by Charibert, and was probably present at the panegyric declaimed in the king's presence in Paris in 567. She was highly regarded by the church for her saintly devoutness; see *Vita S. Balthildis* 18, ed. B. Krusch, MGH SRM 2 (Hanover, 1888), pp. 505-506.

SELECT BIBLIOGRAPHY

Since this is a bibliography for a text in translation, references to primary sources have been made to texts in translation where available and appropriate.

Primary sources

Ausonius, ed. and tr. H. G. Evelyn White, 1-2 (Loeb, London, 1968).
Caesarius of Arles, *Regula sanctarum virginum* and *Ad sanctimoniales epistolae*, PL 67 (Paris, 1865).
    Rules for nuns of St. Caesarius of Arles, tr. Mother M. C. McCarthy, Catholic University of America, Studies in Medieval History, N. S. 16 (Washington, 1960).
Catullus, Tibullus and Pervigilium Veneris, ed. and tr. F. R. Cornish (Loeb, London, 1962).
Claudianus, ed. and tr. M. Platnauer, 1-2 (Loeb, London, 1922).
Corippus, *In laudem Iustini Augustini minoris*, ed. and tr. A. Cameron (London, 1976).
Dracontius, *Opera*, ed. F. Vollmer, MGH AA 14 (Berlin, 1905).
Ennodius, *Opera*, ed. F. Vogel, MGH AA 7 (Berlin, 1885).
Epistolae aevi merowingici collectae, ed. W. Gundlach, MGH *Epist.* 3, *Merowingici et Karolini* 1 (Berlin, 1902).
Epistolae Austrasicae, in *Epistolae aevi merowingici collectae*, ed. W. Gundlach, MGH *Epist.* 3, *Merwingici et Karolini* 1 (Berlin, 1902), pp. 110-153.
Fredegar, *Chronicorum libri IV cum continuationibus*, ed. B. Krusch, MGH SRM 2 (Hanover, 1888), pp. 1-193.
Gregorius I Papa, *Registrum Epistolarum* 1, ed. P. Ewald and L. M. Hartmann, MGH *Epist.* 1-2 (Berlin, 1891).
Horace, *Opera*, ed. E. C. Wickham (Oxford, 1975).
    Commentary on Horace Odes, Book 1, R. G. M. Nisbet and M. Hubbard (Oxford, 1970).

Inscriptiones Latinae Christianae veteres 1-3, ed. E. Diehl (Berlin, 1925-1927).
Jerome, *Epistolae* 1-8, ed. with French tr., J. Labourt (Paris, 1949-1963).
Leges Burgundionum ed. L. R. de Salis, MGH *Legum Sect.* 1. 2/1 (Hanover, 1892).
Lex Salica, ed. K. A. Eckhardt, MGH *Legum Sect.* 1. 4/2 (Hanover, 1969).
Liber historiae Francorum, ed. B. Krusch, MGH SRM 2 (Hanover, 1888).
Martin of Bracara, *Martini Episcopi Bracarensis Opera omnia*, ed. C. W. Barlow, (Yale, 1950).
Menander Rhetor, ed. and tr. D. A. Russell and N. G. Wilson (Oxford, 1981).
Merobaudes, *Opera*, ed. F. Vollmer, MGH AA 14 (Berlin, 1905).
Panégyriques latins 1-3, ed. E. Galletier (Paris, 1949).
XII Panegyrici Latini, ed. R. A. B. Mynors (Oxford, 1964).
Paulinus of Nola, *Epistolae* and *Carmina*, Corpus scriptorum ecclesiasticorum Latinorum 29 and 30, ed. J. Hartel (Vienna, 1894); Ancient Christian Writers 35 and 36, ed. and tr. P. G. Walsh (Maryland, 1964).
Poetae Latini 1-5, ed. E. Baehrens (Leipzig, 1883).
Poetae Latini Aevi Carolini, ed. K. Strecker, MGH *Poetarum Latinorum*, vol. 4 fasc. ii (Berlin, 1923).
Procopius, *Bella* 1 - 4, ed. J. Haury (Leipzig, 1962).
Prudentius, *Carmina*, Corpus Christianorum series Latina 126, ed. M. P. Cunningham (Turnhout, 1964).
Sidonius Apollinaris, ed. and tr. W. B. Anderson, 1-2 (Loeb, London, 1963).
Statius, *Silvae*, ed. and tr. J. H. Mozley (Loeb, London, 1928).
Sulpicius Severus, *Libri qui supersunt*, Corpus scriptorum ecclesiasticorum Latinorum 1, ed. C. Halm (Vienna, 1866) - ,*Vita Martini* and *Epistolae*, ed., tr. with commentary, J. Fontaine, SChr. 133-135 (Paris, 1967-1969).
Vergil, *Opera*, ed. F. H. Hirtzel (Oxford, 1900).
Vita Droctovei Abbatis Parisiensis, ed. B. Krusch, MGH SRM 3 (Hanover, 1896).
Vita S. Balthildis, ed. B. Krusch, MGH SRM 2 (Hanover, 1888).

Secondary sources

Aigrain, R., "Un Latin en Germanie", *Bulletin de la Societé d'Antiquaires de l'Ouest* 1 (1916), pp. 19-31.
- , *Sainte Radegonde vers 522-587* (3rd. edn., Paris, 1924).
- , "Le voyage de Saint Radegonde à Arles", *Bulletin philologique et historique du Comité des travaux historiques et scientifiques* (1926-1927), pp. 1-9.

Alföldi, A., tr. H. Mattingley, *A conflict of ideas in the late Roman empire* (Oxford, 1952).

Auerbach, E., *Mimesis: the representation of reality in Western literature*, tr. W. R. Trask (Princeton, 1953).
- , *Literary language and its public in late Latin antiquity and the middle ages*, tr. R. Manheim (London, 1965).

Baader, G., "Early medieval adaptations of Byzantine medicine in western Europe", *Dumbarton Oaks Papers* 34 (1985), pp. 251-259.

Baldwin-Smith, E., *Architectural symbolism of imperial Rome and the midde ages* (New York, 1978)

Beaunier, J., and Besse, J. M., *Abbayes et prieurés de l'ancienne France* 1-10 (Paris, 1905-1941).

Beck, G. H. J., *The pastoral care of souls in South East France during the sixth century* (Analecta Gregoriana 51, Rome, 1950).

Benko, S., "Vergil's fourth eclogue in Christian interpretation", in H. Temporini and W. Haase (eds.), *Aufstieg und Niedergang der romischen Welt* 2, 31.1 (Berlin, 1980).

Besse, J. M., "Les premiers monastères de la Gaule méridionale", *Revue des questions historiques* 71 (1902), pp. 395-464.
- , *Les moines de l'ancienne France, période gallo-romaine et mérovingienne* (Paris, 1906).

Beumann, H., "Gregor von Tours und der *sermo rusticus*", in *Spiegel der Geschichte: Festgabe für Max Braubach*, ed. K. Repgen and S. Skalweit (Münster, 1964), pp. 69-98.

Beyerle, F., "Das legislative Werk Chilperichs I", *Zeitschrift Savigny-Stiftung für Rechtsgeschichte*, Germanische Abteilung 78 (1961), pp. 1-38.

Bezzola, R., *Les origines et la formation de la littérature courtoise en Occident 500 -1000*, 1 (Bibliothèque de l'École des Hautes Études, 286, Paris, 1944).

Blanchet, A. and Dieudonné, A., *Manuel de numismatique française* 1 (Paris, 1912).

Blomgren, S., "Zur Construktion *resilire alicui*", *Eranos* 51 (1953), pp. 160ff.

-, "In Venantii Fortunati carmina adnotationes novae", *Eranos* 69 (1971), pp. 104-150.

-, "Fortunatus cum elogiis collatus. De cognatione quae est inter carmina Venantii Fortunati et poesin epigraphicam Christianam", *Eranos* 71 (1973), pp. 95-111.

-, "Ad Aratorem et Fortunatum adnotationes", *Eranos* 72 (1974), pp. 143-155.

Bonnard, L., *La navigation intéieure de la Gaule a l'époque gallo-romaine* (Paris, 1913).

Bonnet, M., *Le latin de Grégoire de Tours* (Paris, 1902).

Born, L. K., "The perfect prince according to the Latin panegyrics" *American Journal of Philology* 53 (1934), pp. 20-35.

Brennan, B., "Senators and social mobility in sixth century Gaul", *Journal of Medieval History* 11 (1985), pp. 145-161.

- , "Venantius Fortunatus: Byzantine agent?", *Byzantion* 65 (1995), pp. 7-16.

Brown, P. R. L., "Aspects of the Christianisation of the Roman aristocracy", *Journal of Roman Studies* 51 (1961), pp. 1-11.

- , *The world of late antiquity from Marcus Aurelius to Muhammad* (London, 1971).

- , *Relics and social status in the age of Gregory of Tours*, Stenton Lecture, 1976 (Reading, 1977).

- , *The cult of the saints: its rise and function in Latin Christianity* (Chicago, 1981).

- , *The body and society: men, women and sexual renunciation in early Christianity* (New York, 1988).

Buchner, R., *Die Provence im merowingischer Zeit: Verfassung - Wirtschaft -Kultur* (Stuttgart, 1933).

Burdeau, F., "L'empereur d'après les panégyriques latins", in F. Burdeau et al. (eds.), *Aspects de l'empire romain* (Paris, 1964).

Burgess, T. C., "Epideictic literature", *Studies in classical philology* 3 (1902), pp. 89 -142.
Butler, C, "Numerological thought", in A. Fowler (ed.), *Silent Poetry* (London, 1970).
Cameron, Alan, *Claudian: poetry and propaganda at the court of Honorius* (Oxford, 1970).
- , *Circus factions: Blues and Greens at Rome and Byzantium* (Oxford, 1976).
Cameron, Averil, "The Byzantine sources of Gregory of Tours", *Journal of Theological Studies* 26 (1975), pp. 421- 426.
- , "The empress Sophia", *Byzantion* 45 (1975), pp. 5-21.
- , *Continuity and change in sixth century Byzantium* (London, 1981), ch. 6, "Corippus' poem on Justin ll: a terminus of antique art?"; ch. 10, " The early religious policies of Justin"; ch. 14, "A nativity poem of the sixth century A.D."; ch. 16, "The Theotokos".
- and Kuhrt, A. (eds.), *Images of women in antiquity* (Beckenham, 1983).
- , *Christianity and the rhetoric of empire. The development of Christian discourse* (California, 1991).
Carcopino, J., *Virgile et le mystère de la lVe Eclogue* (Paris, 1943).
Carlot, A., *Étude sur le domesticus franc*, Bibilothèque de la Faculté de Philosophie et Lettres de l'Université de Liège 13 (Liège, 1903).
Cassel, R., *Untersuchungen zur Griechischen und Romischen Konsolationsliteratur* (Munich, 1958).
Chadwick, H., *Boethius: the consolations of music, logic, theology and philosophy* (Oxford, 1981).
Chadwick, N., *The Celts* (Penguin, 1971).
Chase, A. H., "The metrical lives of St. Martin by Paulinus and Fortunatus and the prose life by Sulpicius Severus", *Harvard Studies in Classical Philology* 43 (1932), pp. 51-76.
Clark, G., *Women in antiquity: pagan and Christian lifestyles* (Oxford, 1993).
Claude, D., *Untersuchungen zum frühfränkischen Comitat*, Zeitschrift der Savigny-Stiftung für Rechtsgeschichte, Germanistische Abteilung 81, (1964), pp. 1-79.

Clerici, E. "Note sulla lingua di Venanzio Fortunato", *Rendiconti dell'Instituto Lombardo, Accademia di Scienze e Lettere: Classe di lettere e scienze morali e storiche* 104 *(1970), pp. 219-251.*

- , "Due poeti, Emilio Blossio Dracontio e Venanzio Fortunato", *Rendiconti dell'Instituto Lombardo, Accademic de Scienze e Lettere: Classe di lettere e scienze morali e storiche* 107 (1973), pp. 108-150.

Cloche, P., "Les élections épiscopales sous les Mérovingiens", *Moyen Âge* 26 (1924), pp. 203-254.

Collins, Richard, "Observations on the form, language and public of the prose biographies of Venantius Fortunatus in the hagiography of Merovingian Gaul", in H. B. Clarke and M. Brennan (eds.), *Columbanus and Merovingian mentality* (Oxford, 1981), pp. 105-131.

Collins, Roger., "Theodebert 1, *Rex Magnus Francorum*" in P. Wormald (ed.), *Ideal and reality in Frankish and Anglo-Saxon society* (Oxford, 1983), pp. 7-33.

Conway, M., "St. Radegund's reliquary at Poitiers", *The Antiquaries Journal* (1923), pp. 1-12.

Cordoliani, A., "Fortunat, l'Irlande et les Irlandais". *Études mérovingiennes, Actes des journées de Poitiers* 1952 (Paris, 1953), pp. 35- 43.

Coudanne, L., "Baudonivie, moniale de Sainte-Croix et biographe de Saint Radegonde", *Études mérovingiennes, Actes des journées de Poitiers* 1952 (Paris, 1953), pp. 45-51.

Courcelle, P., "Les exégèses Chrétiennes de la quatrième Eclogue", *Revue des études anciennes* 79 (1957), pp. 294-319.

- , *Histoire littéraire des grandes invasions germaniques* (Paris, 1964).

- , *Late Latin writers and their Greek sources* (Cambridge, Mass., 1969).

Cumont, F., *Afterlife in roman paganism* (Harvard, 1962).

Dalton, O. M., *The history of the Franks by Gregory of Tours,*, tr. with introduction (repr. Oxford, 1971).

Davis, G., "Ad sidera notus: strategies of lament and consolation in Fortunatus' De Gelsuintha", *Agon* 1 (1967), pp. 118-134.

Deichmann, F. W., *Bauten und Mosaiken von Ravenna* (Wiesbaden, 1958)
- , *Ravenna, Geschichte und Monumente* (Wiesbaden, 1969).
- , *Ravenna, Hauptstadt des spätantiken Abendlandes* 1 - 2 (Wiesbaden, 1974 and 1976).
- , *Rom, Ravenna, Konstantinopel, Näher Osten: Gemammelte Studien zur spatantiken Architektur, Kunst und Geschichte* (Wiesbaden, 1982).
Delaruelle, E., "Sainte Radegonde, son type de sainteté et la chrétienté de son temps", *Études mérovingiennes, Actes des journées de Poitiers* 1952 (Paris, 1953), pp. 65-74.
Delehaye, H., "Saint Martin et Sulpice Sévère", *Analecta Bollandiana* 38 (1920), pp. 5-136.
de Maillé, G., *Recherches sur les origines chrétiennes de Bordeaux* (Paris, 1959).
Derens, J., and Fleury, M., "La construction de la cathédrale de Paris par Childebert 1 d'après le *De ecclesia Parisiaca* de Fortunat", *Journal de savants* (1977), pp. 177-253.
Dill, S., *Roman society in Gaul in the Merowingian age* (London, 1926).
Dronke, P., *Women writers of the middle ages* (Cambridge, 1984).
Duffy, J., "Byzantine medicine in the sixth and seventh centuries: aspects of teaching and practice", *Dumbarton Oaks Papers* 34 (1985), pp. 21-27.
Ewig, E., "Kirche und Civitas in der Merowingerzeit", *Settimane de studio del Centro Italiano di Studi sul l'alto Medioevo* 7 (1960), pp. 45-71.
- , "Studien zur Merowingischen Dynastie", *Frühmittelalterliche Studien* 8 (1974), pp. 15-59.
- , "Zum christlichen Königsdanken im Frühmittelalter", in H. Alsma (ed.), *Spätantikes und Frankisches Gallien* 1 (Munich, 1976), pp. 3-71.
Fabre, P., *Saint Paulin de Nole et l'amitié chrétienne* (Paris, 1957).
Favez, C., *La consolation latine chrétienne* (Paris, 1957)
Favreau, R., *Les inscriptions médièvales* (Turnhout, 1979).
Fontaine, J., "Un clé littéraire de la *Vita Martini* de Sulpice Sévère: la typologie prophétique", in *Mélanges offerts à Mlle. Christine Mohrmann* (Utrecht and Anvers, 1963), pp. 84-95.

- , "Hagiographie et politique, de Sulpice Sévère à Venance Fortunat", *Revue d'histoire de l'Église de France* 62 (1976), pp. 113-140.

- , "Verite et fiction dans la chronologie de la *Vita Martini*", in *Saint Martin et son temps*. *Studia Anselmiana*, 46, pp. 189-236.

Gabe, S., "Radegundis: sancta, regina, ancilla. Zum Heiligheitsideal der Radegundisviten von Fortunat und Baudonivia", *Francia* 16 (1989), pp. 1- 10.

Gaiffier d'Hestroy, B. de, "S. Venance Fortunat, évêque de Poitiers: les témoignages de son culte", *Analecta Bollandiana* 70, fasc. 3/4 (1952), pp. 252 ff..

- , "Les deux poemes de Fortunat en l'honneur de Saint Vincent", *Études mérovingiennes, Actes des journées de Poitiers* 1952 (Paris, 1953), pp. 127- 134.

Ganzenmuller, W., *Das Naturgefühl im Mittelalter* (Leipzig-Berlin, 1914).

Garaud, M., "Les classes sociales dans la cité de Poitiers a l'époque mérovingienne", *Études mérovingiennes, Actes des journées de Poitiers* 1952 (Paris, 1953), pp. 137-146.

Gauthier, N., *L'évangélisme des pays de la Moselle* (Paris, 1980).

George, J. W., "Variations on themes of consolation in the poetry of Venantius Fortunatus". *Eranos* 86 (1988), pp. 53-66.

- , "Poet as politician: Venantius Fortunatus' panegyric to King Chilperic", *Journal of Medieval History* 15 (1989), pp. 5-18.

Gilliard, F. D., "The senators of sixth century Gaul", *Speculum* 54 (1979), pp. 685 - 697.

Godman, P., *Alcuin: the Bishops, Kings and Saints of York*, ed. and tr., (Oxford, 1982).

- , *Poetry of the Carolingian Renaissance* (London, 1985).

Goffart, W., "Byzantine policy in the west under Tiberius ll and Maurice", *Traditio* 13 (1957), pp. 77-118.

- , *Barbarians and Romans, A.D. 418-584: the techniques of accomodation* (Princeton, 1980).

- , *The narrators of barbarian history (A.D. 550-800)* (Princeton, 1988).

Graver, M., "Quaelibet audendi: Fortunatus and the acrostic", *Transactions of the American Philological Association* 123 (1993), pp. 219-245.
Green, R. P. H., *The poetry of Paulinus of Nola* (Brussels, 1971).
Grenier, A., *Manuel d'archéologie gallo-romaine* 1-4 (Paris, 1931-1960).
Griffe, E., "Saint Martin et le monachisme Gaulois", in *Saint Martin et son temps, Analecta Anselmiana* 46 (1961), pp. 3-24.
Gussone, N., "Adventus-Zeremoniell und Translation von Reliquien: Victricius von Rouen, De laude Sanctorum" *Frühmittelalterliche Studien* 10 (1976), pp. 31-44.
Haarhoff, T. J., *Schools of Gaul: a study of pagan and Christian education in the last century of the Western Empire* (Oxford, 1920).
Hardie, A., *Statius and the "Silvae": poets, patrons and epideixis in the Graeco-Roman world* (Liverpool, 1983).
Heather, P, *Goths and Romans 332-489* (Oxford, 1991)
Herrin, J., *The formation of Christendom* (Oxford, 1987).
Higounet, C., "Les saints mérovingiens d'Aquitaine dans la toponymie", *Études mérovingiennes, Actes des journées de Poitiers* 1952 (Paris, 1953), pp. 157-167.
Hoeflich, M. F., "Between Gothia and Romania; the image of the king in the poetry of Venantius Fortunatus", *Res publica litterarum* 5 (1982), pp. 123-136.
Holum, K. G., and Vikan, G., "The Trier ivory, adventus ceremonial and the relics of St. Stephen", *Dumbarton Oaks Papers* 33 (1979), pp. 113-133.
Hunt, R. W., and Lapidge, M., "Manuscript evidence for knowledge of the poems of Venantius Fortunatus in late Anglo-Saxon England", *Anglo-Saxon England* 8 (1979), pp. 279-295.
Jackman, G., *Die Vierte ekloge Virgils* (Cologne 1953).
Jackson, R., *Doctors and diseases in the Roman empire* (London, British Museum Publications, 1988).
James, E., *The Merovingian Archaeology of South-West Gaul*, British Archaeological Reports, Suppl. Ser. 2/5, i and ii (Oxford, 1977).
- , (ed.), *Visigothic Spain: new approaches* (Oxford, 1980).
Janson, T., *Latin prose prefaces* (Stockholm, 1964)

Joret, C., *La rose dans l'antiquité et au moyen âge* (Statkine Reprints, Geneva, 1970).
Jullian, C., "Notes gallo-romaines, XLVII: La jeunesse de Saint Martin", *Revue des études anciennes* 12 (1910), pp. 260-280.
- , "Notes gallo-romaines, XCIII-XCIV-XCV: Remarques critiques sur les sources de la Vie de Saint Martin", *Revue des études anciennes* 24 (1922), pp. 37-47, 123-128, 229-235.
- , "Notes gallo-romaines, XCVI-XCVII-XCVII-XCIX: Remarques critiques sur la vie et l'œuvre de Saint Martin", *Revue des études anciennes* 24 (1922), pp. 306-312, and 24 (1923), pp. 49-55, 139-143, 234-250.
Kassel, R., *Untersuchungen zur griechischen und romischen Konsolationsliteratur* (Munich, 1958).
Kelly, J. N. D., *Jerome, his life, writings and controversies* (London, 1979).
Kennedy, G. A., *Classical rhetoric and its Christian and secular tradition from ancient to modern times* (London, 1980).
Keydell, R., "Epithalamium", in *Reallixikon für Antike und Christentum* 5 (Berlin, 1960), cols. 927-943.
Klingshern, W., "Caesarius' monastery for women in Arles and the composition and function of the *Vita Caesarii*", *Revue Bénédictine* 100 (1990), pp. 441-481.
Kopp, S., *Ein neues elogium von Venantius Fortunatus* (Wurzburg, 1939).
Kurth, G., *Études franques* 1-2 (Paris-Brussels, 1919).
Laistner, M. L. W., *Thought and letters in Western Europe, A.D. 500-900* (London, 1957).
- , *The intellectual heritage of the early middle ages: selected essays*, ed. C. G. Starr (Ithaca, New York, 1957).
Langosch, K., *Profile der lateinischen Mittelalters* (Darmstadt, 1967).
Laporte, J., "Le Royaume de Paris dans l'œuvre hagiographique de Fortunat", *Études mérovingiennes, Actes des journées de Poitiers* 1952 (Paris, 1953), p.169-177.
Lasko, P., *The kingdom of the Franks* (London, 1971).
Latouche, R., "Grégoire de Tours et les premiers historiens de France", *Association Guillaume Budé, Lettres d'humanité* 2 (1943), pp. 81-101.

- , *Les grandes invasions et la crise de l'Occident au Ve siècle* (Grenoble, 1946).
- , *Gaulois et Francs* (Grenoble, 1965).

Lattimore, R., *Themes in Greek and Latin epitaphs*, Illinois Studies in Language and Literature 28 (Urbana, 1942).

Latzke, T., "Der Fürstinnenpreis", *Medieval lateinische Jahrbuch* 14 (1979), pp. 22- 65.

Leach, E. R., "Melchisedech and the emperor: icons of subversion and orthodoxy", *Proceedings of the Royal Anthropological Institute of Great Britain and Ireland for 1972* (London, 1973), pp. 5-14.

Lebecq, S., *Les origines franques, Ve - IXe siècle* (Paris, 1990).

Le Blant, E., *L'epigraphie chrétienne en Gaule et dans l'Afrique romaine* (Paris, 1890).

- , (ed.) *Nouveau receuil des inscriptions chrétiennes de la Gaule anterieures au VIIIe siècle* (Paris, 1892).

Lelong, C., *La vie quotidienne en Gaule a l'époque mérovingienne* (Paris, 1963).

Leo, F., "Venantius Fortunatus, der letzte römische Dichter", *Deutsch Rundschau* 32 (1882), pp. 414- 6.

- , "Der gelegenheitsdichter Venantius Fortunatus" in K. Langosch (ed.), *Mittellateinische Dichtung* (1969), pp. 57-90.

Levison, W., *Deutschlands Geschichtsquellen im Mittelalter* 1 (Weimar, 1952).

Lewis, A. R., "The Dukes in the Regnum Francorum, A.D. 550- 51", *Speculum* 51 (1976), pp. 381-410.

Lot, F., "Les migrations saxonnes en Gaul et en Grande Bretagne du IIIe au Ve siècle", *Revue historique* 119 (1915), pp. 1-40.

- , "A quelle époque a-t-on cessé de parler latin?", *Archivum Latinitatis Medii Aevi* 6 (1937), pp. 97-159.

- , *Les invasion germaniques* (3rd. edn., Paris, 1944).

- , *La naissance de la France* (Paris, 1948).

- , *La fin du monde antique et le debut du moyen âge* (rev. ed. Paris, 1951).

McDermott, W. C., "Felix of Nantes: a Merovingian bishop", *Traditio* 31 (1975), pp. 1 - 24.

Mâle, E., *La fin du paganisme en Gaule et les plus anciennes basiliques chrétiennes* (Paris, 1950).

Manitius, M., "Zu spätlateinischen Dichtern", *Zeitschrift für österreichischen Gymnasien* (1886), pp. 250-251
- , *Geschichte der christlich - lateinischen Poesis bis zur Mittel des 8. Jahrhunderts* (Stuttgart, 1891).
- , *Geschichte der lateinischen Literatur des Mitteralters* 1 (Munich, 1911).
Marie, G., "Sainte Radegonde et le milieu monastique contemporain", *Études mérovingiennes, Actes des journées de Poitiers* 1952 (Paris, 1953), pp. 219- 225.
Mariner Bigorra, S., "Prudencio y Venancio Fortunato: influencia de un metro", *Helmantica* 26 (1975), pp. 333 ff.
Markus, R. A., *From Augustine to Gregory the Great* (repr. London, 1983).
Marrou, H. I., *Histoire de l'éducation dans l'antiquité* (Paris, 1948).
Martindale, J. R., *The prosopography of the later Roman empire 2, A.D. 395-527* (Cambridge, 1980).
Matthews, J., "Anicius Manlius Severinus Boethius", in M.Gibson (ed.) *Boethius* (Oxford, 1981), pp. 15-43.
Meneghetti, A., "La latinità di Venanzio Fortunato", *Didaskaleion* 5 (1916), pp. 195-298; 6 (1917), pp. 1-166.
Meunier, R. A., *Grégoire de Tours et l'histoire morale du Centre-Ouest de la France* (Poitiers, 1946).
- , "L'intérêt politique de la correspondance de saint Fortunat", *Études mérovingiennes, Actes des journées de Poitiers* 1952 (Paris, 1953), pp. 239- 248.
Mommsen, T., "Schlussbericht über die Herausgabe der *Auctores antiquissimi* (1898)", *Gesammelte Schriften* 7 (Berlin, 1909), pp. 691-694.
Monod, G., *Études critiques sur les sources de l'histoire mérovingienne* 1-2 (Paris, 1872-1885).
Morelli, C., "L'epitalamio nella tarda poesia latina", *Studi Ital.* 18 (1910), pp. 319- 432.
Morghen, R., "Introduzione alla lettura di Gregorio di Tours", *Convegni del Centro di studi sulla spiritualità medievale* 12 (Todi, 1979).
Musset, L., *The Germanic invasions: the making of Europe, A.D. 400-600*, tr. E. and C. James (London, 1975).

Muthesius, A., "From seed to samite: aspects of Byzantine silk production", in L. Monnas and H. Granger-Taylor (eds.), *Ancient and medieval textiles: studies in honour of Donald King* (Textile history 20, Pasold research fund, 1989). pp. 135-149.

Navarra, L., "Venanzio Fortunato; stato degli studi e proposte di ricerca", *La cultura in Italia fra tardo Antico e alto Medievo: Atti del convegno tenuto a Roma: consiglio Nazionale delle Ricerche, dal 12 al 16 Nov. 1979,* 2 (Rome, 1981), pp. 605-610.

- , "A proposito del De navigio suo de Venanzio Fortunato in rapporto alla Mosella di Ausonio e aglo Itinerari di Ennodio", *Studi storico-religiosi* 3, part 1 (1979), pp. 79-131.

Nelson, J., "Royal saints and early medieval kingship" in D. Baker (ed.), *Sanctity and Secularity: the Church and the world,* Studies in Church History 10 (Oxford, 1973), pp. 39-44.

- , "Queens as Jezebels: the careers of Brunhild and Balthild in Merovingian History", in D. Baker (ed.), *Medieval Women,* Studies in Church History, subsidia 1 (Oxford, 1978), pp. 31-77.

Nissen, T., "Historisches Epos und Panegyrikos in der Spätantike", *Hermes* 75 (1940), pp. 298-325.

Norberg, D., "Ad epistolas varias merovingici aevi adnotationes", *Eranos* 35 (1937), pp. 111 ff.

- , *Introduction à l'étude de la versification latine médiévale* (Stockholm, 1958).

Nutton, V., "From Galen to Alexander: aspects of medicine and practice in late antiquity", *Dumbarton Oaks Papers* 34 (1985), pp. 1-14.

O'Donnell, J. J., *Cassiodorus* (Berkeley, 1979).

- , "Liberius the patrician", *Traditio* 37 (1981), pp. 31-72.

Oldoni, M., "Gregorio de Tours e i Libri Historiarum", *Studi medievali,* ser. 3, 13, (1972), pp. 563-700.

Pearce, J. W. E., *The Roman Imperial Coinage 9, Valentinian I - Theodosius I,* ed. H. Mattingley, C. H. V. Sutherland, and R. A. G. Carson (London, 1951).

Pearsall, D. and Salter, E., *Landscapes and seasons in the medieval world* (London, 1973).

Percival, J., *The Roman villa: a historical introduction* (London, 1976).
Peter, H., "Der Brief in der römischen Literatur", *Abhandlungen der philologisch-historischen Classe der Königlich Sachsischen Gesellschaft der Wissenschaften* 47. 3 (Leipzig, 1901), pp. 178 ff.
Poucelle, A., tr. F. Pheasant, *Porneia: on desire and the body in antiquity* (Oxford, 1988).
Poupardin, R., *Recueil des Chartes de l'abbaye de S. Germain-des-Près* 1 (Paris, 1909), pp. 5 ff.
Prinz, F., *Frühes Monchtum im Frankenreich* (Munich, 1965).
- , "Zur geistigen Kultur des Monchtums im spätantiken Gallien und im Merowingerreich", in *Monchtum und Gesellschaft im Frühmittelalter* (Darmstadt, 1976).
Prou, M., *Les monnaies mérovingiennes: catalogue des monnaies françaises de la Bibliothèque Nationale* (Paris, 1982).
Raby, F. J. E., *A history of Christian Latin poetry* (Oxford, 1953).
- , *A history of secular Latin poetry* (Oxford, 1957).
Randers - Pehrson, J. D., *Barbarians and Romans: the birth struggle of Europe, A.D. 400-700* (London, Canberra, 1983).
Riché, P., "La femme dans la societé germanique païenne" and "La femme a l'époque barbare" in P. Grimal (ed.), *Histoire mondiale de la femme* (Paris, 1965), pp. 27-34 and 35-46.
Roberts, M., "The use of myth in Latin epithalamia from Sidonius to Venantius Fortunatus", *Transactions of the American Philological Association* 119 (1989), pp. 321-348.
- , "The description of landscape in the poems of Venantius Fortunatus: the Moselle poems", *Traditio* 49 (1994) pp. 1-22.
Rogers, B. J., "The poems of Venantius Fortunatus: a translation and commentary", Ph.D. thesis (Rutgers, 1969).
Rouche, M., "Francs et Gallo-Romains chez Grégoire de Tours", in *Gregorio di Tours,* pp. 141- 69, Convegni del Centro di studi sulla spiritualità medievale 12 (Todi, 1979).
Roux, J. L., "Un troubadour devenu évêque de Poitiers: Saint Fortunat", *Picton* 8 (1978), pp. 5-56.
Salin, E., "Les conditions de vie au temps de Radegond et de Fortunat, d'après le temoignage des sepultures", *Études mérovingiennes, Actes des journées de Poitiers* 1952 (Paris, 1953), pp. 269-272.

Sasel, J., "Il viaggio di Venanzio Fortunato e la sua attività in ordine alla politica bizantina", *Antichità altoadriatiche* 19 (1981), pp. 359-375.

Scarborough, J., *Roman medicine* (London, 1969).

Scheibelreiter, G., "Königstochter im Kloster. Radegund (d. 587) und der Nonnenaufstand von Poitiers (589)", *Mitteilungen des Instituts für österreichische Geschichtsforschung* 87 (1979), pp. 1-17.

Standacher, K., "Das Reisegedicht des Venantius Fortunatus", *Schlern* 15 (1934).

Stein, E., *Studien zu Geschichte des byzantischen Reiches, vornehmlich unter den Kaisern Justinus II und Tiberius Constantinus* (Stuttgart, 1919).

- , *Histoire du Bas empire* 1-2, tr. J. R. Palanque (Paris - Brussels, 1949-1959).

- , *Opera minora selecta* (Amsterdam, 1968).

Steinmann, K., *Die Gelesuintha-Elegie des Venantius Fortunatus (Carm. VI. 5): Text, Übersetzung, Interpretationen* (Zurich, 1975).

Struthers, L. B. "The rhetorical structure of the encomia of Claudius Claudian", *Harvard Studies in Classical Philology* 30 (1919) pp. 49-81.

Syme, R., "The fame of Trajan", in *Emperors and biography* (Oxford, 1971), pp. 89-112.

Szöverrfy, J., *Venantius Fortunatus and the earliest hymns to the Holy Cross*, Classical Folia 20 (New York, 1966).

- , *Weltliche Dichtungen des lateinischen Mittelalters 1, Von den Anfängen bis zum Ende der Karolingerzeit* (Berlin, 1970).

- , "A la source de l'humanisme chrétien médiéval: *Romanus* et *barbarus* chez Venance Fortunat", *Aevum* 65 (1971), pp. 71-86.

Thomson, E. A., *The early Germans* (Oxford, 1965).

- , "The conversion of the Spanish Suevi to Catholicism", in E. James (ed.) *Visigothic Spain: new approaches* (Oxford, 1980), pp. 77-92.

- , *Romans and barbarians: the decline of the West* (Wisconsin, 1982).

Thompson, J. W., *The literacy of the laity in the middle ages* (New York, 1960).
Thraede, K., "Zwischen Gebrauchstext und Poesie: Zur Spannweite der antiken Gattung "Brief", in J. Vereman and F. Decreus (eds.), *Acta Colloquii Didactici classici Octavi*, Didactica Classica Gandensia 20 (1980), pp. 190 ff.
Thurlemann, M., *Der historische Diskurs bei Gregor von Tours: Topos und Wirklichkeit* (Berne - Frankfurt, 1974).
Todd, M., *The early Germans* (Oxford, 1992).
Trilling, L., *Sincerity and authenticity* (London, 1974).
Vercanteren, F., "Le "Romanus" des sources franques", *Revue belge de philologie et d'histoire* 2 (1982), pp. 77 ff..
Vieillard-Troiekouroff, M., "Les monuments religieux de Poitiers", *Études mérovingiennes, Actes des journées de Poitiers 1952* (Paris, 1953), pp. 178-191.
- , *Les monuments religieux de la Gaule d'après les oeuvres de Grégoire de Tours* (Paris, 1976).
von Simpson, O., *Sacred fortress, Byzantine art and statecraft in Ravenna* (Chicago, 1948).
Wallace-Hadrill, J. M., *The barbarian West, 400-1000* (London, 1952, repr. 1977)
- , *The long-haired kings and other studies in Frankish history* (London, 1962).
- , "Gregory of Tours and Bede: their views on the personal qualities of kings", *Frühmittelalterliche Studien* 2 (1968), pp. 125-133.
- , *Early Germanic kingship in England and on the continent* (Oxford, 1971).
- , *Early medieval history* (Oxford, 1975).
- , *The Frankish church* (Oxford, 1983).
Walsh, P. G., "Venantius Fortunatus", *The Month* 120 (1960), pp .292-302.
Wareman, P., "Theudechildis Regina", *Classica et Mediaevalia* 37 (1986), pp. 199- 201.
White, C, *Christian friendship in the fourth century* (Cambridge, 1992).
Wieruszowski, H., "Die Zusammensetzung der gallischen und franksichen Episcopats bis zum Vertrag von Berdun (843) mit

besonderer Berucksuchtigung der Nationalität und des Standes", *Bonner Jahrbuch* 127 (1922), pp. 16-29.
Wightman, E. M., *Roman Trier and the Treveri* (London, 1970).
Wilson, E. F. "Pastoral and epithalamium in Latin literature", *Speculum* 23 (1948), pp. 35-47.
Wood, I., *Early Merovingian devotion in town and country,* Studies in Church History 16 (Oxford, 1979), pp. 61-76.
- , "Ecclesiastical politics in Merovingian Clermont", in P. Wormald (ed.), *Ideal and reality in Frankish and Anglo-Saxon society* (Oxford, 1983).
Wopfner, H., "Die Reise des Venantius Fortunatus durch die Ostalpen", in *Festschrift für Ehren E. von Ottenhals* (Innsbruck, 1925).
Zeuss, J. C., *Die Deutschen und die Nachbarstämme* (München, 1837).

Index

Aaron, Old Testament priest, 82
Abel, son of Adam, 81
Abraham, Old Testament patriarch, 81, 86
Achaia, 18
Achilles, Greek hero, 28
Adam, 81, 83
African, 114
Agatha, Christian martyr, 12
Agnes, Christian martyr, 12
Agnes, Mother Superior (see Biographical notes), 20, 70-71, 95, 103-104, 106-110, 119-121
Albinus, Provençal noble, 55
Albinus, saint, 108
Allobroges, 118
Alps, 49
Amalfrid, Radegund's cousin, 116-117
Andalusia, 50
Andernach, 101
Andrew, Christian apostle, 18
Apollonius, Roman writer, 53
apples, 22, 51-52, 120
Arab, 13
Aracharius, 6
Arcadius, 6
Aregius, Abbot of Limoges, 53
Arles, 20
Artachis, possibly Amalfrid's' son, 116-117
Athanagild, king of the Visigoths, 31
Athens, 62
Atticus, 5
Audulf, Fortunatus' messenger, 119
Augusti (a), as imperial title, 83, 111, 113-114
barbarian, 34, 64, 115

Bartholomew, Christian missionary, 18
Basques, 77, 113, 115
Batavians, 50, 115
bees, 25, 57
belt of honour, 60, 66
Berny-Rivière, 73
Berthar, Radegund's father, 117-118
Britain, 113
Britons, 46, 64, 77, 115
Brumachius, 7
Brunhild, queen of the Franks (see Biographical notes), 25, 27-33, 49, 97- 99, 118-1199
Caesar, as title, 26
Caesarius, Bishop of Arles, 20
Cantabrians, 113
Cantusblandus, villa of Aregius, 53
Cariacum, 108
Cato, Roman censor, 59
Charibert l, son of Lothar (see Biographical notes, 34- 35, 75
Childebert l, brother of Lothar (see Biographical notes), 35, 36, 51-52, 78
Childebert ll, son of Sigibert and Brunhild (see Biographical notes), 97-99, 118-119
Chilperic, son of Lothar (see Biographical notes), 47, 73-80, 83-86
Chlodobert, son of Chilperic and Fredegund, 88
Chlodosind, daughter of Brunhild and Sigibert, 119
Clovis, father of Lothar and Childebert l, 88-89
Conda, *domesticus*, 65
Constantine the Great, emperor, 114
consuls, Roman, 59
Council of Chalcedon, 113
count, 50, 66
Cupid, 27-28, 41
Dacians, 46, 113
Dagaulf, husband of Vilithuta, 9
Daedalus, 106
Dagobert, son of Chilperic and Fredegund, 88
Dalmatians, 113

Danes, 60, 77
Daniel, Old Testament prophet, 82
Danube, river, 113
David, Old Testament kind, 37, 63, 82, 85-86
Domitianus, Bishop of Angers, 108
domesticus, 65-66
dukes, 26, 59
Dynamius of Marseilles, Provençal noble (see Biographical note), 55-56
Egypt, 60
Elbe, river, 113
Elijah, Old Testament prophet, 12, 19, 83
Enoch, son of Cain, 12, 83
Eomund, friend of Fortunatus and Radegund, 108
Ethiopians, 18
Eusebia, 14-15
Eve, 80
Fabius, Roman general, 37
Flaccus (see Horace)
flowers, 13, 70-71,105
Fortunatus, 20, 47, 72, 80, 118
Fredegund, queen and wife of Chilperic (see Biographical note), 78-80, 85-87
Frisians, 77
Galicia, 17-21, 113
Galsuinth, daughter of Athanagild and Goiswinth, 40-50
Gelonians, 41
Genesius, Christian martyr, 20
Germanus, Bishop of Paris (see Biographical note), 69
Gideon, Old Testament leader, 82
Gogo, Sigibert's *major domus* (see Biographical note), 54-58
Goiswinth, queen of the Visigoths, 41-45, 49-50
Goths, 46, 77, 118
Greeks, 64
Gregory, Bishop of Tours (see Biographical note), 21-23, 71-72, 89-90, 94-95
Gregory of Nazianzus, 89
Helena, empress, 114

Herminfrid, Radegund's uncle, 117-118
Hilary, Bishop of Tours, 46, 47
Horace (Flaccus), Roman poet, 91
Homer, Greek poet, 32, 62
honey, 52, 57, 63, 121
Illyrians, 18
Indians, 18, 46, 74
Isaac, son of Abraham, 81
Isaiah, Old Testament prophet, 82
Jacob, son of Isaac, 18, 81
Japheth, son of Noah, 81
Job, Old Testament prophet, 81, 85-86
John, apostle, 19
John the Baptist, 83
Jonah, Old Testament prophet, 82
Joshua, Old Testament leader, 82
Justin ll, Emperor (see Biographical note), 111-115
Justina, niece of Gregory of Tours, 95
Jutes, 77
Latin language, 37
Lerins, 20
Loire, river, 46
Lothar l, son of Clovis, 29, 36, 66, 74, 77-78, 88
Lupus, duke, 59, 62-64
Maccabees, 85
Mars, 26
Marseille, 55
Martin, Bishop of Galicia, 17-21
Martin, Bishop of Tours, 18, 47
Mary, mother of Christ, 12, 51, 103
Matthew, apostle, 18
Melchisedec, Old Testament king and priest, 81
Metz, 1, 53, 99
Minerva, 15
Mopsus, 93
Moses, Old Testament leader, 82
Moselle, river, 1, 99, 101
Narbonne, 46

Nauriacum, 54
Nile, river, 60
Noah, builder of ark, 81
oath of allegiance, to Frankish queen, 47
Orpheus, 57
Pannonia, 19
Papulus, count, 54
Paradise, 2, 6, 13, 106
Paris, 9, 34
Paul, Christian missionary and theologian, 18-19, 83, 103, 112
Persian, 18, 46
Peter, apostle and martyr, 3, 12, 18-20, 51, 83, 103, 112
Phoebus, 62
Phrygians, 113
Pindar, Greek poet, 91
Poitiers, 46
Pompey, Roman general, 59
Pyrenees, 30, 46, 49
Radegund (see Biographical note), 12, 20, 47, 69-70, 79, 95, 103, 106-110, 114-115, 119-121
Rhine, river, 50, 101-102, 113
Rhone, river, 46, 113
Rome, 59
Romans, 9, 34, 38, 60, 64, 112, 115
Romulus, founder of Rome, 17, 115
Rouen, 47
royal tutor, 66 (see also Gogo)
Samson, Old Testament figure, 82
Samuel, Old Testament prophet, 82
Sapphic verses, 89-91, 93
Sappho, Greek poet, 90, 94
Saxons, 32, 60, 67, 77
Saxony, 66
Scipio, Roman general, 59
Scythians, 18, 46, 113
Seine, river, 46
senator(ial), 6
Seth, son of Noah, 81

Shem, son of Noah, 81
Sigamber, 37
Sigibert 1, son of Lothar (see Biographical note), 25, 27-33, 59-60, 66, 75
silk, 117
Solomon, Old Testament king, 37, 82, 86
Sophia, empress of Byzantium (see Biographical note), 111, 114-115
Sophocles, Greek dramatist, 72
Spain, 44, 49, 58, 119
Spaniard, 30-31
Stephen, Christian martyr, 12, 51
Suebi, 77, 87
Tejo, river, 50
Thecla, Christian martyr, 12
Thessalians, 113
Theudebald, son of Theudebert 1, 66
Theudebert 1, son of Theuderic 1 (see Biographical note), 29, 39, 66
Theudechild, daughter of Theuderic (see Biographical note), 38
Theuderic 1, son of Clovis (see Biographical note), 39, 65
Thomas, Christian apostle, 18
Thracians, 46, 113
Thuringia, 29, 32, 114, 116
Tincillac, 108
Titiana, Fortunatus' sister, 103
Toledo, 40, 43
Tours, 21, 46
Trajan, Roman emperor, 37
Trajan's forum, 62
tribnune, 65
Trier, 99
Trinity, the Holy, 17, 111-112
Ultrogotha, wife of Childebert 1 (see Biographical note), 35, 51-52
Venus, 15, 28-30
Vergil, Roman poet, 32, 62, 71
Victory, 32
Vienne, river, 46, 72
Vilicus, Bishop of Metz, 1-2, 53
Vilithuta, 9-14
villa, Fortunatus', 72

TRANSLATED TEXTS FOR HISTORIANS
Published Titles

Gregory of Tours: Life of the Fathers
Translated with an introduction by EDWARD JAMES
Volume 1: 176pp., 2nd edition 1991, ISBN 0-85323-327-6

The Emperor Julian: Panegyric and Polemic
Claudius Mamertinus, John Chrysostom, Ephrem the Syrian
edited by SAMUEL N. C. LIEU
Volume 2: 153pp., 2nd edition 1989, ISBN 0-85323-376-4

Pacatus: Panegyric to the Emperor Theodosius
Translated with an introduction by C. E. V. NIXON
Volume 3: OUT OF PRINT

Gregory of Tours: Glory of the Martyrs
Translated with an introduction by RAYMOND VAN DAM
Volume 4: 150pp., 1988, ISBN 0-85323-236-9

Gregory of Tours: Glory of the Confessors
Translated with an introduction by RAYMOND VAN DAM
Volume 5: 127pp., 1988, ISBN 0-85323-226-1

The Book of Pontiffs (*Liber Pontificalis* to AD 715)
Translated with an introduction by RAYMOND DAVIS
Volume 6: 175pp., 1989, ISBN 0-85323-216-4

Chronicon Paschale 284-628 AD
Translated with notes and introduction by
MICHAEL WHITBY AND MARY WHITBY
Volume 7: 280pp., 1989, ISBN 0-85323-096-X

Iamblichus: On the Pythagorean Life
Translated with notes and introduction by GILLIAN CLARK
Volume 8: 144pp., 1989, ISBN 0-85323-326-8

Conquerors and Chroniclers of Early-Medieval Spain
Translated with notes and introduction by KENNETH BAXTER WOLF
Volume 9: 176pp., 1991, ISBN 0-85323-047-1

Victor of Vita: History of the Vandal Persecution
Translated with notes and introduction by JOHN MOORHEAD
Volume 10: 112pp., 1992, ISBN 0-85323-127-3

The Goths in the Fourth Century
by PETER HEATHER AND JOHN MATTHEWS
Volume 11: 224pp., 1992, ISBN 0-85323-426-4

Cassiodorus: *Variae*
Translated with notes and introduction by S. J. B. BARNISH
Volume 12: 260pp., 1992, ISBN 0-85323-436-1

The Lives of the Eighth-Century Popes (*Liber Pontificalis*)
Translated with an introduction and commentary by RAYMOND DAVIS
Volume 13: 288pp., 1992, ISBN 0-85323-018-8

Eutropius: Breviarium
Translated with an introduction and commentary by H. W. BIRD
Volume 14: 248pp., 1993, ISBN 0-85323-208-3

The Seventh Century in the West-Syrian Chronicles
introduced, translated and annotated by ANDREW PALMER
including two Seventh-century Syriac apocalyptic texts
introduced, translated and annotated by SEBASTIAN BROCK
with added annotation and an historical introduction by ROBERT HOYLAND
Volume 15: 368pp., 1993, ISBN 0-85323-238-5

Vegetius: Epitome of Military Science
Translated with notes and introduction by N. P. MILNER
Volume 16: 182pp., 2nd edition 1995, ISBN 0-85323-910-X

Aurelius Victor: De Caesaribus
Translated with an introduction and commentary by H. W. BIRD
Volume 17: 264pp., 1994, ISBN 0-85323-218-0

Bede: On the Tabernacle
Translated with notes and introduction by ARTHUR G. HOLDER
Volume 18: 224pp., 1994, ISBN 0-85323-378-0

Caesarius of Arles: Life, Testament, Letters
Translated with notes and introduction by WILLIAM E. KLINGSHIRN
Volume 19: 176pp., 1994, ISBN 0-85323-368-3

The Lives of the Ninth-Century Popes (*Liber Pontificalis*)
Translated with an introduction and commentary by RAYMOND DAVIS
Volume 20: 360pp., 1995, ISBN 0-85323-479-5

Bede: On the Temple
Translated with notes by SEÁN CONNOLLY,
introduction by JENNIFER O'REILLY
Volume 21: 192pp., 1995, ISBN 0-85323-049-8

Pseudo-Dionysius of Tel-Mahre: *Chronicle*, Part III
Translated with notes and introduction by WITOLD WITAKOWSKI
Volume 22: 192pp., 1995, ISBN 0-85323-760-3

Venantius Fortunatus: Personal and Political Poems
translated with notes and introduction by JUDITH GEORGE
Volume 23: 192pp., 1995, ISBN 0-85323-179-6

For full details of Translated Texts for Historians, including prices and ordering information, please write to the following:

All countries, except the USA and Canada: Liverpool University Press, Senate House, Abercromby Square, Liverpool, L69 3BX, UK (*tel* 0151-794 2233, *fax* 0151-708 6502).

USA and Canada: University of Pennsylvania Press, Blockley Hall, 418 Service Drive, Philadelphia, PA 19104-6097, USA (*tel* [215] 898-6264, *fax* [215] 898-0404).